The first comprehensive map of Pennsylvania's "improved parts and extensive frontiers" was produced in 1759 by Nicholas Scull, the Commonwealth's surveyor-general. This 1776 version, produced in London for an "American Atlas" during the American Revolution, distinctly shows the lonely Forbes Road west of the Susquehanna River.

# PENNSYLVANIA'S
# FORBES TRAIL

GATEWAYS *and* GETAWAYS *along the* LEGENDARY ROUTE
*from* PHILADELPHIA *to* PITTSBURGH

Burton K. Kummerow    Christine H. O'Toole    R. Scott Stephenson

Preface by Fred Anderson
Edited by Laura S. Fisher

Illustrations by Gerry Embleton and Richard Schlecht
Principal photography by Harriet Wise

Taylor Trade Publishing
An imprint of the Rowman and Littlefield Publishing Group
Lanham  |  Boulder  |  New York  |  Toronto  |  Oxford

# This book has been made possible by the Colcom Foundation

French and Indian War 250, Inc. also acknowledges with gratitude the generous support of the Katherine Mabis McKenna Foundation, the Richard King Mellon Foundation, C.J. Queenan, Jr., Pennsylvania's Department of Community and Economic Development, and Pennsylvania's Department of Conservation and Natural Resources.

© 2008 by French and Indian War 250, Inc.
Deborah L. Corll, Production Manager
French and Indian War 250, Inc. is an initiative of the Allegheny Conference on Community Development.

Printed in the United States of America
Design and Printing by The YGS Group | www.theygsgroup.com
Cover design by Diana Dugina Riebling

Distributed by National Book Network

ISBN 1-58979-388-9
ISBN 13 978-1-58979-388-0

FRENCH & INDIAN WAR
COMMEMORATION
*250 years*

SFI
CERTIFIED
SOURCING

FIBER USED IN THIS PRODUCT LINE
MEETS THE SOURCING REQUIREMENTS
OF THE SFI PROGRAM
WWW.SFIPROGRAM.ORG

The Sustainable Forestry Initiative
(SFI) program promotes responsible
environmental behavior and sound
forest management.

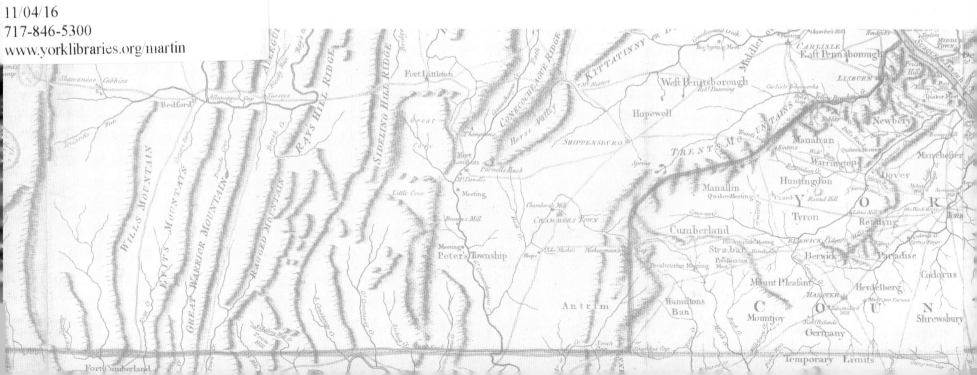

*Gratitude to:* **Cordelia S. May**

*and the*

**Richard King Mellon Foundation**

*Exemplary Stewards of Our Nation's
Natural and Historic Resources*

# Forbes Campaign Chronology

**December, 1757**—The British decide on a three-pronged attack against the French in North America at Louisbourg, Nova Scotia; New York's Hudson River Valley; and across Pennsylvania to Fort Duquesne on the Forks of the Ohio.

**March 4, 1758**—John Forbes is appointed brigadier general in command of the Pennsylvania campaign.

**March 15**—Teedyuscung, leader of the eastern Delawares, continues peace negotiations with Pennsylvania Governor William Denny in Philadelphia.

**April 18**—General Forbes arrives in Philadelphia to take command and decides on a methodical, protected advance with well-supplied forts every fifty miles.

**May 24**—Lieutenant Colonel Henry Bouquet arrives in Carlisle as Forbes' deputy commander.

**June 2**—Work begins on the Forbes Road west of Fort Loudoun.

**Mid-June**—Ships arrive in Philadelphia with siege artillery and Colonel Montgomery's Highland Battalion of troops.

**June 14**—Colonel Bouquet meets with Cherokee and Catawba warriors at Fort Loudoun.

**June 24**—Colonel Bouquet arrives at Raystown (later Fort Bedford) with advance troops to begin work on a base camp.

**July 4**—General Forbes arrives in Carlisle.

**July 15**—Envoy Christian Frederick Post and Delaware leader Pisquetomen leave Philadelphia on a peace mission to the Ohio Indians after Governor Denny has another council with Teedyuscung.

**July 23**—Pennsylvania Colonel John Armstrong sets out to mark a road across Pennsylvania to Loyalhanna (later Fort Ligonier). Virginia Colonel George Washington, then at Fort Cumberland, Maryland begins arguing for the route of the old Braddock Road.

**August 2**—General Forbes orders Colonel Bouquet (and Washington) to open a road across the Allegheny Mountains to Loyalhanna.

**August 14**—General Forbes arrives at Shippensburg.

**September 3**—Pennsylvania Colonel James Burd and a large detachment arrive at Loyalhanna and begin building a fort.

**September 5**—Colonel Bouquet leaves Raystown for Loyalhanna.

**September 6**—General Forbes arrives at Fort Loudoun.

**September 14**—Highland Major James Grant and 850 men are badly defeated while reconnoitering Fort Duquesne. Major Grant is captured.

**September 15**—General Forbes arrives at Raystown.

**October 5**—Colonels Bouquet and Washington meet with General Forbes at Raystown.

**October 7-26**—Christian Frederick Post and Pisquetomen return east for the Indian council that leads to the Treaty of Easton, Pennsylvania. Negotiations result in an Indian agreement to cut their alliance with the French in exchange for no European settlements in Ohio Country.

**October 12**—French and Indians attack Loyalhanna and are repulsed by Colonel Burd.

**October 23**—Colonel Washington and his Virginia troops arrive at Loyalhanna.

**November 2**—General Forbes arrives at Loyalhanna.

**November 8**—Post and Pisquetomen bring news to Loyalhanna of the Treaty of Easton and soon take letters from General Forbes to the western Delaware villages.

**November 11**—A Council of War at Loyalhanna, with all senior British and provincial officers present, results in the decision to wait until spring to attack Fort Duquesne.

**November 12**—Virginia troops accidentally attack each other in a friendly fire incident near Loyalhanna. A prisoner reports that Fort Duquesne is short of troops and supplies. General Forbes immediately orders an attack on the French.

**November 15**—Colonel Washington and Virginia troops are cutting a road through Chestnut Ridge, leading a three-pronged assault on Fort Duquesne.

**November 18**—General Forbes, Colonel Bouquet and the army main force follow Washington on the new road.

**November 24**—The British are only twelve miles from Fort Duquesne. French Commander Lignery blows up the French fort and escapes on the rivers with his garrison.

**November 25**—The British army takes formal possession of Fort Duquesne.

**November 26**—General Forbes names the site of the ruined French fort Pittsburgh, in honor of William Pitt, the British Secretary of State, and declares a day of public thanksgiving.

**December 4**—General Forbes and most of the army leave Pittsburgh. Colonel Washington leaves soon after, resigns his commission and marries Martha Custis. Colonel Bouquet meets with western Delaware Indian leaders and then marches east, leaving a small winter garrison under the command of Pennsylvania Colonel Hugh Mercer.

**January 17, 1759**—General Forbes arrives in Philadelphia.

**March 11**—General Forbes dies and is buried, with full military honors, in the chancel of Christ Church, Philadelphia.

# CONTENTS

# Preface

Even at highway speeds, people who gaze out from car windows as they follow Route 30 across Pennsylvania have no trouble finding tranquility in the companionable countryside that unfolds between Lancaster and Pittsburgh. For the Scots-Irish, German, Scots, and English farmers who lived there in the mid 18th century, however, the region seemed anything but tranquil. From the fall of 1755 through the end of 1758, in particular, they saw it as a landscape of terror.

Indian attacks made it so, and the fear that consumed the region's settlers during those years arose from the chaotic way that whites had intruded into Indian country in the previous decades. For a quarter-century after the founding of Pennsylvania, William Penn had purchased lands between the Delaware and the Susquehanna Rivers from the area's native chiefs in a fair, peaceful, and orderly fashion, then re-sold it to farmers through his land office. This policy, which encouraged immigration and produced the highest population growth rate ever seen in North America, lasted from 1683 until 1712, when Penn's health crumpled under a series of strokes. He died six years later, and his heirs squabbled over who would control the province for another sixteen; during that whole time the orderly acquisition of land from the Indians fell into abeyance. Meanwhile immigrants continued to arrive in unstoppable waves, and simply appropriated whatever lands suited them. By the mid-1720s they were carving farms out of Indian hunting grounds west of the Susquehanna, where William Penn had solemnly promised that whites would never settle.

Over the next quarter-century squatters created farmsteads in isolated "coves" throughout the maze of central Pennsylvania's valleys. Indian warriors allied with the French first raided those vulnerable farmsteads in the autumn of 1755, following General Edward Braddock's failed attempt to drive the French from their stronghold at the Forks of the Ohio, Fort Duquesne. Panic radiated outward with the refugees as they fled farms, hamlets, and trading posts, spreading eastward to York and Lancaster; soon it gripped Philadelphia itself. For three long years thereafter, Indian warriors appeared like wraiths from the forest to attack and burn farmsteads, and even the forts that the province had erected to protect them. With the exception of a single counterstroke in the summer of 1756 – an assault on Kittanning, an Indian town on the Allegheny River, which merely intensified retaliatory raids thereafter – the government of Pennsylvania was helpless to respond.

This was the military situation that Brigadier General John Forbes met when he arrived in Philadelphia in April 1758. A fifty-year-old Scot whose fortune could be better reckoned in ambition than pounds sterling, Forbes had served as regimental surgeon in the Scots Greys (the Second Royal North British Dragoons) before he purchased a cavalry commission in that same regiment in 1735. Since then he had grown into an experienced and prudent commander.

Above all he was determined not to repeat the catastrophe that General Braddock had suffered three years before.

Braddock's great errors, Forbes thought, had been to scorn Indian allies and to hasten his march against Fort Duquesne. The former had denied him scouts, and hence intelligence concerning the French and their native allies; the latter meant that he was roughly a hundred miles from the nearest English fort when an Indian and French force half the size of his own destroyed his command on July 9, 1755. Forbes, therefore, intended to make his march across Pennsylvania in the form of a "protected advance," building a road to carry matériel and reinforcements forward and studding it with blockhouses and four substantial forts – Loudoun, Littleton, Bedford, Ligonier – where his troops could regroup in the event they suffered a blow like the one that had fallen on Braddock.

No less important than this protected advance, however, was Forbes' determination to build and utilize alliances with Indians in support of his expedition. To everyone's surprise he did this by forging an alliance with Israel Pemberton, a Quaker grandee who had withdrawn from Pennsylvania politics rather than violate his pacifist principles. In 1756 Pemberton had founded the *Friendly Association for Regaining and Preserving Peace with the Indians by Pacific Measures* to open a diplomatic channel to French-allied Indians on the Ohio, in the hope of encouraging them to make peace. In this he had worked with Teedyuscung, the chief of a Delaware band at Shamokin (modern Sunbury) who had left the warpath in 1757, and with a Moravian missionary named Christian Frederick Post who had married into the Delaware people. Teedyuscung approached the French-allied Delawares on the Ohio, inviting them to send a chief to a peace conference sponsored by Pennsylvania at Easton in the fall of 1758. At Easton that chief, Pisquetomen, agreed to ask his people to withdraw from their alliance with the French in return for Britain's promise to prohibit white settlement beyond the Alleghenies. The preliminary terms of the Treaty of Easton were completed on October 25; soon thereafter Pisquetomen and Post returned to the Ohio in order to urge the Indians there to ratify the agreement.

Meanwhile Forbes continued to build his road, complete with forts and blockhouses, westward from Lancaster. Impetuous subordinate officers did everything they could to speed up what seemed to them a glacial pace: Colonel George Washington of the First Virginia Regiment urged Forbes to abandon his chosen route for Braddock's old road, and Major James Grant launched an unauthorized surprise attack on Fort Duquesne and suffered a stunning defeat as a result. Notwithstanding these insubordinations Forbes remained steadfast, moved all the more deliberately, and waited for Pisquetomen and Post to complete their diplomatic overtures. When they at last succeeded, the French had no choice but to withdraw. John Forbes finished his road and quietly took possession of the ruins of Fort Duquesne on November 25. Three months later, he was dead.

He had been dying by degrees since June, from what may have been stomach cancer. During the last stages of the advance he became so weak that he had to be carried to Fort Duquesne on a litter. His fortitude earned him the admiration of his subordinates, and this comment in the *Pennsylvania Gazette's* obituary:

> As an Officer, he was quick to discern useful Men, and useful Measures, generally seeing both at first View, but open to Information and Council; in Command he had Dignity, without Superciliousness, and tho' perfectly Master of the Forms, never hesitated to drop them, when the Spirit, and more essential Parts of the Service, required it.

Most of all he had not hesitated to drop the conventional view that wars can, or should, be decided by force alone. Because he had had the courage to trust pacifists and Indians who wanted peace, the wisdom to pursue diplomacy, and the persistence to continue building his road, Forbes won his greatest victory without firing a shot.

Forbes' success in 1758, of course, did not produce an enduring peace. The thousands of settlers who streamed west over the road after the war scorned the promises made at Easton to leave the land beyond the Alleghenies to the Indians. Their aggressive behavior helped provoke Pontiac's War and yet another devastation of the Pennsylvania frontier. During the Revolution western Pennsylvania would suffer yet another calamitous Indian war. Eight decades later a farm town near Forbes' road, Gettysburg, became the site both of the battle that marked the turning point of the Civil War and the address by which Abraham Lincoln gave that conflict transcendent meaning. Finally, when United Flight 93 crashed less than three miles from the original trace of the road in the borough of Shanksville, on September 11, 2001, Americans stood reminded that even the most placid landscape can still become, in all too brief a moment, a scene of shocking destruction and terror.

These events can perhaps provide a productive context for understanding Forbes' achievements today. Because he understood the terrorist violence that confronted him less as a problem that could be resolved by killing his enemies than by understanding them, he took enormous care to investigate what course to pursue before he set out on it, learning from past experience and ruling out nothing as a potential solution. Fundamentally his answer was to approach his enemies as human beings to be understood, not savages to be annihilated. As a result he found a way to conclude a conflict that was impossible to resolve by military force alone.

What happened after Forbes accomplished his mission illustrates the ironies of historical outcomes. The last thing he intended for his road was that it should become the main avenue along which white settlers would pour into the West and dispossess Indians of their lands, but that was precisely what happened, and Pittsburgh became the jumping-off point for the conquest of the Ohio Valley. He could not have imagined that Britain's post-war attempts to control its unruly settlers and impose fiscal and territorial order on its newly expanded empire would drive hitherto-patriotic colonists into rebellion, but that was what happened, too. The result of that rebellion – a new nation united by common allegiance to political values of equality and freedom – would surely have struck Forbes as the most astonishing outcome of all.

The Revolution that Forbes' old subordinate George Washington led transformed British colonists into Americans and created a nation where the pursuit of happiness and the quest for power intertwined at every stage of its subsequent development. It was Lincoln's genius, at Gettysburg, to define the struggle to preserve the Union at its moment of greatest peril as a defense of the Revolutionary principles of liberty, equality, and government by the consent of the people. And it remains our struggle today to confront the challenge of a new war in such a way as to preserve our national security without sacrificing the principles that have made us the people we are.

In this sense there may be no better time than the present to visit the Forbes Road and the sites of memory that line its path through some of the loveliest countryside in Pennsylvania, and indeed in the nation. In doing so we can acquaint ourselves with a man of extraordinary moral courage, who ended an intractable frontier war by building a road to his enemies' homeland and offering them peace. Perhaps we who travel that route can find cause there to hope that the troubles of the present day, so seemingly intractable, may also be susceptible of resolution. If so, John Forbes could have no more fitting memorial than the road that bears his name.

Fred Anderson
University of Colorado, Boulder

# The Cast Of Characters in 1758

## British Military Leaders

**Brigadier General John Forbes, 50 (1707-1759)** British generals have long considered Forbes one of the best staff officers in the army, but the perceptive, hard-working Scot now has his own command in Pennsylvania. Trained as a physician, he suspects his health may cast a shadow over this career-making opportunity.

**Lieutenant Colonel Henry Bouquet, 39 (1719-1765)** Swiss-born professional soldier Bouquet has been fighting for European armies from Holland to Sardinia. Now, he is hired out to the British and will become a frontier hero.

**Sir John St. Clair, (d. 1767)** The energetic Scottish quartermaster has been in America for three years, collecting men, equipment and supplies for the British army. Sir John may be a peer of the realm but he lacks the tact and common sense to get things done.

**Major James Grant, 38 (1720-1806)** A portly and popular veteran Highland officer, Grant, the Laird of Ballindollach, is a Scottish aristocrat. His vaunted military experience will fail him in the Pennsylvania forest.

## Colonial Military Leaders

**Colonel George Washington, 26 (1732-1799)** Bold, charismatic, and robust, Washington has been a frontier soldier for four years. After this campaign, he plans to retire from military service, marry a rich widow and become a prosperous Virginia planter.

**Colonel John Armstrong, 41 (1717-1795)** An engineer and surveyor by trade, Armstrong is one of the immigrant Irish and Scottish leaders in frontier Cumberland County. He and several brothers have settled in the growing village of Carlisle and are fighting the French and Indians.

**Colonel James Burd, 32 (1726-1793)** Shippensburg is the home base of this Scottish immigrant who has married into the influential Shippen family and is managing their frontier properties. A capable engineer, Burd has built roads and forts for the war effort and will play a major role in the Forbes Campaign.

**Colonel Hugh Mercer, 32 (1726-1777)** A physician who fled his troubled Scottish homeland, Mercer has found a haven tending sick on the Pennsylvania frontier. Now fighting French and Indians, Mercer is destined to move to Virginia and join a future rebellion.

## Native Americans

**The Delaware Nations** Split by colonial settlements on ancestral lands, there are two nations of Delaware Indians. Villages in the east are on lands north of Philadelphia while more villages are in the Ohio Valley of western Pennsylvania.

> **Teedyuscung, 58 (ca.1700-1763)** Big and impressive, Teedyuscung has recently burst on the scene as a self-proclaimed "King." Allied with the peace-seeking Quakers, he is negotiating a permanent reserve for his eastern Delawares on a branch of the Susquehanna River.

> **Three Brothers**
> **Pisquetomen (b. ca. 1700)**
> **Tamaqua (Beaver) (d. 1769)**
> **Shingas (d. 1763-64)**
> The three principal leaders of the Western Delawares moved to the Ohio Valley decades ago to escape European settlers. Recently allied with the French in fierce attacks on frontier settlements, they are rumored to be seeking peace talks with the English.

**The Cherokee Nation** Powerbrokers among Indian nations in southeastern America, Cherokee war parties have come to Pennsylvania to help the British fight the French and traditional Indian enemies. Their long, bumpy relationship with the redcoats will soon erupt into all out war.

**The Iroquois Confederacy** The six allied nations across western New York have the dominant Native American Council Fire in the region. Officially neutral in the French and Indian struggle, the Iroquois want their chain of influence to continue among client Indian nations in Pennsylvania.

## Pennsylvanians

**Benjamin Franklin, 52 (1706-1790)** The Philadelphia Renaissance man is a printer, politician, scientist, city father and, briefly, a colonel in the French and Indian War. Franklin has recently sailed to London and will spend much of the rest of his long career as a diplomat in Europe.

**Israel Pemberton, Jr., 43 (1715-1779)** Philadelphia Quaker merchants have controlled Pennsylvania politics for generations. Now, led by the high-minded and fervent Pemberton, they are seeking peace with all the Indian nations.

**Christian Frederick Post, 48 (1710-1785)** The unassuming German-born Moravian missionary is a true friend of Native Americans. He will soon be chosen for a dangerous, history-changing mission to Indian Country.

**Conrad Weiser, 62 (1696-1760)** The German immigrant is a revered founder of the Pennsylvania County of Berks and Borough of Reading. After decades of tireless efforts to promote peace between settlers and Native Americans, Weiser is caught up in the brutal frontier war both as a soldier and a diplomat.

**George Croghan, 38 (1720-1782)** Well-known on the Pennsylvania frontier as a shifty Indian trader and agent, Croghan is the master of the land deal. The tough and determined Irish immigrant, however, is unmatched as an Indian negotiator.

**The Reverend Thomas Barton, 28 (ca. 1730-1780)** The idealistic Anglo-Irish missionary has come to Pennsylvania to spread the Anglican faith among settlers and, hopefully, Indian nations. Instead, for the moment, he is an army chaplain and keen observer of the Forbes Campaign.

## A French Frontier Commander

**François-Marie le Marchand de Lignery, 55 (1703-1759)** The son of a respected frontier soldier, Lignery is, himself, a French Canadian veteran of campaigns throughout the Great Lakes and Ohio Valley. His perilous task is to defend a humble fort at the edge of the French Empire in North America.

*Two major characters in the 1758 General Forbes Campaign meet in September at Fort Cumberland, Maryland. Virginia Colonel George Washington, here with Lieutenant Colonel George Mercer, gives army chaplain and diarist Thomas Barton "a very polite reception and generous, hospitable entertainment."*

# How to Use this Book

*Pennsylvania's Forbes Trail* is a map to America's first road west. Following the famous route through the state's ridges and valleys, its geography and history, its wild places and its unique cities, it's also a compelling contemporary story.

In 1758, General John Forbes and his fearless troops—including a young George Washington—hacked their way through mountains and wilderness to claim North America for the British. The 18th and 21st centuries are the bookends for this unique historic travel guide. Two maps begin and end the tale, showing how Forbes' 300-mile path helped define Pennsylvania. The Scull map, on the inside front cover, directed pre-Revolutionary settlers along the British army's route from the sophisticated city of Philadelphia to the wild Forks of the Ohio, now Pittsburgh. The satellite image on the inside back cover shows the original Forbes route today, now linking major cities, college towns, and county seats.

Forbes followed existing roads west as far as Carlisle. There, his army proceeded by clearing a path through dense woods to the Forks. Throughout this book, the **Forbes Trail** refers to General Forbes' route from Philadelphia to the Forks; the **Forbes Road** refers to the actual path cut from Carlisle west by General Forbes' army in 1758.

All the riches of the Forbes Trail can be discovered within a few miles of the Pennsylvania Turnpike and its predecessor, the Lincoln Highway (Route 30). Lancaster and Carlisle, Fort Loudoun and Fort Littleton, and Bedford and Ligonier were outposts for Forbes troops two centuries before they became exits from the highway. Today, they are gateways to the state's most surprising corners. Ideas for weekend getaways and family adventures accompany reports on seven destinations. Chapter maps with icons keyed to attractions help travelers plan itineraries that link the living history of 1758 with museums, outdoor fun, shopping and dining within a short distance. Suggestions for one-of-a-kind inns and restaurants in each area offer a change of pace from standard national brands.

Moving from east to west, each chapter plunges into Pennsylvania in 1758. The historical narrative contains numerous quotes from the 18th century participants, and tells of army life, provincial and international intrigues, and the dangers of "the dark and terrible woods." Vivid illustrations bring to life a cast of memorable characters: Washington learning to be a leader with the British army; Indian leaders like Teedyuscung and Pisquetomen bargaining to save their land; military commanders like Forbes himself, mortally ill but shrewdly guiding a challenging campaign; and diplomats like Christian Frederick Post, the humble German immigrant crisscrossing the frontier to forge a peace treaty.

Another important character in *Pennsylvania's Forbes Trail* is the majestic landscape itself. This guide introduces state parks and forests where

Pennsylvania's rivers and mountains stretch past the horizon, virtually unchanged since Forbes passed by. It directs visitors to places where the original road remains, and tells how today's residents protect its woods, streams and wildlife. *Pennsylvania's Forbes Trail* brings the state's human history and its natural history together.

Over time, many place names have been simplified, with the result that period and modern spelling can differ. For example, the modern town of Fort Loud<u>on</u> was named for the Earl of Loud<u>oun</u>; Fort <u>Little</u>ton was once called Fort <u>Lyttel</u>ton. While maps in the book use the exact spelling of the modern road system for the sake of driving accuracy, within the text we have used consistent spelling to avoid confusion. Careful scholarship, contemporary reporting and superb artwork combine to make *Pennsylvania's Forbes Trail* a lively introduction to the state's past and present.

*Brigadier General John Forbes gave his name to a challenging military campaign and to a remarkable road. As his health failed him, the General "made a willing sacrifice of his own life to what he valued more, the interest of his King and country."*

# Introduction

Before its naming in 1758, Pittsburgh was known as the Forks of the Ohio. The Forks were a spectacular slice of landscape where two rivers, the Allegheny and the Monongahela, joined together and became the mighty Ohio. They were about as far from familiar civilization as Europeans could imagine. They were inhabited by Native Americans who had lived and hunted in the region for thousands of years. Then, in the mid 18th century, with unimaginable consequences, the Forks caught the attention of two warring European empires.

This is the story of how a union of rivers became Pittsburgh. It is a story of how a military road, a trail through rugged mountain forests, created a gateway to the American interior and a path to American independence.

In 1758, Europe was experiencing the Age of Enlightenment. Reason and science were replacing the religious conflicts of previous centuries. An industrial revolution would soon usher in the modern era. There was an explosion of art, music and literature. Denis Diderot was writing his *Encyclopedie* and Samuel Johnson's *Dictionary of the English Language* was three years old. Wolfgang A. Mozart was two, only three years from creating his first musical composition. George Friederic Handel's sixteen-year-old *Messiah* was already a concert standard. Painter William Hogarth was busy lampooning both rich and poor in Georgian England. Francisco Goya, perhaps Spain's greatest painter and an unrelenting chronicler of war's horrors, would begin his career in two years.

The world, in turn, was enduring an age of empire. France and England were in the middle of a hundred year war. The two monarchies had different world views. England was a protestant alliance of king and parliament. Catholic France remained an absolute monarchy. By 1758, their conflict had spread around the globe. The latest collision, called the Seven Years' War in Europe, and known as the French and Indian War in America, became the first world war. Before it was over, both countries and their allies would clash on the high seas, in India, Africa, the Caribbean, and even the Philippines.

This conflict began, unlike its predecessors, in North America. Both France and England had planted far-flung settlements that were now many generations old. The thriving British colonies in America were pinned to the Atlantic coast by a great mountain and forest barrier. French Canada had penetrated and claimed the waterways of the American interior but its population remained small and scattered. A score of Native American nations increasingly felt trapped between the European rivals.

As the English colonies continued to grow and spread, France moved to prevent their access to the west. A fortified life line, from Montreal to the Ohio Valley and down the Mississippi to New Orleans, blocked the British from the American interior. In 1754, the Virginia Colony, intending to establish settlements around the Forks of the Ohio, collided with the French. That summer, a twenty-two-year-old Virginia officer named George Washington was soundly defeated in the nearby mountains. The incident on the American frontier sparked a world war.

Fort Duquesne anchored French interests at the Forks. The English countered in 1755, before the French and Indian War was officially declared, with a 2,000 man army determined to raise the British flag in the Ohio Country. After hacking and scraping a hundred mile road through the mountains, General Edward Braddock and his redcoats suffered a humiliating defeat just eight miles from their Fort Duquesne goal. Braddock was killed and the survivors fled back to the English settlements.

The next two years were ruinous for the British cause in America. Pennsylvania and Virginia, left all but unprotected by Braddock's defeat, suffered a "reign of terror" from French and Indian raiding parties. Setbacks in New York and New England included massacres and more failed campaigns. The French seemed to own all the good leadership, Indian allies, luck and victories. One British general sarcastically admitted that "this part of the world does not abound in good news."

By the end of 1757, English King George II and his ministers had heard enough bad news. A new, effective Secretary of State, William Pitt, the Elder, took up the war efforts. Pitt, the Great Commoner, planned the next steps with his astute, 78-year-old, army commander-in-chief, Lord Ligonier. They focused on America, changing the military leadership and designing an ambitious three-pronged attack on French Canada. One seaborne invasion would go after the great Fortress of Louisbourg at the northern tip of Nova Scotia. Another would press north from Albany, capture French Fort Carillon (Ticonderoga) and continue through Lake Champlain toward Montreal. The southern prong would again cross Pennsylvania with elusive Fort Duquesne and the Forks of the Ohio as its objectives. The Pennsylvania commander, Brigadier General John Forbes, had explicit orders to "clear this province [Pennsylvania] of the enemy." Would 1758 be a year of miracles or would it bring more disappointments?

*Fort Pitt in 1761 at the Forks of the Ohio.*

# *Philadelphia*
## April 22, 1758

*British Commander Brigadier General John Forbes welcomes the first contingent of Highland troops landing at the busy Philadelphia docks. The Highlanders will soon march west to join the army preparing to attack the French at Fort Duquesne.*

# General Forbes Takes Command

Brigadier General John Forbes

Philadelphia's teeming waterfront was attracting even more attention than usual. On Saturday, April 22, 1758, it was worth a walk down the cobblestones of Market Street to gaze at the sight unfolding on the wharf.

Three companies of His Majesty's Highlanders, raw-boned Scots, were stepping on dry land for the first time in months. At the 1746 Battle of Culloden, many of these men had been defeated and branded wild barbarians for rebelling against the British Crown. They were arriving from Scotland by way of Ireland, the first contingent of the 1st Highland Battalion, sent to join the army marching west.

The Highlanders did not arrive in time to be covered by Thursday's edition of the *Pennsylvania Gazette*. Buried on the fourth page of the paper, a single sentence announced the Philadelphia arrival of the "Honourable General John Forbes from New York" on the previous Tuesday, April 18. Forbes was back at the docks on April 22, watching the Highlanders disembark. They, along with the rest of the battalion yet to arrive, would be the backbone of his attack force.

After several years of frontier war, many Philadelphians were eager for a victory over the French. Starting up Market Street from the hustle and bustle of the city docks, the General led his troops past the London Coffee House Tavern and through the raucous crowds in a series of produce, meat, and seafood stands known as the Jersey Stalls. They marched through the Second Street intersection, decorated by the city stocks and dominated by the courthouse and an old Quaker meeting house. They headed toward

the Pennsylvania State House (today's Independence Hall) sporting a brand new (Liberty) bell hanging in its tall brick belfry. Two months later, the General was crossing the Schuylkill River, heading west with his troops. General Forbes and his troops were at the start of a long trail that would change American history.

## Brigadier General John Forbes

Brigadier General John Forbes, a sober and respected staff officer, was assigned the daunting task of chasing the French out of the Ohio Valley. The first attempt, led by General Edward Braddock in 1755, had ended in disaster. Forbes was a practical man with a full plate of responsibilities. He was a field commander, strategist, logistician and diplomat and kept a constant stream of letters flowing to a wide circle of correspondents. John Forbes had the right experience for the job.

He was a child of Scotland, the youngest son of the laird or master of Pittencrieff Estate, near Edinburgh. After studying medicine, the twenty-five-year-old Forbes followed the path of many younger sons and purchased a junior officer's slot in the Scot's Greys Cavalry Regiment. During the 1740s, he proved himself a brave and loyal officer. He fought against his rebellious country men at the Battle of Culloden and his skills as a staff officer and quartermaster caught the attention of the British generals. By 1750, Forbes was a lieutenant colonel. He served on the staffs of Lord Loudoun, Lord Ligonier, even the King's son, the Duke of Cumberland.

In 1757, when his comrade-in-arms, the Earl of Loudoun, was commanding in America, Forbes became colonel of the 17th Regiment of Foot and served as Loudoun's adjutant general in New York. Early in 1758, British army commander Lord Ligonier and Secretary of State William Pitt promoted John Forbes again and tasked him with the final assault on the French in Pennsylvania. A month later, General Forbes was headed for his new command in Philadelphia.

*A blue-coated Royal Artillery officer oversees soldiers and Philadelphia dock workers unloading tons of cannons, ammunition, and equipment from English supply ships.*

## Ben Franklin's City

Twenty-five thousand Philadelphians proudly lived in one of the largest cities in the British Empire. The key to Philadelphia's success was its mile long waterfront, a gateway down the Delaware River to the world. The docks and wharves were a tangle of warehouses, ship's chandlers, rope walks, and distilleries. The benefits of all this seaborne wealth changed the Philadelphia skyline in the 1750s. New spires gave the city a touch of European grandeur.

The Society of Friends (Quakers), dominating Pennsylvania and Philadelphia politics, labored mightily to keep the doors open to all comers. Throngs of Scots-Irish immigrants were moving to the frontier. A flood of Germans, close to 60,000 by the 1750s, began to upset English colonists. Local leader Benjamin Franklin complained "Unless the stream of their importation could be turned they will soon outnumber us. We will not be able to preserve our language." In spite of Franklin's concerns, Germans continued to arrive and a dozen languages could be heard around the city.

Tapping Mr. Franklin's energy, the community was making Philadelphia a modern city. Franklin thought the unpaved streets were a disgrace. "In dry weather the dust was offensive. [After a rain] I saw with pain the inhabitants wading in mud." Using his persuasive gifts, Franklin convinced the city to cover Market Street with paving stones. Whale oil streetlamps soon followed. The city's first citizen sponsored better fire departments, fire insurance, an academy that became the University of Pennsylvania, a charity hospital, a public library, and science clubs. Skilled local craftsmen were among the best in the thirteen colonies. Georgian-style row houses were filling out the lots in Society Hill. The lively arts, painting, social dancing, drama, and instruction in gentlemen's fencing, were the rage while Quakers chided citizens for "embracing all the afflictions of worldliness."

## The Royal Artillery

On June 13, 1758, two long-awaited store ships arrived from England. Dock workers began to offload bronze artillery pieces and hundreds of boxes and barrels of ammunition and equipment. General Forbes needed these supplies to lay siege to French Fort Duquesne.

Eighteenth century artillery pieces were cast from either iron or bronze. The preferred lighter bronze cannons formed the bulk of Forbes' artillery train in 1758. Long-barreled cannons fired either solid iron shot against fortifications or containers of smaller iron balls that produced a devastating shotgun effect against massed troops. Artillerists fired mortars and howitzers at high trajectories, lobbing explosive iron shells over the walls of forts. Howitzers could also be fired horizontally at attacking troops. Eighteenth century European armies categorized their artillery pieces according to ammunition—either by the weight of the solid iron shot in the case of cannons or the diameter of the hollow explosive iron shells fired by howitzers and mortars. The stores that arrived in Philadelphia included four bronze 12-pounder and six bronze 6-pounder fieldpieces, along with a dozen mortars firing a round, explosive, 4½ inch iron shell. A fieldpiece could throw a cannon ball 2000 yards.

An 18th century artillery train was a formidable sight. One hundred and twenty wagons, pulled by five hundred horses, were required to move the Forbes Expedition's artillery, ammunition, and equipment. This essential branch of the army was supervised and manned by a detachment of 37 officers and men of the Royal Regiment of Artillery, founded in 1722. Additional men, trained especially for the task, were drawn from Pennsylvania's provincial troops.

*Not everyone in his army is as enthusiastic about the upcoming campaign as General Forbes.*

*Large Indian council meetings are held outdoors and crowds listen attentively to long, well-crafted speeches, often translated for multi-lingual audiences by interpreters.*

## The Pennsylvania Quakers Search for Peace

William Penn had been persecuted for his Quaker beliefs in 17th century England. As a colonial proprietor with broad powers granted by King Charles II, he brought utopian plans to settle a free colony for all mankind in America. In 1681, Pennsylvania became a pacifist commonwealth that promoted universal brotherhood.

The English called local native people the Delawares, but the Indians called themselves Lenni Lenape, the Real People. They became the first test of Quaker idealism. With great ceremony in 1682, Penn signed a treaty with the Lenni Lenape that would last "as long as the water flows and the sun shines and grass grows." He was determined to treat all Native Americans with fairness. Seventy-five years after the Great Treaty, the Penn family was still in power as European settlers moved west and drove the Indians off their land. The sons of William Penn were involved in the infamous 1737 Walking Purchase, defrauding Delawares of much of their land north of Philadelphia. Many Indians moved to the Ohio Country, dividing the Delaware nation between west and east.

No one illustrated the Quaker world view more than Israel Pemberton, Junior. Thirty-five at mid-century, he was idealistic and hardworking. The charity-minded Mr. Pemberton felt that, with all his merchant wealth, he still lacked the "humility [that is] the foundation of every true Christian's work of religion." Attracted to politics, he was devoted to government by Quaker principles. He remained adamant about Pennsylvania's unique commitment to pacifism. One royal governor remarked that the Society of Friends "measured their merit by the extent of suffering for conscience sake." Philadelphia Friends claimed their just treatment of Indians was working. Thanks to careful diplomacy, they could point to a long peace. Frontier trade was flourishing. Pacifism and brotherly love trumped the need for costly defense.

## Forest Diplomacy

Pennsylvania councils between Indian, British and colonial leaders often took place at public spaces in the State House (later Independence Hall), county courthouses, and open fields. Hundreds of Indian men, women and children traveled from their homes to witness these events. They also drew throngs of colonial onlookers. Native diplomats insisted that their languages and customs be used in council. The most striking visual elements of this diplomacy were wampum and the tobacco peace pipes.

Wampum beads were assembled from the shells of the Quahog clam (for purple) and the Atlantic whelk (for white). Originally produced by Indians living along the coast of Long Island Sound and Narragansett Bay, by the 1750s colonial traders were making wampum in New Jersey and southeastern Pennsylvania for Indian councils and trade. Council speakers exchanged strings of wampum to reinforce talking points. During a March, 1758 meeting with Pennsylvania officials, Delaware Indian leader Teedyuscung presented "a belt of ten rows, which had in the center of it two figures of men taking one another by the hand." The two figures portrayed Teedyuscung and Pennsylvania Governor William Denny. Figures at each end of the belt were "the sun rising and the sun set." The figures of eight men in between were Indian nations that had agreed to make peace.

At the opening of this council, Teedyuscung employed the calumet or peace pipe. The pipes had elegantly-carved stone bowls and elaborately-decorated yard-long wooden stems. After filling the bowl of a calumet sent by western nations seeking peace with the British, the Delaware leader lit it and smoked before passing it to Governor Denny. Indians believed that the curling wisps of smoke rising to the room's ceiling would drive away the clouds that threatened peace.

## Braddock's Defeat Threatens the Pennsylvania Frontier

In 1755, General Edward Braddock's redcoat army marched confidently west to claim the Forks of the Ohio but found death and destruction at the hands of the French and Indians. As chastened military survivors hastened east to Philadelphia, a flood of French and Indian attacks on frontier settlements followed them. Pennsylvania Royal Governor Robert Hunter Morris squabbled with the Provincial Assembly about how to meet the threat. A band of terrified, angry settlers threatened to march on the capital, spurring the government to action.

Benjamin Franklin helped guide an emergency frontier defense. He cajoled the Assembly into passing a militia bill, a very American solution that advocated short term enlistments, elected officers, and built a chain of forts. Franklin was suddenly in the "military business though I did not conceive myself well-qualified for it." He led some troops out to the frontier north of Philadelphia and designed wooden stockades with his usual probing intellect, calling his forts "contemptible, [but] sufficient defense against Indians who have no cannon." Franklin, soon to sail to England, generally enjoyed the short time of his "colonelship" except when his troops saluted him by firing their muskets outside his house, breaking some of his glass scientific instruments.

All of these calls to defense did not sit well with the Quakers. Israel Pemberton despaired as events "produced a greater and more fatal change among us as a society than seventy preceding years." He could not conceive of a situation that made peace negotiations impossible.

The French-led surprise frontier attacks, cruelly effective in spreading terror, continued in 1756. Settlers were randomly captured and scalped without warning. They withdrew to their emergency shelters, only to see their homes and crops ravaged. Pennsylvania's long chain of rude stockade forts, many just palisades around log cabins, was fatally ineffective. Philadelphia and Lancaster filled up with refugees. The war zone was vast and dangerously unpredictable and few trained troops were available. Who was to pay for the growing cost of colonial defense? The situation was destructive, intractable and depressing.

## The Quakers Find an Indian Partner

While the Pennsylvania government was offering bounties for Indian scalps, Israel Pemberton searched for anyone who could give him hope for peace. He found that man in Conrad Weiser, a veteran Pennsylvania Indian agent. Weiser suggested some Indian diplomats who might take peace offers to the eastern Delawares north of Philadelphia. Pemberton invited Indian leaders to a series of dinner parties at his home. He gave them a large white wampum belt of peace with the wish that "your people [the Indians] still have a love and regard for their old friends [the Pennsylvanians]."

Pemberton soon heard that an unsung Delaware headman named Teedyuscung was in the Moravian settlement of Bethlehem waiting to talk to the governor. The Quakers wasted no time seizing on the hopeful signs. In early July, 1756, a Friends meeting created a new organization, the *Friendly Association for Regaining and Preserving Peace with the Indians by Pacific Measures.* After dragging his feet and risking a lost opportunity, the indecisive Governor Morris traveled north to meet with Teedyuscung later in July. The Quakers, forty strong with wagonloads of presents, were already there.

*As a short-lived army colonel, the ever-curious Ben Franklin carefully measures how long it will take to cut down trees for a fort stockade wall.*

*Delaware leader Teedyuscung eagerly discusses his complaints about Pennsylvania's Indian policy with his new found Quaker ally, Israel Pemberton, Jr.*

## Indian Councils at Easton

Teedyuscung, afraid of a trap, moved the meeting to Easton at the Forks of the Delaware River. Governor Morris was suspicious of this Indian leader, who called himself the King of Ten Nations. Ben Franklin, another skeptic who attended the meeting, believed there would never be "a firm peace with the Indians till we have drubbed them."

A much larger council met in November, 1756, with local crowds gaping at the outdoor spectacle. Iroquois leaders attended to investigate the upstart Delaware. The meeting also featured a new Pennsylvania governor. William Denny was an army officer said to have three moods, "a little peevish, peevish, and excessively peevish." Denny saw clearly that the Pennsylvania frontier was in a deplorable situation. Rumors were flying that the Indians would cause trouble, so he rode to Easton with a large military escort.

This week-long second Easton meeting followed the Indian ritual of ceremony, speeches, and pauses for reflection. Emboldened by support from the Quakers, Teedyuscung claimed that the 1737 Walking Purchase had stolen Delaware land. It was a risky ploy, but Pennsylvania wanted peace with the Indians. With piles of gifts, colonial leaders promised to consider trade and restoring hunting lands.

## Delaware "King" Teedyuscung

No one in Philadelphia had heard of Teedyuscung before 1756. Born about 1700, he lived with the eastern or Wyoming Delawares on a branch of the Susquehanna River. Caught between the powerful Iroquois nations to the north, and depending more and more on white settlers who had invaded their lands, the eastern Delawares needed nimble diplomacy to survive the frontier war that erupted in 1755.

Filled with swagger and braggadocio, Teedyuscung impressed colonial leaders. One Quaker said his name meant "He who makes the Earth tremble" and he lived up to that billing. The Delaware leader was imposing, lusty and well spoken. The Quakers were certain they had found a partner for peace. Teedyuscung rode boldly to meetings wearing long boots, a billowing brown coat with gold lace and checkered breeches. Other Indians complained that he was turning into a white man. He took to calling himself the King of Ten Nations much to the surprise of the Iroquois and other Indian neighbors.

Teedyuscung, however, had a potentially fatal flaw. One Indian agent who found Teedyuscung "haughty and very desirous of respect and command" also reported that "he can drink three quarts or a gallon of rum a day without being drunk." He was known to carry a bottle in each pocket of his breeches. Often in his cups, he could be surly and incomprehensible. He was an unreliable ally but, without him, Pennsylvania had little chance for peace with the Delaware Nation.

*Redcoat Highland soldiers bring curious customs, like wrapping themselves in kilts of heavy plaid wool, to the Pennsylvania frontier.*

## The Highland Scots

The citizens of Philadelphia were treated to an unusual sight on Tuesday, June 13, 1758. The newly-arrived battalion of more than one thousand British redcoats went through the maneuvers of loading, firing, and marching. The low rumbling of drums, the shouting of sergeants, and the martial airs of the soldiers impressed the spectators.

The *Pennsylvania Gazette's* reference to "the novelty of their dress" hinted at the unusual character of Lieutenant Colonel Archibald Montgomery's 1st Highland Battalion, raised in Scotland the previous year. Together with another Highland regiment, the 42nd "Black Watch," Montgomery's corps contained many men for whom English was a second language. Most Highlanders still spoke the ancient Gaelic language of their forbearers. Unlike other British soldiers, these troops were clothed in a version of the traditional Highland military dress: short coats, kilts and bonnets. Their arms included a heavy, iron-hilted sword fashionable among their countrymen. The high-pitched skirl of bagpipes urged them on to fight on the battlefield.

It was no accident that Britain's Highland regiments were in North America in 1758. Highland Scots were politically suspect, having participated in several rebellions against the crown since 1688. One English general advocated their service in America because they were "hearty, intrepid, accustomed to a rough country, and no great mischief if they fall. How can you better employ a secret enemy than by making his end conducive to the common good?" Such sentiments were unfair, for Highland Scots had risked their lives to defend King George II. Many of these same men would lose their lives in the upcoming struggle to take possession of the Forks of the Ohio.

*An officer of His Majesty's Highland troops fully-dressed for General Forbes' review.*

## Preparing for War in the City of Brotherly Love

As Indian negotiations continued into 1758, General John Forbes was in urgent need of colonial funds, troops, wagons and supplies for his campaign. The General wrote royal governors seeking their support. After a week in Philadelphia, he was feeling very alone in "this damned troublesome place." He was waiting for orders and was "almost wore out in writing, as I am here entirely alone, without any assistance." Forbes began a series of informative letters to English Secretary of State William Pitt, the architect of the American offensive so "no time may be lost in informing His Majesty of the progress of his affairs."

## The Forbes Team

At 6,000 plus, the planned Forbes strike force was triple the size of General Braddock's 1755 army. When it came together out at Raystown (Fort Bedford), it would be one of the largest communities in Pennsylvania. The backbone would be the royal troops. Colonel Archibald Montgomery's 1st Highland Battalion would be joined by soldiers from the Royal Americans, the 60th Regiment of Foot. Three companies of the Royal Americans assigned to Pennsylvania during the past two years were now headed for New York. Four other Royal American companies, with Lieutenant Colonel Henry Bouquet in command, were coming to Pennsylvania from South Carolina. The rest of the army was being cobbled together from provincial troops raised for the campaign. Pennsylvania would provide three battalions, Virginia two, with Maryland, Delaware and North Carolina providing a few hundred men each.

The team effort required for the campaign was massive. The most direct and practical route would be selected through grueling terrain. Tons of supplies would be moved in stages to a collecting point as close as possible to Fort Duquesne. The maximum number of men would march through the hostile environment, often facing bad weather, to the best point of attack. Finally, the clock was ticking. Winter could halt the 1758 assault on the Forks of the Ohio.

## General Forbes Sets Some Priorities

General Forbes had two priorities to avoid the fatal mistakes of the Braddock Campaign. The first was a careful, methodical advance. General Braddock had used an 18th century version of a quick strike. Dividing his force, he carved out a hundred mile frontier road with a portion of the army he called his flying column. Braddock's defeat, however, was so complete that panic set in, leaving the frontier totally unprotected. Forbes had been studying the work of the French officer Comte Turpin de Crisse, who advocated a protected advance in his 1754 book, *Essay on the Art of War*. The new General would gradually advance his army between stockaded camps forty miles apart, leapfrogging supplies with small wagons and packhorses.

## Indian Allies

The other priority was recruiting Indian allies. General Braddock had failed in his attempts to attract friendly Delawares to his side. Effective Indian scouts and fighters were life-savers in the woods. The unfortunate truth for the British was that few Indians in the region were allies.

General Forbes had two options. The first was Cherokee war parties from South Carolina already ranging in Pennsylvania. In spite of past differences, a recent treaty was bringing Cherokee warriors from the south to help the British war effort. The Cherokees, however, had different cultural attitudes toward war-making. They were frustrated with a British campaign that was agonizingly slow.

Another option was a calculated risk. Following the Easton councils of 1756, there was a well-attended Indian conference at Easton during the hot summer of 1757. The talks ended with a dramatic exchange of the white wampum belts of peace between the Pennsylvania Governor and Teedyuscung. Israel Pemberton and Forbes held meetings after the General arrived in Philadelphia. Pemberton explained that he, the Quakers' Friendly Association and Governor Denny had been busy promoting peace with Teedyuscung. Pemberton wanted to build the peace breakthrough into a diplomatic mission to the Ohio Valley Indian nations. Forbes listened carefully. On May 3, 1758, the General told Governor Denny that Teedyuscung "has the public faith for the making of such a settlement [with the Ohio Valley Indians]."

## War or Peace?

In late June, two men arrived unheralded in Philadelphia. Pisquetomen was a veteran western Delaware leader. He had joined the French in their attacks on Pennsylvania settlements but was now in the east to discuss peace. His companion was Christian Frederick Post, a German Moravian missionary who had lived and married within the Indian nations. Together, this unusual team would soon bolster Teedyuscung's claims that the English could find peace with all the Delaware Indians.

Another military commander, over 300 miles to the west, was also concerned about Indian allies. François de Lignery was the commander of Fort Duquesne, the four-year-old outpost at the Forks of the Ohio. The garrison was always undermanned and the supply lines from Montreal and Illinois were long and precarious. Indian allies had been a key to the fort's success. Using their authority along with gifts and trade, the French had created an alliance with nations in the upper Great Lakes. Every season, Indian allies paddled and carried their canoes hundreds of miles to reinforce the Ohio Valley defenses. Lignery was more concerned about the local Shawnee and Delaware nations that appeared to be tiring of the French occupation. Could this tiny fort on the edge of the French Empire withstand another British assault?

*Indian warriors, allies of the French from the Great Lakes, wear war paint and decoration said by one British observer to have "something in it both romantic and terrible."*

# Finding the Forbes Road

General Forbes' itinerary first carried him and his entourage along the 18th century Great Road from Philadelphia to the burgeoning country town of Lancaster. Two and a half centuries of growth and development have transformed Philadelphia and its hinterland, but one can still follow Forbes' footsteps in this area. Known as Lancaster Avenue or Old Lancaster Road, the historic route now traverses the affluent Main Line suburbs of Ardmore, Haverford, and Bryn Mawr. Today's travelers will note many stately stone taverns along the route, some of them dating back to the early 18th century —a sure sign that one has not strayed from Forbes' path in 1758.

After passing the Susquehanna River at Harrisburg (site of the 18th century ferry crossing established by Indian trader John Harris) and driving west from Carlisle, today's historic road-hunters who keep a close eye on the landscape can see how topography shaped the route that Forbes' army ultimately took to the Forks of the Ohio River. A leisurely drive along the Forbes Trail from Fort Loudoun to Bedford, in particular, reveals the formidable challenge of laying out a road that snaked its way over and around the numerous ridges of the Allegheny Mountains. Cowans Gap State Park (www.dcnr.state.pa.us/StateParks/parks/cowansgap.aspx), located just a short drive from Fort Loudoun, is a great place to park the car and take a hike in a forested settling that evokes 1758. The army's 1758 route passed through Cowans Gap at this spot, roughly following the present day Stumpy Lane and State Route 1005.

Travelers rushing west on the Pennsylvania Turnpike can catch a dramatic bird's eye view (weather permitting) of the seemingly endless Allegheny Mountains as they crest the ridge just east of Breezewood, the famous "Town of Motels." In 1758, Forbes' army crossed the ridge at this precise point, although many feet higher. Toll road construction in the mid 20th century created an artificial gap in the mountain here, but the view of the mountainous landscape would be familiar to Forbes' army.

In western Pennsylvania, many sections of the Forbes Road are still in use as township or secondary roads, like the one running through the center of Westmoreland County's Historic Hanna's Town site. History buffs can walk along an undeveloped, carefully preserved section of the Forbes Road in Allegheny County's Boyce Park. Recently marked by a group of dedicated volunteers from the Allegheny Foothills Historical Society (www.plumhistory.org), this deeply rutted road scar can be accessed by turning off Pierson Run Road near the Carpenter Log House.

*pg. 22, left to right, Past generations have erected signs and monuments marking the route of the Forbes Road. This marker is in the Laurel Highlands near Ligonier; over the last 2½ centuries, the 1745 General Warren Inne has been welcoming travelers on the Forbes Trail. General Forbes passed by and may have stopped here in 1758. Many colonial buildings still survive and prosper on the trail the General followed across Pennsylvania.*

*pg 23, top two images, Remnants of the twenty-foot wide Forbes Road and eroded dirt redoubts are still visible in the Laurel Highlands. bottom image, Three generations of roads have climbed over Ray's Hill in the Allegheny Mountains at this spot. In 1758, the Forbes Road needed switchbacks to get over the steep slope. In the 1900s, U.S. Route 30, just visible through the trees, was replaced by the Pennsylvania Turnpike that cuts straight through the mountain toward Breezewood, the Juniata River Crossing, and the mountain gaps that lead to Bedford.*

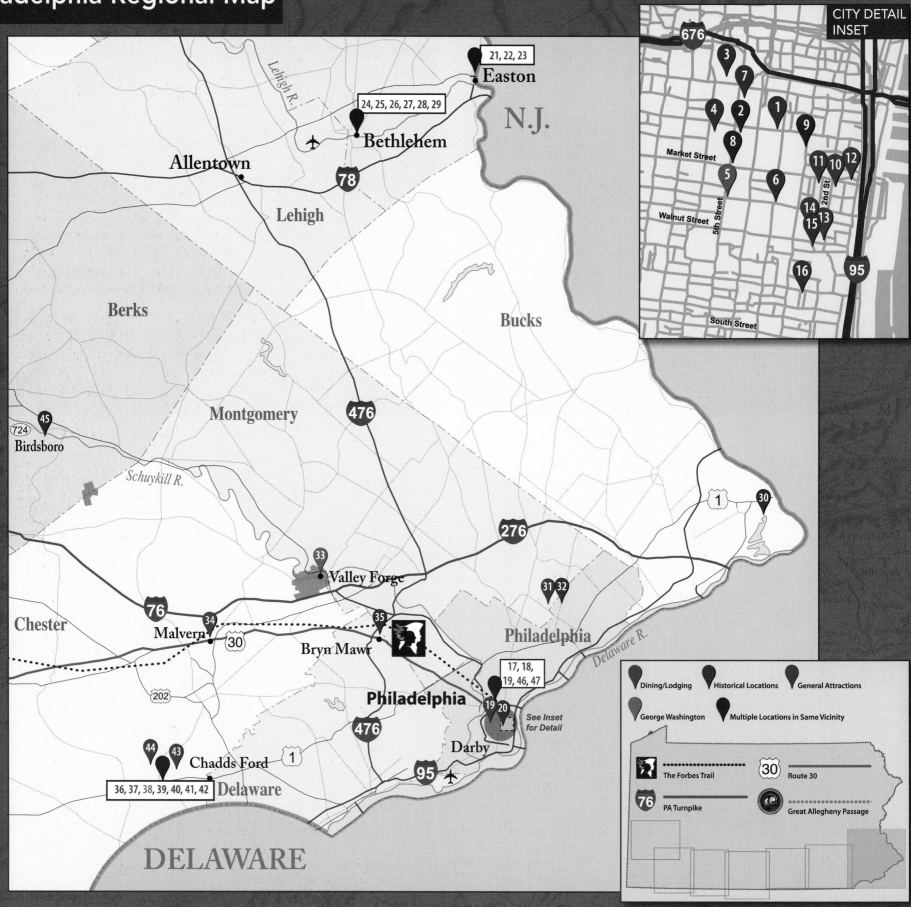

# Philadelphia Regional Map

**CITY DETAIL INSET**

N.J.

Easton — 21, 22, 23

24, 25, 26, 27, 28, 29 — Bethlehem

Allentown

Lehigh

78

Berks

Bucks

724 — 45

Birdsboro

Schuykill R.

Montgomery

476

1

30

276

33 — Valley Forge

31 32

76

34

Malvern

30

35

Bryn Mawr

Philadelphia

Philadelphia

Delaware R.

17, 18, 19, 46, 47
See Inset for Detail

202

19 20

Darby

476

95

44 43 — Chadds Ford

36, 37, 38, 39, 40, 41, 42 — Delaware

Chester

1

DELAWARE

## City Detail Inset

676

3
7
4 2 1
9
8
11 10 12
Market Street
5 6
5th Street
2nd St
14
15 13
Walnut Street
16
95
South Street

## Legend

- Dining/Lodging
- Historical Locations
- General Attractions
- George Washington
- Multiple Locations in Same Vicinity

- The Forbes Trail
- 30 — Route 30
- 76 — PA Turnpike
- Great Allegheny Passage

## Visiting Philadelphia

When General Forbes landed in Philadelphia in 1758, it was already one of the largest cities in the British Empire. Today it's a vibrant city of 1.4 million, but it has never forgotten its roots. Thanks to the original street grid, it's still easy to find your way by foot at the beginning of the Forbes Trail. The Old City along the Delaware River is a surprising, living neighborhood that rewards investigation.

Before independence, Philadelphia was a prosperous city with a Quaker flavor. You can see the landmarks that Forbes would have passed—and the one where he remains—starting at Front and Market Streets.

*The spire of Christ Church rises over Old City Philadelphia.*

# See 1758 Today

The **Delaware Chief Tamanend** still stands regally, in statue form, here at the waterfront on Market Street, with his back to the attractions of Penn's Landing. Revered in the days before independence as "the patron saint of America," he shared his friend William Penn's vision of peace between the Indians and the English (his admirers founded the society later known, more notoriously, as Tammany Hall). Dozens of Quaker meeting houses still stand in the region. Among the oldest is the spacious **Arch Street Friends Meeting House**[1] (320 Arch Street, Philadelphia; 215-627-2667; www.archstreetfriends.org). Still in regular use, the meeting house profiles Pennsylvania's founder in "Penn the Peacemaker." The small permanent exhibit explains how Penn's ideals shaped not only the thinking of the Founding Fathers, but even the language of the Declaration of Independence. The **Liberty Bell**[8], now on display next to **Independence Hall**[5], emphasizes Penn's impact. It was cast in 1751 to honor his Charter of Privileges, and rung at the first public reading of the Declaration of Independence on July 8, 1776. Get an overview of Penn's visionary urban design for the city at **Welcome Park**[15]: the plaza at Second and Walnut Streets offers a one-block version of the plan, along with a timeline of Penn's tumultuous life. The famous three-story inn just across the street is **City Tavern**[13], the city's social center in the 1770s (138 South Second Street, Philadelphia; 215-413-1443; www.citytavern.com). Today, the authentically restored tavern still serves colonial fare like venison and rabbit.

Among the low red brick structures of Old City, it's easy to pick out the tall white steeple of **Christ Church**[9], at Second Street north of Market (20 North American Street, Philadelphia; 215-922-1695; www.christchurchphila.org). Walk through its shady churchyard and into the sanctuary, and the story of the Forbes Expedition comes full circle.

Upon his death in Philadelphia on March 11, 1759, John Forbes was buried with full military honors beneath the sanctuary. His remains lie near the wall plaque that praises the general, who "in defiance of disease and numberless obstructions, brought to happy issue a most extraordinary campaign." Other notables like Benjamin Franklin are buried here and at the Church's larger **Burial Ground**[2], two blocks north. Founded in 1695, the Anglican church was a meeting place for Philadelphia's most powerful and well-connected early residents, including the Washingtons and skeptic Ben Franklin. One wag describes Christ Church as "the great non-Quaker yuppie church of 18th century Philadelphia." Now an Episcopalian church, its doors are open to all.

Grocers have sold fresh food at the corner of Second and Pine Streets since 1745; General Forbes probably passed under these brick arcades. Originally dubbed "The Shambles," meaning butcher's lane, it is still used as a Sunday farmers market in good weather. Now better known as **Head House Square**[16], for the nearby 1805 firehouse, this is one of the city's coolest pub and dining scenes. South Street anchors the neighborhood, offering rock shows, boutiques, and cheese steaks.

Follow General Forbes by heading west along Market Street to cross the Schuylkill River. Lancaster Avenue is the primary route through the Main Line, the suburbs named for the passenger railroad along Route 30. The road passes **Harriton House**[35], a 1704 Quaker estate that was an early tobacco plantation (500 Harriton Road, Bryn Mawr; 610-525-0201; www.harritonhouse.org). Continue to the village of Malvern and the **General Warren Inne**[34] (16 Village Way, Old Lancaster Road, Malvern; 610-296-3637; www.generalwarren.com). When Forbes rode by, this hostelry was already thirteen years old. Today it operates as an elegant small hotel and restaurant, still displaying its original 1745 deed.

*pg. 26, Philadelphia's Elfreth's Alley is the nation's oldest continually inhabited street.*

## George Washington Was Here

Philadelphia's Old City was the scene of George Washington's greatest victories and most notable defeats. It is still a living part of downtown, creating an irreverent mix of old and new. International tourists mingle with kids on skateboards, commuters on bikes, and locals clad in woolen jackets, perukes and knee breeches. The latter are interpreters at Independence National Historical Park, which comprises a dozen historic sites in the neighborhood. To visit landmarks like Independence Hall and the National Constitution Center, start your visit right between them, at the **Independence Visitor Center**[4] (1 North Independence Mall West, Sixth and Market Streets, Philadelphia; 800-537-7676; www.independencevisitorcenter.com). This wonderful free resource welcomes visitors with short films and exhibits, information kiosks, maps, and helpful staff. Pick up timed admission tickets for Independence Hall (reserve online in advance), or board guided city tours here. Popular interactive exhibits fill the vaulting spaces of the **National Constitution Center**[7], with separate ticketing from Park attractions (525 Arch Street, Philadelphia; 215-409-6600; www.constitutioncenter.org).

The **Independence Living History Center**[6], facing the First Bank of the United States, is a lab for recent archeological finds, including excavations at the site of the President's House near Independence Hall (143 South Third

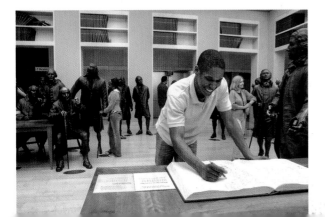

Street, Philadelphia; 215-965-2305; www.nps.gov/inde/ilhc.htm). Artifacts from 1790 focus on Washington's nine household slaves.

Washington's neighborhood haunts include City Tavern and Christ Church, where visitors can sit in the president's family pew. Just steps from the ornate chancel where his former commander, John Forbes, was interred, it offers a place to meditate on the connections between Washington's youthful experiences with the British army and his adult years leading the new nation.

From his summer home as president in Germantown to military encampments at Valley Forge and the Brandywine River, Washington's footsteps extend throughout the region. The visitor center at the **Brandywine Battlefield Historic Site**[38] (1491 Baltimore Pike, Chadds Ford; 610-459-3342; www.ushistory.org) interprets Washington's tactical strategies during the largest engagement of the War for Independence. On September 11, 1777, Washington and James Grant, fellow officers in the Forbes Expedition, faced each other again—as adversaries. Follow the path of the battle through driving tours outlined on the web site.

At **Valley Forge National Historical Park**[33], a short film and interpretive displays at the Welcome Center orient visitors to the 3,600-acre park, the winter encampment, and the war (1400 North Outer Line Drive, King of Prussia; 610-783-1077; www.nps.gov/vafo). Trolley tours depart from the center, which also distributes directions for self-guided driving tours. Look for Blue Spot icons, where visitors can use their cell phones to learn more about their surroundings. Dial and choose from a menu of lively stories, including Washington's political battles and Martha Washington's role here as a hostess.

*pg. 28, The National Constitution Center flanks Independence National Historical Park.*
*pg. 29, clockwise from lower left, The Peter Wentz homestead in Montgomery County served as Washington's headquarters in 1777; Washington summered at Germantown's Deshler-Morris House as president; General Forbes' memorial plaque in Christ Church; the view from the Washington family pew at Christ Church.*

### George Washington and the Long Shadow of the French and Indian War

The Forbes Expedition marked young George Washington's final military command until June 1775 when the Second Continental Congress, meeting in Pennsylvania's State House in Philadelphia, appointed the now 43-year old Washington to command the fledgling Continental Army.

How ironic that just twenty years before, young Washington had wished desperately to become a British officer, laboring tirelessly through five campaigns to instill an *esprits de corps* in his beloved Virginia Regiment. "Discipline is the soul of an army," he reminded his officers shortly before the Forbes Expedition. "It makes small numbers formidable, procures success to the weak, and esteem to all." Faced with the monumental task of transforming the Continental Army into a disciplined fighting force able to stand its ground against the British Army, Washington drew heavily on his French and Indian War experience in the War of American Independence.

The Continental Army included many French and Indian War veterans. Charles Scott, William Woodford, and George Weedon, for example, had all served under Washington in 1758 and later commanded brigades during the Philadelphia Campaign and Valley Forge encampment (1777-78). Washington's general orders of January 28, 1778, during the depths of the Valley Forge winter, struck a familiar chord with men like Scott, Woodford, and Weedon. "Exact discipline and the strictest obedience to orders," Washington exhorted in words that echoed his youthful commands, "(Discipline) is the Soul of an Army and foundation of success." The French and Indian War cast a long shadow, indeed.

BRIG. GEN.
JOHN FORBES
Colonel of the 17th Regt. of Foot
and
Commander of His Majesty's Troops
in the Southern Provinces of
North America.
Born in Petincrief, Fifeshire, Scotland 1710.
Died in Philadelphia March 11th 1759.

Interred in this Chancel.

By a steady pursuit of well conducted
measures in defiance of disease and
numberless obstructions, he brought to
a happy issue a most extraordinary
campaign resulting in the evacuation of
Fort Duquesne, and made a willing sacrifice
of his own life to what he loved more, the
interest of his King and Country.

Erected by the Society of Colonial Wars
in the Commonwealth of Pennsylvania.

# History: Bethlehem, Easton and the Moravians

By 1758, Easton and Bethlehem were established settlements where Indians and Europeans mingled, promised peace—and sometimes clashed. Sixty miles north of Philadelphia, the two neighboring towns, Easton on the Delaware River and Bethlehem on the Lehigh, played major roles in Pennsylvania's pre-revolutionary history.

Thirteen Moravian missionaries arrived in Bethlehem in 1741, naming the town on Christmas Eve. The eight-pointed Moravian

*left to right, The Sun Inn, Bethlehem's 18th century landmark; the Central Moravian Church, built in 1803.*

star tops doorways and shop windows all along Main Street, where walking tours of the community begin at the **Welcome Center**[24] (501-505 Main Street, Bethlehem; 610-691-6055; www.historicbethlehem.org). Turning onto Church Street feels like entering a medieval European village, dominated by the massive domed church.

The German-speaking Moravians were completely self-sufficient, operating 35 industries and producing crafts along the Monocacy Creek to supply their missions. Huge dormitories still stand here, with a distinctive style of brick eyebrow window arches and herringbone-style doors. The **Moravian Museum**[27] tells the story of these dedicated settlers (66 West Church Street, Bethlehem; 800-360-8687; www.historicbethlehem.org). The five-story log house has been used continuously since 1741, and included a residence for Christianized Indians. Walk through the adjacent cemetery, with two-hundred-year-old trees and well-tended flat stone markers. Dubbed "God's Acre," it includes the graves of 56 Indians buried peacefully alongside whites.

Most Native Americans were not converted. The Indian massacre of nearby missionaries on November 24, 1755 is commemorated each November with specially themed walking tours. The attack horrified the peace-loving Moravians and Quakers and prompted negotiations in Easton that began in 1756 and culminated in a peace treaty two years later.

Other 1740s buildings now host Bethlehem's **Moravian College**. On the south bank of the Lehigh River, **Lehigh University** rises up a massive hillside. The student bodies mingle along a lively Main Street dominated by the **Hotel Bethlehem**[25], an elegant 1922 inn (437 Main Street, Bethlehem; 800-607-2384; www.hotelbethlehem.com). The business district includes a superb selection of casual eateries. See the full list at www.lehighvalleypa.org. Browse the wood-floored **Moravian Book Shop**[26] (428 Main Street, Bethlehem; 888-661-2888; www.moravianbookshop.com). Founded in 1743, it's the world's oldest bookstore. The next-door expansion includes a café and Christmas store selling all sizes of Moravian stars.

Nine miles east of Bethlehem, quiet **Easton** (pop. 26,000) lures visitors by focusing on more recent history. The museums at **Two Rivers Landing** face Centre Square, on the site where Native Americans and colonists signed the Treaty of Easton in 1758.

## Family Fun

**Franklin Square**[3] is a shady Old City oasis (200 North Sixth Street, Philadelphia; 215-592-7273; www.onceuponanation.org). Voted the city's best play space for kids, it groups a classic carousel, picnic benches, a café, and a mini-golf course around a cool fountain. Some golf course obstacles are Philadelphia icons. Hit a ball across a scale model of the Ben Franklin Bridge or up the steps of its Museum of Art.

Whether by trolley, horse-drawn carriage, or Segway transporters, Philadelphia's tours let the whole family keep up with city explorations. Trips along the Benjamin Franklin Parkway offer overviews of the city's finest museums. Stop for photo opportunities at the "Rocky" statue en route to the **Philadelphia Museum of Art**[17] (26th Street and Benjamin Franklin Parkway, Philadelphia; 215-763-8100; www.philamuseum.org). Afterwards, visit the Parkway's other gems.

The venerable **Franklin Institute**[46] is a science museum for all ages (222 North 20th Street, Philadelphia; 215-448-1200; www.franklininstitute.org). The nearby **Please Touch Museum**[47] welcomes young children (210 North 21st Street, Philadelphia; 215-963-0667; www.pleasetouchmuseum.org).

A trip north to the Bethlehem region offers more family fun. In Easton, two small museums share a building and an inventive approach to family entertainment. Two Rivers Landing pairs **The Crayola Factory**[22] and the **National Canal Museum**[23] in a renovated four-story building (30 Centre Square, Easton; 610-515-8000; www.crayola.com/factory; 610-559-6613; www.canals.org).

The Crayola Factory explodes with color. Craft stations, ball mazes, computer-generated images tell the company story. The Crayola Store next door supplies a rainbow of chalk, clay, markers, and more.

The National Canal Museum pulls kids into the era of mule-drawn barges in ingenious ways. Floating model boats through a 90-foot water channel with working locks, kids learn how families worked on barges. They harness mules, build model aqueducts, and climb aboard a life-sized barge. In summer, they can help steer a real barge ride on the Josiah White from **Hugh Moore Park** on the restored Lehigh Canal. Excellent short videos and computer timelines enhance this outstanding small museum.

To travel between Bethlehem, Northampton County, and Philadelphia, choose scenic Route 32. The two-lane road winds within sight of the river and the canal, past charming towns like Lumberville and New Hope. Nearby is **Pennsbury Manor**[30]. William Penn's country estate is a state historic site (400 Pennsbury Memorial Road, Morrisville; 215-946-0400; www.pennsburymanor.org).

*top to bottom, Carriages ply the narrow streets of Old City Philadelphia; Franklin Square's mini-golf course includes pint-sized landmarks.*

# Great Houses and Gardens

At 9,200 acres, **Fairmount Park** is one of the largest parks in the world, with several fine 19th century homes (215-683-2000; www.fairmountpark.org). A few miles northwest of the park, Europeans attracted by Penn's promise of religious and economic freedom settled Germantown in 1683. They lived alongside English Quakers whose homes still welcome visitors. Look for the distinctive gray stone facades of these house museums. Wyck, built in 1690, maintains a 175-year-old rose garden. Stenton, which dates to the 1720s, was the home of James Logan, William Penn's secretary. Damage from the Battle of Germantown in 1777 is still evident

*left to right, Cedar Grove, built in 1748, is one of Fairmount Park's historic homes; gardeners tend plots at Bartram's Garden.*

at Cliveden, a National Trust property. George Washington returned to this hilltop community in 1790 for a summer stay at the Deshler-Morris House. Later, local Quakers sheltered slaves on the Underground Railroad. Get details on all sites from the **Germantown Historical Society**[32] (5501 Germantown Avenue, Philadelphia; 215-844-0514; www.germantownhistory.org). A steep uphill climb along cobblestoned Germantown Avenue brings you to **Chestnut Hill**, a chic shopping district. **Morris Arboretum**[31], the University of Pennsylvania's 92-acre garden nearby, focuses on rare and woody plants in a Victorian setting (100 East Northwestern Avenue, Philadelphia; 215-247-5777; www.upenn.edu/arboretum).

One of the city's most venerable gardens lies southwest, a few miles from Philadelphia International Airport. Despite its surroundings—

the Philadelphia Gas Works and other flat and charmless industrial sites—this site is a landmark in the history of botany. **Bartram's Garden**[20] the 18th century home of the naturalist Bartram Family, is a Delaware River plantation that preserves native species (5400 Lindbergh Boulevard, Philadelphia; 215-729-5281; www.bartramsgarden.org). John Bartram, who purchased 100 acres here in 1728, traveled as far as Canada and Florida collecting American plant life; his son William's *Travels* is a classic work of natural history. The view of downtown Philadelphia from these peaceful fields is a stunner, but review complicated directions to the site in advance. **Schuylkill River boat rides**[19] carry visitors from center city to Bartram's Garden in good weather (215-222-6030; www.schuylkillbanks.org).

# Great Outdoors

Within 20 miles of downtown Philadelphia, wide-open spaces beckon. Valley Forge, to the northwest, and the Brandywine Valley, on the Delaware border, put the "natural" in history. Bike easy paths, float down a famous river, or share views that artists have cherished for a century.

Home to English Quakers since the 1680s, the bucolic Brandywine Valley maintains their peaceful spirit. The Brandywine's peace was shattered only once. The British and Continental armies clashed in 1777 on what is now called "America's first September 11." Near the spot where Cornwallis' troops first forded the river, float along on kayaks, canoes or inner tubes from the **Northbrook Canoe Company**[44] (1810 Beagle Road, West Chester; 800-898-2279; www.northbrookcanoe.com). The cool current eases through an unhurried and unspoiled landscape, where herons and turtles bask. Two state-approved bike routes, marked L and S, follow quiet level roads. Square stone Quaker meeting houses stand at many crossroads through the fields. And in Chadds Ford, the **Brandywine River Museum**[41] displays the work of the Wyeth family (1 Hoffman Mill Road, Chadds Ford; 610-388-2700; www.brandywinemuseum.org). The museum is perfectly sited in a grist mill with a view of the river. Don't be surprised to see a fisherman float past, reclining in an inner tube.

**Valley Forge National Historical Park**[33] offers six miles of superb biking trails and 90-minute bike tours on summer Saturdays—an excellent introduction to the region's rolling topography (1400 North Outer Line Drive, King of Prussia; 610-783-1077; www.nps.gov/vafo). Bike rentals are available weekends in good weather at the Welcome Center parking lot. Two sizes of kids' bikes, buggies and tagalongs (half-bikes) are offered along with 21-gear adult models.

*Top to bottom, The gristmill is the symbol of the Brandywine River Museum; Valley Forge Park offers miles of rolling bike paths.*

## Uniquely Philadelphia

Throughout Independence National Historical Park and Valley Forge, the 18th century literally comes to life through **Once Upon a Nation**. With storytellers, free programs for kids, and colonial townspeople strolling the streets, this unique open-air program targets children and adults alike. Free events are offered April through October at thirteen Old City sites marked by circular benches; gather round. Once Upon a Nation also offers wonderful ticketed programs, like the evening Tipplers Tours of local historic taverns or live presentations by George Washington or Thomas Jefferson. An absorbing evening program at Valley Forge shows what nights were really like for the Continental soldiers under Washington's leadership. On summer Saturdays, visitors dine with the troops before being entertained by soldier tales (215-629-4026; www.onceuponanation.org).

## Did You Know?

Legendary frontiersman **Daniel Boone**[45] was born to a Quaker family in Birdsboro in 1734. The homestead is now a state museum (400 Daniel Boone Road, Birdsboro; 610-582-4900; www.danielboonehomestead.org). In 1755, Boone traveled from North Carolina to join the Braddock Expedition as a teamster. He narrowly avoided death in the catastrophic battle.

## Plan a Visit

### Annual Regional Events

**Mummers Parade,** January 1
www.phillymummers.com

**Philadelphia Flower Show,** March
www.theflowershow.com

**Bethlehem Bach Festival,** May
www.bach.org

**Devon Horse Show and County Fair,** May
www.thedevonhorseshow.com

**July Fourth Festival,** July
www.americasbirthday.com

**Battle of Brandywine reenactment,** September
www.ushistory.org/brandywine/index.html

*clockwise from lower left, Birdsboro's Boone Homestead; Once Upon a Nation at Washington's Headquarters, Valley Forge; City Tavern in Old City; the Waterworks Restaurant overlooks the Schuylkill River.*

## Old City

For more information:
Greater Philadelphia Tourism Marketing
1 North Independence Mall West, Philadelphia
 (800) 537-7676 | www.gophila.com

### DINING
**City Tavern**[13]
138 South Second Street at Walnut Street,
Philadelphia
(215) 413-1443 | www.citytavern.com
• Not to be missed. Traditional menu in the
  most popular tavern of the late 18th century.

**The Waterworks Restaurant**[18]
640 Waterworks Drive, Philadelphia
(215) 236-9000
www.thewaterworksrestaurant.com
• Fine dining and great views along famous
  Boathouse Row, near the Philadelphia
  Museum of Art.

**Snow White Restaurant**[11]
200 Market Street, Philadelphia
(215) 923-2342
• Scrapple, that Philadelphia favorite, comes
  with breakfasts at this 50-year-old diner.

**Franklin Fountain**[10]
116 Market Street, Philadelphia
(215) 627-1899 | www.franklinfountain.com
• A bust of Ben presides over old-fashioned
  ice cream treats. Near Independence Mall.

### LODGING
**Thomas Bond House**[14]
129 South Second Street, Philadelphia
(800) 845-2663
www.thomasbondhousebandb.com
• An antique-furnished B&B inside
  Independence National Historical Park,
  this was the home of Dr. Bond, an 18th
  century physician.

**Penn's View Hotel**[12]
Front and Market Streets, Philadelphia
(800) 331-7634
www.pennsviewhotel.com
• European-style hotel with bar and trattoria.

## Valley Forge

For more information:
Valley Forge Convention and Visitors Bureau
600 West Germantown Pike, Plymouth Meeting
(610) 834-1550 | www.valleyforge.org

### DINING AND LODGING
**General Warren Inne**[34]
16 Village Way, Old Lancaster Road, Malvern
(215) 296-3637 | www.generalwarren.com
• Restored 1745 inn; eight guest suites and
  restaurant.

## Bethlehem and Easton

For more information:
Lehigh Valley Convention and Visitors Bureau
840 Hamilton Street, Allentown
(800) 747-0561 | www.lehighvalleypa.org

Historic Bethlehem
501-505 Main Street, Bethlehem
(800) 360-8687 | www.historicbethlehem.org

### DINING
**Pott's Doggie Shop**[29]
114 West Fairview Street, Bethlehem
(610) 865-6644
• A favorite of the college crowd (and
  everyone else). Take-out only.

**Apollo Grill**[28]
85 West Broad Street, Bethlehem
(610) 865-9600 | www.apollogrill.com
• Casual award-winning bistro near historic
  district.

**Pearly Baker's Ale House**[21]
11 Centre Square, Easton
(610) 253-9949 | www.pearlybakers.net
• Friendly, family-style pub.

### LODGING:
**Hotel Bethlehem**[25]
437 Main Street, Bethlehem
(800) 607-2384 | www.hotelbethlehem.com
• Downtown's most popular hotel, with
  excellent restaurant and tap room.

## Brandywine River Valley

For more information:
Delaware County's Brandywine Conference
and Visitors Bureau
One Beaver Valley Road, Chadds Ford
(800) 343-3983 | www.brandywinecvb.org

### DINING
**Simon Pearce Restaurant**[43]
1333 Lenape Road, West Chester
(610) 793-0948 | www.simonpearce.com
• Contemporary dining alongside
  the Brandywine River; glassblowing
  demonstrations and shop.

**Dilworthtown Inn**[37]
1390 Old Wilmington Pike, West Chester
(610) 399-1390 | www.dilworthtown.com
• This 1753 structure has been a tavern
  since 1780. Extensive wine list; Zagat-
  rated.

**Hank's Place**[40]
Routes 1 and 100, Chadds Ford
(610) 388-7061 | www.hanks-place.net
• Casual home-style café.

**Jimmy John's**[36]
1507 Wilmington-West Chester Pike
Route 202, West Chester
(610) 459-3083
• A local institution for hot dogs and
  burgers. Drop a quarter in the slot to
  operate the massive model train display.

### LODGING
**Brandywine River Hotel**[39]
Routes 1 and 100, Chadds Ford
(800) 274-9644
www.brandywineriverhotel.com
• Convenient to battlefield and museum.

**Pennsbury Inn**[42]
883 Baltimore Pike, Chadds Ford
(610) 388-1435 | www.pennsburyinn.com
• On the National Register of Historic
  Places; eight-acre property and B&B.

## The Environment: Preserving Priceless Resources

Imagine a world that has too much space. Eighteenth-century colonists looked west and saw a vast, threatening wilderness, ready made for conquest and exploitation by the boldest among them. After centuries of settlement, populations grew and a formerly limitless world suddenly had boundaries. People started thinking preservation when polluted urban neighborhoods multiplied and small church graveyards filled up. New, larger cemeteries, like Philadelphia's 1836 Laurel Hill, became urban parks where visitors could commune with their ancestors in a natural setting. At the same time, a few visionaries went a step further in the biggest cities. Philadelphia set aside Fairmount Park along the Schuylkill River in 1855 and New York created Central Park, carved out of rocky, stagnant swampland, three years later.

Today, Fairmount may not be quite as famous as Central but it is just as important in the life of a major city. Originally created to protect Philadelphia's increasingly polluted water supply, the park turned old country estates overlooking the river and city into a 9,200 acre public oasis that is more than ten times as large as its New York counterpart. Stretched over 63 neighborhoods, it takes in ten percent of Philadelphia's land and includes the Franklin D. Roosevelt Park, recovered from marshes around heavy industry and the old Philadelphia Navy Yard, at Fairmount's south end. The park's patchwork features city squares, 18th century country houses, vintage exposition buildings, a zoo, a working farm, rowing clubs, river excursions, a beautiful and historic water works, neighborhood recreation areas and plenty of open space.

Once endless forests were disappearing at an accelerating rate, victims of a late 19th century countrywide housing boom. At the time, many preached that America, with its frontier closing, was quickly exploiting its natural resources and they would soon run out. Others wanted the country's most beautiful places forever protected as wilderness. Future Pennsylvania Governor Gifford Pinchot teamed up with President Theodore Roosevelt in 1905 to champion national forest conservation. The Keystone State was already a leader in saving forestland with a commission chartered in 1895. Today's Pennsylvania Department of Conservation and Natural Resources (DCNR) preserves 2.1 million acres, about twelve percent of the 17 million acres that survive as forest land. In addition, it manages 117 state parks dotted around Pennsylvania, rural and suburban descendants of Philadelphia's old Fairmount Park.

After more than a century of countrywide conservation efforts, a new phenomenon dubbed suburban sprawl has entered the picture. As automobiles and roads spread out American cities, efforts have accelerated to save farmland and once remote historic houses now surrounded by development. A group called the Rural History Confederation has collected 19 museums and historic sites throughout the suburbs west and north of Philadelphia. Anchored around Valley Forge National Historical Park, this new vision for heritage tourism has created oases, some almost overwhelmed by subdivisions, which echo past campaigns to set aside Fairmount Park and Laurel Hill Cemetery. In scores of smaller communities on the Forbes Trail from Pittsburgh to Philadelphia, the Pennsylvania Downtown Center is determined to spark revitalization along beloved old main streets under siege from the centrifugal forces of our busy lives.

Fairmount Park Commission
Philadelphia's Park System
(215) 683-0200 | www.fairmountpark.org

Pennsylvania Department of Conservation and Natural Resources
www.dcnr.state.pa

Information on Pennsylvania State Parks
(888) PA-PARKS [888-727-2757]

General Information on Pennsylvania
(800) VISITPA [800-847-4872]

Rural History Confederation
www.ruralhistoryconfederation.org

Pennsylvania Downtown Center
(717) 233-4675 | www.padowntown.org

*pg. 36, The Mill at Anselma, grinding wheat since 1747, undoubtedly ground flour for the Forbes Campaign. Saved in 1982 as a rural and historic resource in the French and Pickering Creek watersheds, it still operates as one of the best preserved grist mills in America.*
*pg. 37, clockwise from lower left, The graveyard at Philadelphia's St. Mary's Catholic Church, in use since 1759, illustrates the crowded urban church burial grounds that evolved into large cemetery parks during the mid 19th century; one of the most spectacular properties in Fairmount Park is the 18th century Belmont Estate. Visitors can still see an unparalleled view of downtown Philadelphia once enjoyed by Ben Franklin and George Washington; the William Keith House, dating to 1722, is the only surviving Pennsylvania home of a colonial governor. Later called Graeme Park, the house and grounds are a part of the Rural History Confederation created to preserve historic structures and open space in the Philadelphia suburbs.*

# Lancaster

**July 2, 1758**

With Lancaster's skyline looming in the background, General John Forbes, travelling to Carlisle with his staff and light cavalry escort, stops on the side of the road as a parade of supply wagons and beef cattle passes by. The nearby farm recalls the 1719 Hans Herr House still standing in the county.

# General Forbes Hits the Trail

General John Forbes waited almost two months in Philadelphia for royal troops, guns and supplies. The 1st Highland Battalion finally arrived on June 8 and the siege cannons and supplies soon followed. Forbes could now join his already troubled campaign. Cherokee Indian allies, tired of waiting for the English army, were deserting him. Supply wagons contracted in Pennsylvania were still scarce. With troops and supplies gathering from all directions, the bad roads were slowing everyone down.

By June 30, the General was traveling to Carlisle by way of Lancaster. Forbes' military staff, headed by patient and loyal Major Francis Halkett, a veteran of Braddock's defeat, was a large entourage of advisors and personal attendants. A proper English general expected certain comforts, even on a back country campaign. A general's field equipage — tents, desks, tables, beds, and mess gear — was transported in wagons and carts. A horse-drawn carriage, rare in colonial America, was another symbol of rank. In 1755, General Braddock had been jolted and jostled from Alexandria to Fort Cumberland, finally abandoning his coach as his army carved a new road through the Allegheny Mountains.

## Traveling on the King's Highway

General Forbes spent the next few days riding through hot summer weather. Leaving Philadelphia, crossing the Schuylkill River on flat barges at the Upper Ferry, the General and his staff, with a cavalry escort, were on the King's Highway. American roads were all dust, mud, tree stumps and bone-jarring potholes. The Lancaster Road was a heavily-traveled, two decades old link between the Quaker City and inland farms sending goods east.

On the seventy-mile ride to Lancaster, the redcoats passed through the richest farm country in British North America. Welsh settlers, English Quakers and German farmers created communities that today are the bustling Philadelphia suburbs. Further west, in the neighborhood that became Paoli and Malvern, the column rode into the forests and fields of the rolling piedmont region.

General Forbes and his staff entered Lancaster County at the headwaters of Octoraro Creek. They saw neat and orderly German communities as they crossed the old St. Peter's Road, pointing southeast toward Delaware. Riding by the roadside taverns of Bird-in-Hand and Cross Keys (later Intercourse), they crossed the Great Conestoga Creek and skirted the Dark Hazel Swamp. Rows of log, half-timber, brick and stone houses announced Lancaster. Trotting on the wide expanse called King Street, the military parade passed the brick courthouse dominating the center square.

## Pennsylvania's First Cavalry Troop

Pennsylvanians are proud of the 1st Troop, Philadelphia City Cavalry, widely considered to be the oldest continuously active U.S. military unit. Formed in November 1774, the Light Horse of the City of Philadelphia played a prominent role in the Revolutionary War campaigns of 1776 and 1777. Members of the unit, now part of the National Guard, have served in all of America's wars.

Philadelphia's First Troop was not Pennsylvania's first cavalry unit. General John Forbes persuaded colonials to raise two troops of good men, mounted on light serviceable horses, for the 1758 expedition. The Pennsylvania Light Horse picked provincial soldiers fit for hard duty on the frontier. Their duties included scouting, escorting convoys, pursuing deserters, and carrying dispatches.

The provincial troopers were to be equipped with horsemen's weapons and equipment, their green uniforms supplemented with leather caps and green cloaks. After reviewing the troop at Carlisle on July 8, Forbes protested that the unit's poor quality accoutrements were rendered useless already. When a detachment arrived at the Raystown advanced base a few days later, Colonel Henry Bouquet observed that the troop's swords, their principal weapon "are a joke —they could not kill a chicken with this tiny knife."

In spite of these challenges, the Pennsylvanian horsemen, together with a troop drawn from Colonel George Washington's Virginia Regiment, rendered valuable service. Pennsylvania and Virginia troopers formed an escort for General Forbes. They were also the first British troops to reach the Forks of the Ohio.

*As soldiers collect forage near Carlisle, a Pennsylvania light cavalryman inspects the weapon he's been issued, a sword that Colonel Bouquet predicts cannot kill a chicken.*

## The New Town Called Lancaster

Almost three decades old, Lancaster was something new for the American colonists still hugging the seacoast. Lacking a waterway to float goods to buyers, it was a homegrown market, a hub for roads to all the points of the compass. Philadelphia was its major partner and outlet. Thousands of wagons rolled along the King's Highway. Lancaster Town had close to 3,000 residents and was America's first inland city, a "back country emporium" for the whole region.

The new borough was the seat of Pennsylvania's earliest western county. One 1755 visitor commented: "You will not see many inland towns in England so large as this, and none that are so regular." Lancaster was a link with the frontier fur trade beyond the Susquehanna River. It was a busy local market place for produce from surrounding farms and villages. A fast moving brook in town was powering mills. Lancaster's best asset, however, was a smart plan that helped it grow quickly. James Hamilton, Lancaster's proprietor, drew up a balanced grid of streets and lots on his 500 acre grant. He gave investors one year to build houses on their lots. He welcomed any and all economic pursuits and built a permanent marketplace building. He promoted responsible and popular government with an impressive courthouse at town center. Mr. Hamilton also welcomed German immigrants.

The result was a distinctive cultural blend. German farmers and artisans from the Rhineland and Switzerland poured into the region. Without the wars and religious troubles they faced in Europe, the immigrants prospered. They brought a swirl of Protestant sects; ninety-percent were Lutherans and Reformed (now the United Church of Christ) while the rest were Brethren, Mennonites, Moravians, Dunkers, Schwenkfelders, and Amish. Mennonites had settled on the frontier along Conestoga Creek in the early 1700s. The Moravians moved west from their main settlement at Bethlehem and founded Lititz. By the 1750s, two-thirds of Lancaster households were German. They called themselves Deutsch but the English called them "Dutch" and "Swissers." The "Engellanders," a mix of English Anglicans, Quakers and Scots-Irish, thought the meticulous Dutchmen were dull, even comical. Immigrant Germans struggled to find a balance between cherished Old Country ways and an evolving American culture. No one, however, could fault them as skilled farmers and craftsmen or reliable neighbors.

## Back Country Business

Lancaster quickly became a busy commercial center. Important players from many backgrounds came to town. Scandal brought merchant Edward Shippen, the well-bred former Philadelphia mayor, to the community in 1752. Mr. Shippen, with interests in the fur trade and frontier land, immediately became a first citizen. He helped his new son-in-law, James Burd, open a fine wine store, featuring "Madeira, Teneriffe, Malaga and Jamaica Spirits." A German physician, Adam Simon Kuhn, was another town leader as was Jewish merchant Joseph Simon who partnered with others to build many shops and warehouses. John Cameron, determined to undersell everyone, set out to create a great shop of retail goods, causing howls of protest from his competitors.

Lancaster's economic backbone, however, was the scores of quality craft shops lining its streets. Close to forty trades were working in town by the 1750s. William Henry, a popular local gunsmith, metal worker and inventor, persuaded teen-aged visitor Benjamin West to pursue an artistic career, launching one of the great painters from colonial America. Lancaster's pride in craft — practical and problem-solving but also art from the hands of skilled artisans — shaped two historic local products. The Conestoga Wagon and Pennsylvania Rifle were vital ingredients in the American story for more than a century.

*German and Swiss immigrants, ancestors of today's Pennsylvania Dutch, have their own unique dress, decorations, furnishings, and customs they brought to the New World.*

## The Royal American Regiment

The first contingent of British troops from Forbes' army, two hundred soldiers and officers from the 60th or Royal American Regiment, marched west with Colonel Bouquet in late May 1758. This unique corps, raised specifically for service in North America, was already familiar to many Pennsylvanians. After Braddock's 1755 defeat, British officials authorized a new regular regiment of four battalions (four thousand men in all), hoping to tap the large pool of colonial manpower.

The Royal American Regiment was led by a diverse group of European officers. The rank and file included European recruits, drafts from existing British regiments, mixed with native-born and immigrant colonial recruits. British commander Lord Loudoun, the colonel of the Royal Americans, called America "the best recruiting country we have." The corps was filled with men who spoke English and German in a bewildering variety of dialects. After a three or four year enlistment, Royal American recruits were promised bounties of land at war's end. One regimental officer observed that young indentured servants, receiving free passage from Europe in exchange for years of hard service under colonial masters, were "glad to go into the army to get rid of their slavery, [and made] the best soldiers we get in America."

Four companies from the 1st Battalion of the Royal American Regiment served in the 1758 expedition under Lieutenant Colonel Henry Bouquet. The entire battalion was reunited in Pennsylvania the following year and served as the primary British garrison in Pennsylvania through the mid 1760s. The modern British Army's elite Rifle Regiment traces its descent from the Royal American Regiment.

### A Frontier Buffer

French and Indian war parties ravaged the Pennsylvania frontier after General Braddock's 1755 defeat. The assault caused "great horror and confusion" and sent a flood of settlers scurrying across the Susquehanna River to safe havens. Edward Shippen saw potential disaster ahead "…if the [French and Indian] enemy should take possession of this town [Lancaster] and destroy the people, who can dare to stay on their plantations betwixt here and Philadelphia." Scores of armed watchmen spent restless nights braced for trouble.

*The 60th Regiment of Foot is being recruited in America to fight the French. As the Royal Americans, they wear red faced with royal blue.*

In 1756, Pennsylvania's leaders sputtered into action, building an arc of stopgap forts north and west of Lancaster. The community quickly became a magnet for military affairs. With Lancaster on the main road to and from Philadelphia and points west, governors, diplomats, many colonels and a few generals set up headquarters in town. Express riders galloped through with important dispatches. Whole companies of local recruits for the Royal American and Pennsylvania Regiments were mustered into service and outfitted in the community. They were also paid the King's shilling when they were mustered out. Influential Edward Shippen received praise for his role as a provincial paymaster throughout the emergency.

## Billeting Soldiers

Lancaster and other communities along the military road west were beset with hundreds of uninvited guests. Young soldiers were far from the cream of anyone's society. Away from the frontier, where they shivered in fort barracks, they were assigned to winter in private homes and inns much to the distress of local citizens. A boorish soldier sharing home and hearth could be quite an invasion of a family's privacy.

Philadelphia, faced with the same problem, built a large barracks to accommodate soldiers. A Pennsylvania legislative committee reported that Lancaster was also hard hit by the practice of billeting soldiers. "The military officers have, by force, quartered a large number of soldiers on the private houses, committing great outrages upon the people, by seizing and depriving [them] of their possessions and property, assaulting their persons…" By 1760, the Pennsylvania Colony provided funds to build a Lancaster barracks that housed 500 soldiers.

Quartering soldiers remained a serious issue for colonials when they rebelled against England some twenty years later. Among the many "injuries and usurpations" listed against King George in the Declaration of Independence, Thomas Jefferson took the King to task "for quartering large bodies of armed troops among us." Suspicion of standing armies and trust in citizen militia became founding principles of the United States Republic.

*Rivalries between regular and provincial soldiers and sometimes among provincial soldiers from neighboring colonies, often degenerate into fisticuffs.*

*Inspecting a barrel of spoiled beef in brine can make a quartermaster's job very disagreeable.*

## Mobilizing the Army

In late May 1758, General Forbes, still in Philadelphia, lost patience with Pennsylvania farmers. He and his deputy Colonel Henry Bouquet had the unenviable task of squeezing enough food and supplies out of the colonies to equip and sustain a large army. Demands went out to farmers in Lancaster, York, and Berks Counties for 180 wagons to carry tons of goods to hungry and often ill-equipped soldiers. Forbes was trying to do "everything for the ease of the inhabitants," but he was considering rough measures if His Majesty's subjects did not "do their duty in procuring things easily."

Marshalling reluctant colonials to provide funds, men, and supplies for campaigns was always a challenge. Lancaster, however, was a godsend for army quartermasters. The sizeable brick courthouse became a King's Storehouse, brimming with military equipment. Lancaster businessmen were accused of gouging the government. Local farmers delivered cattle, forage, and flour to military suppliers. Craftsmen were busy assembling muskets and rifles, swords, uniforms, belts and cartridge boxes, shoes, stockings, shipping bags, barrels, and boxes. The gunsmith William Henry, an armourer throughout the war and later in the Revolution, made money fixing old muskets that had been sitting, neglected, in colonial armories. In June of 1758, Colonel George Washington asked Henry "to set about cleaning and putting all the Virginia arms in the best repair you can."

## Finding Wagons

After English military wagons crashed on steep mountain slopes in 1755, General Braddock sent the heavy vehicles home. They were exchanged for smaller, civilian Pennsylvania wagons and pack horses contracted in southern Pennsylvania. The trick was finding farmers willing to transport supplies to a dangerous frontier.

Ben Franklin helped Braddock find wagons in Pennsylvania by using a carrot and a stick. He advertised good pay for each driver, wagon and four horses. A couple of month's service could put considerable cash in a farmer's pocket. The stick was a promise that the redcoats were losing patience with colonial suppliers. They would soon, under the command of the "Hussar" Sir John St. Clair, descend on local farms to get what they needed. German immigrants remembered Hussars as the fierce light cavalry that terrorized the countryside in Europe.

Army quartermasters again struggled to find wagons and horses for General Forbes' 1758 column. Quartermaster Sir John St. Clair, Franklin's so-called Hussar, was still leading efforts to find colonial transport and supplies. The energetic Sir John, unfortunately, was noted more for bombast than efficiency. The British leaders were forced to hire country contractors, led by trader Adam Hoops, to get the job done.

## George Washington Rejoins His Command

At the end of June, 1758, Colonel George Washington was leading Virginia troops through the mountains to Fort Cumberland, Maryland. He was a heroic survivor of Braddock's Defeat, but since 1755, his attempts to defend the Virginia frontier from French and Indian attacks had been frustrating and dangerous. A 1757 trip to Philadelphia had been a bitter disappointment. Hoping to win the approval of the British commander Lord Loudoun, Washington was snubbed. He had done his best during five years of frontier military apprenticeship, but his chances of a regular career in the British Army appeared slim.

Colonel Washington was sick and absent from his post by the end of 1757. Fears of following his father and half-brother to an early death haunted him. In March, 1758, he had written a British army friend: "I have some thoughts of quitting my command and retiring from all public business, leaving my post to be filled by others more capable of the task." Learning from a Williamsburg physician that he may not die after all, he decided to return to his recently-inherited Mount Vernon estate and settle down as a gentleman planter. But first, after winning the heart of a prosperous young widow, he rejoined his troops at Winchester, Virginia, eager to cap off his military career with the Forbes Campaign.

## Colonel Bouquet Hits the Ground Running

Colonel Henry Bouquet, General Forbes' Swiss-born deputy, was in a hurry after landing at Sandy Hook in early May. He marched across New Jersey to Philadelphia with his four companies of the Royal Americans. Stopping briefly to meet General Forbes, Bouquet rode on through Lancaster, arriving in Carlisle, an army base camp, on May 24.

Writing in French to Forbes the following day, he laid out a series of challenges: Pennsylvania was interfering with command and providing supplies too slowly, the creeks and rivers were almost impassable from recent storms, the bad roads needed constant attention, arms and equipment remained scarce, old muskets were bursting in soldiers' hands, no news was coming in from the frontiers, and locals were convinced that the French and Indians would soon attack. Declaring that "slowness in everything will be the death of me," Bouquet was also quick to point out that "we shall have a very fine army here."

On June 3, the Colonel sat down again to catch up on his pile of correspondence. In another long letter to Forbes, he thanked the General for the supplies and equipment now rolling into Carlisle. "You have performed a miracle in obtaining the means to equip the troops." Still burdened with a sea of details, he was planning busy days in the saddle during June, pushing men and supplies through wild mountain country to the next collection point in Raystown (later Bedford).

*Colonel George Washington is a strong and confident four year veteran of frontier fighting.*

## Indian Councils

A year before General Forbes arrived in Philadelphia, Pennsylvania Governor Denny and the Quakers descended on Lancaster. They were continuing peace negotiations with Teedyuscung and his eastern Delawares, hoping to draw in the western Delawares from the back country. A large Iroquois delegation arrived looking to continue their influence over peace talks with the Delawares. Israel Pemberton and one hundred Quaker Friendly Association members were there with gifts, intent on making peace with all the Indian nations. Teedyuscung, afraid of the Iroquois who called him a false king and, worse yet, a "woman," never showed up. When some settlers rode into town with corpses recently killed and scalped by Indian raiders only thirty miles away, a mob gathered and threatened to drag out and shoot the governor and negotiators. The presence of Royal American regulars ended the ruckus but peace talks returned to more neutral ground around Easton.

With trouble all around, perpetual treaties of friendship and protection had been renewed with the local Conestoga Indians in 1755. Once a part of the mighty Susquehannock Nation, the Conestogas were now a handful of Christianized survivors surrounded by white settlements. Five years after the 1758 Forbes Campaign, even the Lancaster jail couldn't protect them. When Indian nations again attacked white settlements in 1763, local anti-Indian sentiments boiled over. Put in the Lancaster jail for their safety, the entire group of Conestoga men, women, and children was massacred by a gang known to history as the "Paxton Boys."

## General Forbes' Deputy Commander

Lieutenant Colonel Henry Bouquet was born to an influential Swiss family in the hotel business. Trained as a soldier, he had spent his entire career serving European monarchies as a mercenary.

After long experience with Dutch and Sardinian armies, Bouquet was hired by the British and sailed to Pennsylvania in 1756. He helped raise and train a new British regiment, the Royal Americans or 60th Regiment of Foot. Most of the recruits were European immigrants so he immediately fit in. He spent 1757 with several companies of the 60th in Charleston, South Carolina, returning to Pennsylvania in early 1758 to serve with General Forbes' campaign. Well-educated, fluent in several languages, sober, patient, efficient, and down-to-earth, Bouquet was the kind of second that Forbes could depend on.

*Lieutenant Colonel Henry Bouquet painted as a frontier hero in 1759.*

## A Very Odd Quartermaster

After an unexceptional military career in Europe, Sir John St. Clair, a baronet from Argyleshire, Scotland, came to the colonies as the quartermaster and advance man for the 1755 Braddock Expedition. His assigned tasks were Herculean. He purchased the food and alcohol that fueled every 18th century army and then hired wagons, packhorses, and drivers to transport thousands of wooden barrels and casks to the frontier. Sir John took on the challenge with unflagging energy. More than one leader referred to him as indefatigable and Braddock himself said "he has done all that could possibly be expected."

Sir John, however, had some serious shortcomings. In a job that required patience and diplomacy, he was quick to anger, impatient with foolishness, and second guessed his commanders. Within months of his arrival, he "stormed like a lion rampant" at Pennsylvania Governor Morris for being slow with a promised road. Badly wounded at Braddock's defeat, he complained that the dead general's efforts were "contrary to his [Sir John's] opinion."

Sir John, now a lieutenant colonel in the 60th Foot, was back in Pennsylvania during 1758 because of his familiarity with the country. General Forbes had wanted the quartermaster job in America and was no fan. Arriving in Philadelphia with Forbes, the mercurial quartermaster rushed on to the frontier to spur the colonials into action. General Forbes and Colonel Bouquet were both uneasy with Sir John's performance. Forbes admitted privately that "He is a very odd man...His only talent [is] for throwing everything into confusion."

*This 1754 portrait captures Sir John St. Clair's contentious personality.*

# General Forbes Rushes to Carlisle

General Forbes' campaign was now in high gear with troops and supplies converging on Carlisle and points west. Even though he was wrestling with a persistent digestive problem, what he ominously called a "Cholera Morbus," Forbes did not have the luxury of slowing down. He was in touch with Pennsylvania Governor Denny about the peace offensive with the Delaware Nation. Denny, still negotiating peace with eastern Indian leader Teedyuscung, would soon send envoy Christian Frederick Post into Ohio Country to talk peace with leaders of the western Delawares.

Forbes and his train rode northwest from Lancaster on the east side of the bluffs overlooking the Susquehanna River. They splashed across the Swatara and Paxtang (Paxton) Creeks, still swollen from recent rains. They passed through frontier Scots-Irish and German settlements that had been ravaged by French-inspired Indian raids. The General and his staff then waited on the banks of the Susquehanna for Harris' Ferry. Safely across the wide and rock-strewn river, they rode toward the distant, shadowy Allegheny Mountains that would soon dominate their lives.

*Hundreds of uniquely American wagons called Conestogas carry tons of food and supplies west with Forbes' army.*

## The Conestoga Wagon

With their bowed blue bodies, tall-wheeled red undercarriages, heavy canvas tops, and four horses in harness, a shouting, whip-wielding teamster mounted on one of the team or walking alongside, Pennsylvania wagons were a non-stop parade on back roads. The 1758 campaign was clogging already busy highways because the military command was eager to move a mountain of supplies west.

Lancaster County craftsmen had adapted English and German farm wagons for rough roads. They were called Conestogas for the creek near Lancaster where they were first mentioned in the 1720s. They were small and sturdy, carrying no more than a ton of freight. They were also beautifully-crafted with subtly-curved beds to keep the load stable on hills, large beveled wheels with iron tires, feed troughs hanging off the back, and hand wrought iron chains and supports. Even the wheel jacks and side tool boxes carried the elaborate iron decorations of owners and makers.

In the 1800s, giant Conestoga Wagons became the eighteen-wheelers of their day. Six matched heavy horses pulled up to five tons of goods over hundreds of miles on the old Forbes and the new National Roads. The sight of these wagons was electric with jingling harness bells and a teamster controlling tons of horse flesh with a single jerk line, shouting gee and haw to turn his team right and left. Railroads ended the Conestoga era although Civil War armies depended on tens of thousands of freight wagons pulled by six mule teams to carry supplies to the fighting.

# The Artisan Tradition

Thank Pennsylvania's earliest immigrants for the tradition of craftsmanship that continues to enrich everyday life. By the mid 18th century, Penn's Woods had already established a reputation for skilled hands. Philadelphia apprentices refined cabinetmaking into a renowned furniture industry. From leather to textiles, from farming to milling and baking, industrious German settlers created industries that supported entire communities in eastern Pennsylvania. Rich seams of iron ore sustained Hopewell, Cornwall, and other villages throughout the eastern part of the state, adding furnace and forge to many town names and attracting skilled ironworkers. With abundant sand and limestone along its rivers, Pennsylvania became a glassmaking power through the 20th century. In the 21st century, handcrafted goods are still a Pennsylvania brand.

Quilts, the fusion of color, motif and patient effort, are enshrined at Lancaster's Quilt and Textile Museum, a project of the city's Heritage Center. Quilt making was a community activity for the Pennsylvania Germans before the Amish adopted the art in the mid 19th century. They contributed the square shape, block patterns, strong colors and motifs, such as tulips and grapevines that are now considered the traditional style. Contemporary quilters may interpret traditional patterns in printed fabrics, although these are not used in Amish homes. Signs at local homes advertise quilts for sale. They are popular items at craft festivals, shops, and even the spring outdoor markets called "mud sales" in the region.

With the invention of the jacquard loom in 1801, textiles moved beyond the limits of geometric design. Among the earliest American patterns for the new looms was one with a classic bush and bird border created by Andrew Kump, a Pennsylvania weaver. Today, those early patterns are reproduced at Family Heirloom Weavers in Red Lion, York County. On rebuilt power looms, the Kline family weaves coverlets and ingrain carpets that replicate 19th century designs. Other examples of the craft are displayed at the National Museum of the American Coverlet in Bedford.

In Lancaster, another European tradition continues. European monks baked "pretiola," with a crossed twist that resembled arms crossed in prayer. Originally given to children as a reward for reverence, the hard-baked version called the pretzel is still manufactured in Pennsylvania Dutch country by Sturgis, Hammond, and other family-owned companies. The tradition of fresh, abundant farm foods is evident in the town markets of central Pennsylvania. The local food movement has renewed interest in artisan cheese-making, a family business in many Amish and Mennonite communities. They are sold seasonally in dairy country, particularly in Cumberland and Franklin counties.

Simple salt-glazed stoneware was a staple of the 18th century homestead, both in England and the colonies. The traditional blue and white wares continue to be produced at Eldreth Pottery in Strasburg, while in Waynesboro, Franklin County, the Renfrew Museum displays the distinctive local redware of the Bell family, now prized by collectors.

Lancaster was a well-known watchmaking center in the late 19th century. The gold Hamilton pocket model manufactured here made trains run on time: it was known as "the watch of railroad accuracy." While the firm has moved overseas, its apprentice tradition continues. At the National Watch and Clock Museum in Columbia, with a 12,000-timepiece collection, the school of horology instructs professionals and hobbyists. The Susquehanna Glass Company, also in Columbia, has been producing fine etched glassware for nearly a century.

To the west, Pittsburgh's glassmaking talent was reflected in stained glass created for middle class homes, grand estates, and churches. Artisans also found work at industrial giants like Pittsburgh Plate Glass, and by the 1920s, the city manufactured over 80 percent of America's glass. Today, it has become a national center for contemporary glass art.

Sustaining Pennsylvania's self-employed craftspeople is the goal of the state's artisan trails designations. The program features local artist galleries, studios, and exhibits along a half-dozen rural routes. The Handmade along the Highway program, with participants chosen by an arts jury, links artisan studios and shops along Routes 30 and 40 to the west. Lancaster and York counties, offering dozens of factory tours, work with companies that interpret their manufacturing history and welcome visitors. The program also designates "living treasures," a Japanese designation for acknowledged masters of their crafts.

*pg. 48, left to right, Patrick Kline of Family Heirloom Weavers; the company's sign in Red Lion; display of textile and pottery items using quilt patterns from the Lancaster Heritage Center. pg. 49, from left, Youghiogheny Station Glass and Gallery in Connellsville showcases the work of glass artists; artisans etch goblets at Susquehanna Glassworks in Columbia; Lancaster's Heritage Center displays hand-pieced quilts; bakers at Hammond's Pretzels produce their specialty.*

For more information:
Lancaster Quilt and Textile Museum
37 Market Street, Lancaster
(717) 299-6440
www.quiltandtextilemuseum.com

Lancaster York Heritage Region
1706 Long Level Road, Wrightsville
(717) 252-0229 | www.lyhr.org

Family Heirloom Weavers
775 Meadowview Drive, Red Lion
(717) 246-2431
www.familyheirloomweavers.com

National Watch and Clock Museum
514 Poplar Street, Columbia
(717) 684-8261 | www.nawcc.org

Pittsburgh Glass Center
5472 Penn Avenue, Pittsburgh
(866) 742-4527
www.pittsburghglasscenter.org

Pennsylvania Artisan Trails
www.visitpa.com/visitpa/artisanTrails.pa

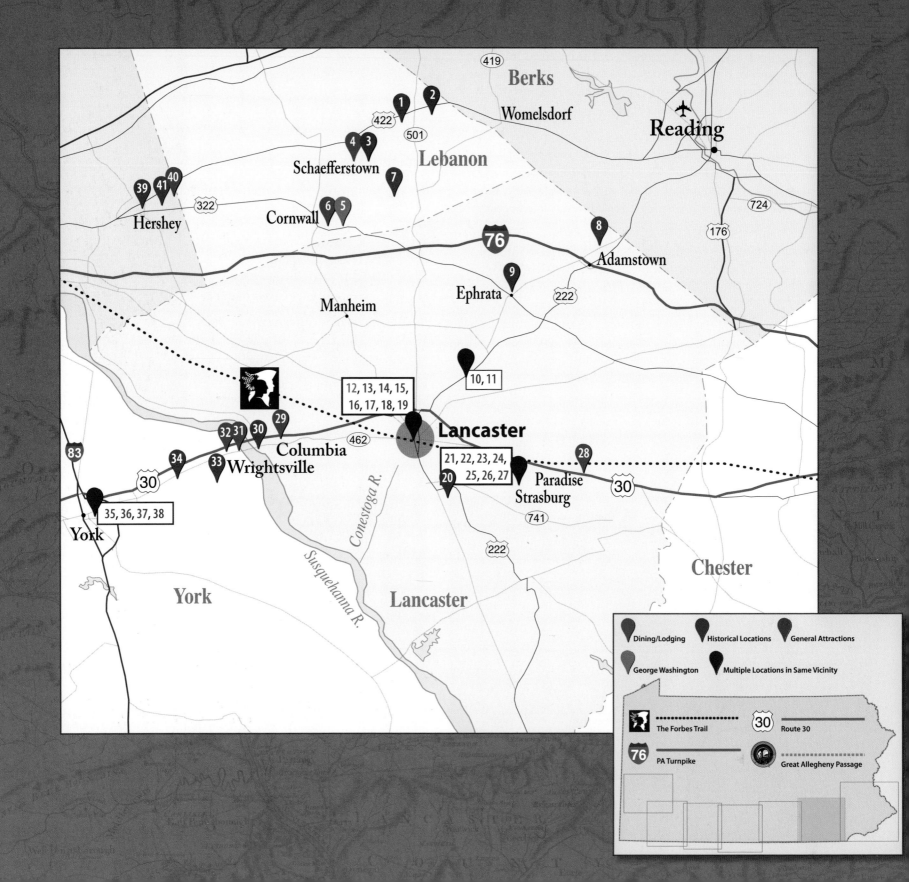

# Lancaster Regional Map

## Visiting Lancaster and Pennsylvania Dutch Country

Despite the city's English name and symbol—the red rose of the House of Lancaster—Lancaster has deep German roots. Amish, Mennonite, Lutheran and Reformed believers accepted Queen Anne's 1701 invitation to settle in the English colony, beginning the traditions of vivid hex signs and German surnames in the region. The Deutsche became known as the Pennsylvania Dutch, and their fine crafts and rich farms met the massive demands of the Forbes Expedition. Nearly three centuries later, both traditions proudly continue.

*Amish family farms thrive in Lancaster County.*

## See 1758 Today

Mennonite Hans Herr and his family were the first Europeans to build a home in Lancaster County. The 1719 **Hans Herr House**[20] and several historic homesteads still stand south of the city (1849 Hans Herr Drive, Willow Street; 717-464-4438; www.hansherr.org). The steeply pitched roof and honey-colored stonework of his home may be familiar to fans of artist Andrew Wyeth: a Herr family descendant, he painted the family home before its restoration in the 1970s.

Lancaster's Penn Square has been a crossroads since 1729. The city center echoes the grid pattern set by the Penns for Philadelphia. General Forbes' troops marched down today's King Street (Route 462) to this central meeting point, now the site of the **Lancaster Heritage Center**[16] (5 West King Street, Lancaster; 717-299-6440; www.lancasterheritage.com). Housed in a cluster of restored buildings, this free public museum, open seasonally, has a German accent. Here's the place to learn about fraktur, the illuminated folk art drawings that record family history, and quilt making. Step next door to browse the **Central Market**[17]. Now housed in a handsome Victorian building, it has sold fresh food continuously since the 1730s. At **Trinity Lutheran Church** on Duke Street, founded in 1730, grave markers in worn German script line the narrow churchyard. Walking tours explore the city's history. It was

the capital for the Continental Congress for one day, on September 27, 1777, and the state capital from 1799 to 1812. Join the tours, conducted April through October, from Southern Market (100 Queen Street; 717-392-1776).

German dissenters built strong communities north of Lancaster. One of the most unusual was the **Ephrata Cloister**[9], where 300 disciples of a charismatic German preacher lived on the banks of the Cocalico Creek (632 West Main Street, Ephrata; 717-733-6600; www.ephratacloister.org). As in the Moravian settlement of Bethlehem in the same era, members devoted themselves to worship and industry. Over a dozen original structures from the 1740s, from dormitories to workshops, are open to the public on the peaceful campus. The visitor center provides an overview of the beliefs and culture of the community. When the last celibate member died in 1813, remaining families formed other local churches.

One of the most famous members of the Cloister was Conrad Weiser. The **Conrad**[2] **Weiser Homestead** lies 15 miles north in Womelsdorf (28 Weiser Lane; 610-589-2934; www.conradweiserhomestead.org). Weiser's amazing gift as a linguist put him at the center of Pennsylvania history for 30 years. Fluent in a half-dozen Indian languages, English, and his native German, he negotiated with the Iroquois in land disputes throughout the 1730s and 1740s and was a key interpreter at the

Treaty of Easton in 1758. While operating a farm of nearly 900 acres, fathering ten children, traveling continuously, and serving as local magistrate and militia leader, he somehow found time to join the Ephrata community for two years. Small, brilliant exhibits in several buildings, open seasonally, bring his remarkable life to light. In 1928, the famed landscape architects, the Olmsted brothers, created sweeping outdoor rooms and a lake on the property for a public park. Weiser is buried here near a statue commemorating his Iroquois friend and companion, Shikellamy.

South of Womelsdorf along Route 419, look for a splash of gold at the Route 501 crossroads. **Historic Schaefferstown**[3] interprets the German heritage of southern Lebanon County with the brightly painted **Gemberling-Rex House**. A 1758 tavern, it retains its 18th century stenciling and Franklin stove. Across Market Street, the **Brendle Museum** interprets the area's German history (111 North Market Street; 717-949-2244; www.hsimuseum.org). The nearby Schaeffer farm, dating from 1736, offers special events. Museum hours are limited. The **Franklin House**[4], built on the town square in 1746, is an old-fashioned restaurant serving German specialties.

*pg. 52, Cornwall Iron Furnace traces early industrial history. pg. 53, clockwise from lower left, Ephrata Cloister rose along the Cocalico Creek in 1732; Schaefferstown commands the crossroads of Routes 419 and 501; Lancaster's Heritage Center explores arts and culture; 18th century interpreters meet at the Conrad Weiser Homestead.*

## George Washington Was Here

George Washington has two known connections here. While commanding the Continental Army at Valley Forge, he rode west to inspect the **Cornwall Iron Furnace**[5], founded in 1742 (94 Rexmont Road, Cornwall; 717-272-9711; www.cornwallironfurnace. org). In the 1750s Pennsylvania smelted one-seventh of the world's iron, despite British attempts to limit colonial production. Cornwall, ten miles north of Lancaster, boasts the only intact charcoal cold blast furnace in the Western Hemisphere. A good small museum interprets the process and the history. The furnace remained in operation until 1883: the unique Gothic Revival buildings from that era resemble red limestone churches rather than factories.

Washington was in Lancaster as president in 1791. The *Pennsylvania Gazette* reported that Washington, returning from a tour of the southern states, crossed the Susquehanna at Wright's Ferry and was feted at the Lancaster courthouse, where no fewer than fifteen toasts were drunk on the 15th anniversary of independence.

Following the July 4 banquet, Washington had a reunion with an old friend. Edward Hand had served as Washington's adjutant general before retiring to his Lancaster farm, Rockford. The Irish-born Hand, like Washington, had served in the British Army as a young surgeon's mate, serving at Fort Pitt. Leaving the British cause in 1774, he followed Washington's command, leading Revolutionary War engagements in Boston, Long Island and Trenton.

Hand's farm, open to the public, is known today as **Rock Ford Plantation**[12] (881 Rock Ford Road, Lancaster; 717-392-7223; www. rockfordplantation.org). Hand hosted his former commander after the 1791 celebration at his home on the banks of the Conestoga River, now part of the city's Central Park. The two-story brick home built on the property in 1794 is an important example of Pennsylvania Georgian architecture.

*Rock Ford Plantation.*

# History: Colonial York

Fifteen miles from Lancaster on the western side of the Susquehanna, York was a power center for the new American colonies and a staging ground for the Battle of Gettysburg in 1863. Founded in 1741, it hosted the Continental Congress in 1777-78, when the Articles of Confederation were enacted. Stroll the city's **Colonial Complex**[38], a core of preserved and reconstructed buildings from this era (157 West Market Street; 717-846-6452; www.yorkheritage.org). Seasonal tours of four structures include the **Golden Plough**, a 1741 tavern, the 1751 **General Horatio Gates House** where Gates lived while attending the Congress, the reconstructed courthouse of 1754, and the **Bobb House**, a log cabin of the 1830s.

York takes its white rose symbol from the British royal house of the 15th century. The city was briefly occupied by Confederate soldiers in 1863, just prior to the battle of Gettysburg. The **York Historical Society Museum**[35], part of the York County Heritage Trust, offers exhibits about daily life through three centuries of settlement (250 East Market Street; 717-848-1587; www.yorkheritage.org).

*The Marquis de Lafayette (statue at right) visited the General Gates House (below, with the Golden Plough Tavern) in early 1778.*

# Family Fun

No place in Pennsylvania is more family-friendly or food-focused than Pennsylvania Dutch country. From chocolate in Hershey to Traintown in Strasburg, there are plenty of attractions to appeal to kids' tastes, all within an easy drive.

North from Lancaster, visit a recreated farm community at the **Landis Valley Museum**[10] (2451 Kissel Hill Road, Lancaster; 717-569-0401; www.landisvalleymuseum.org). With a goal of preserving Pennsylvania German culture, it escorts visitors through a 100-acre site with eighteen buildings. Craftspeople from lacemakers to blacksmiths demonstrate their skills on authentic equipment, and horse-drawn tour wagons pull visitors past fields where historic breeds of geese, horses and cattle still graze. The museum maintains a popular heirloom seed program and operates the Weathervane Museum Store, with a fine collection of handcrafted items. Adjacent to the museum, the **Hands On House**[11] welcomes young children (721 Landis Valley Road, Lancaster; 717-569-5437; www.handsonhouse.org). Pre-schoolers can play dress-up, learn about farms in the "E-I-E-I-O" corner, and tinker in Marty's Machine Shop in this cheerful space, with an outdoor playground and sandbox.

A half-hour drive west, Hershey offers the next-door attractions of **Hershey Park**[39] and **Chocolate World** (100 West Hershey Park Drive, Hershey; 800-437-7439; www.hersheypa.com). For a travelog of the cocoa bean, take the expansive factory tour; for thrills on some of the country's biggest coasters, try the park, rated one of the best in the Northeast. ZooAmerica and pro sports at Hershey Arena are close by.

Antiquing is a contact sport in **Adamstown**, the self-proclaimed Antiques Capital U.S.A. (www.antiquescapital.com). Nearly a thousand dealers operate here, including the massive

**Renninger's**[8], with Sunday markets that attract hundreds of indoor and outdoor sellers (2500 North Reading Road, Denver; 717-336-2177; www.renningers.com). From stained glass to sweaters and sports memorabilia, this is the place to go—and go early.

The village of **Strasburg**, south of Lancaster, is a crossroads with quiet charm and several historic inns. A handful of boutiques on Main Street stay open later on Friday evenings to accommodate weekend visitors. A local specialty is springerle, an anise-flavored cookie baked in intricate molds. The **Springerle House**[21] serves these "picture cookies," a European tradition brought to Lancaster County by its earliest settlers (15 East Main Street, Strasburg; 717-687-8022; www.springerlehouse.com).

Railroad buffs make tracks to the village too. It's the home of the **Strasburg Railroad**[23], the country's oldest short-line, with authentic steam-powered engines (301 Gap Road, Strasburg; 717-687-7522; www.strasburgrailroad.com). Thomas the Tank Engine makes frequent visits. Over 100 locomotives are displayed at the **Railroad Museum of Pennsylvania**[22] (300 Gap Road, Strasburg; 717-687-8628; www.rrmuseumpa.org). Five large train layouts and hundreds of model trains chug the tracks at the **National Toy Train Museum**[25] (300 Paradise Lane, Paradise; 717-687-8976; www.nttmuseum.org). The **Red Caboose Motel**[24] offers 40 rooms in a collection of authentic railcars (312 Paradise Lane, Ronks; 888-687-5005; www.redcaboosemotel.com). Nearby on Route 741 is **Cherry Crest Farms**[26], where the corn maze covers five acres each summer and fall (150 Cherry Hill Road, Ronks; 717-687-6843; www.cherrycrestfarm.com).

*from top, Landis Valley Museum showcases traditional farms and crafts on a farmstead with poultry and livestock; the Strasburg Railroad is a favorite of youngsters.*

# Great Houses and Gardens

It's rare to find a house museum that perfectly captures the spirit of its inhabitants. That is the special attraction of **Wright's Ferry Mansion**[30], which brings to life the redoubtable Susanna Wright (38 South Second Street, Columbia; 717-684-4325; open seasonally). Dubbed "the bluestocking of the Susquehanna," the Quaker intellectual and entrepreneur had this house built in 1738 and lived here until her death in 1784. Restored with an outstanding collection of period arts and furniture that attracts antique connoisseurs, it overlooks the river from its eastern bank in Lancaster County.

The classic English Quaker style of the two-story gray stone house includes original doors, glass, and woodwork. Spacious and light-filled, the rooms have simple whitewashed walls, bare floors, and unadorned windows, echoing the Quaker taste for simplicity. Here Wright entertained business colleagues like Benjamin Franklin. She composed poetry and traded books with Philadelphia intellectuals. She began to record and translate the vocabulary of the local Shawnee people, and established a successful silk production business by raising her own silkworms. Queen Caroline wore Susquehanna silk at the English court, and samples are displayed in Susanna's bedroom.

All of the mansion's antiques date to 1750 or earlier. Fine examples of Philadelphia-made furniture include chairs and chests. Maps, engravings, a pocket sundial, and rare walnut clock suggest Wright's scientific interests, while a collection of kitchen implements show her domestic responsibilities. Ceramics, needlework and metal indicate the prosperous life that Wright and her siblings enjoyed.

Susannah's brother John, for whom Wrightsville is named, operated the western side of the family ferry. Later Wrightsville residents built a covered bridge that

was burned in June 1863 to prevent the Confederates from crossing east: the story is told at **Historic Wrightsville Museum**[32] (309 Locust Street, Wrightsville; 717-252-1169), open Sundays.

Also in Lancaster is the 19th century home of President James Buchanan, **Wheatland**[18] (1120 Marietta Avenue, Lancaster; 717-392-8721; www.wheatland.org). Pennsylvania's only president conducted his front-porch campaign of 1856 from this mansion. Guided tours, exhibits and a short video interpret the life of the 15th president, who served a single term as the storm clouds of the Civil War gathered. The **Lancaster County Historical Society** offers exhibits next door, and the **Tanger Arboretum**[19], with one hundred unusual American specimens, surrounds the site (230 North President Avenue, Lancaster; 717-392-4633; www.lancasterhistory.org).

The 23 acres of **Hershey Gardens**[41] include pockets of interest for children, rosarians, and butterfly enthusiasts (170 Hotel Road, Hershey; 717-534-3492; www.hersheygardens.org). The seasonal garden welcomes spring with over 75,000 tulips and daffodils. Perennial gardens and herb gardens, a rock garden and a Japanese garden are among the highlights. In addition to a formal rose garden with 275 varieties, fifty types of old garden roses (types in production before 1935) bloom in Mrs. Hershey's Rose Garden. The gardens are open year-round except for the outdoor Butterfly House. The elegant **Hotel Hershey**[40], overlooking the property, lends a touch of Moorish grandeur to the scene.

*from top, Visitors meet "James Buchanan" at his estate, Wheatland; the lintel of Hans Herr House bears its date; kitchen at Wright's Ferry Mansion.*

# Great Outdoors

The Lancaster region is flyover country. Located on key migration routes and edged by the broad Susquehanna, the area is a superb spot for bird-watching. The Audubon Society offers an excellent online guide to the Susquehanna River Birding and Wildlife Trail (www.pabirdingtrails.org). **Middle Creek Wildlife Management Area**[7] near Kleinfeltersville attracts thousands of waterfowl to this 5,000-acre preserve (100 Museum Road, Stevens; 717-733-1512; www.pgc.state.pa.us). Follow the sounds of honking snow geese, tundra swans and cormorants to the 400-acre lake. The paved Willow Point hiking path, which is handicapped-accessible, leads to a viewing platform. Six other trails and a trout stream are also available, with seasonal interpretive programs at the visitors center.

At **Samuel Lewis State Park**[33], brisk breezes on a bluff above the Susquehanna offer perfect conditions for kite flying (6000 Mt. Pisgah Road, York; 717-432-5011; www.dcnr.state.pa.us/stateparks/parks/samuelslewis.aspx). Atop **Mt. Pisgah**, the highest point in central York County, an 885-foot ridge offers spectacular views of the river valley and clear night skies. Star-gazing events are frequently held here.

Pennsylvania has over one hundred private fishing lakes. One that welcomes fishermen of all ages is **Limestone Springs Preserve**[1] in Lebanon County (930 Tulpehocken Road, Richland; 717-866-2461; www.limestonespringspreserve.com). This commercial trout hatchery rents gear, cleans the catch, and charges by the pound.

Cyclists can travel nearly 20 miles from Elizabethtown in Lancaster County north to Lebanon along the path of the old Cornwall-Lebanon Railroad. For information on the **Lebanon Valley Rail Trail** visit www.lvrailtrail.com. The **Heritage Rail Trail** runs from the

Mason-Dixon Line 21 miles north, entering York near the Colonial Complex. The route includes two museums in the restored rail stations of the old Northern Central Railroad at New Freedom and Hanover Junction. For details, visit http://ycwebserver.york-county.org/Parks/RailTrail.htm.

*Kite-flying at Samuel Lewis State Park; fishing the Susquehanna at Wrightsville.*

## Uniquely Lancaster

Lancaster's **Central Market**[17] at Penn Square is a noisy, flourishing three-century institution (23 North Market Street, Lancaster; 717-291-4723; www.cityoflancasterpa.com). It's America's oldest farmers market, operating continuously since the 1730s. Opening at dawn each Tuesday, Friday and Saturday, it shows off the bounty of local farms with fresh meats, flowers, baked goods, and much more. As customers wait for orders of freshly ground horseradish, the scent mingles with herbs and exotic spices. International foods, like Panang curry and empanadas flank traditional specialties like shoo-fly pie. There's also a fine selection of cheeses, smoked meats, and candy. While farmers markets are a local food fixture in many central Pennsylvania towns, this bustling, friendly market is the granddaddy of them all.

*Lancaster's Central Market has operated continuously since the 1730s.*

## Did You Know?

In the annals of odd architecture, the **Haines Shoe House**[34] (right) makes an extra-large statement. This unique structure just off Route 30 in Hellam, York County, stands 25 feet high. Built as an ad gimmick by local shoe magnate Mahlon Haines in 1948, it was formerly a guesthouse for honeymooners. It is open seasonally for tours and ice cream (197 Shoe House Road, Hellam; 717-840-8339; www.shoehouse.us).

## Plan a Visit

### Annual Regional Events

**Herb and Garden Faire at Landis Valley,** May
www.landisvalleymuseum.org

**FlavorFest,** May
www.padutchountry.com

**Kutztown Folk Festival,** July
www.kutztownfestival.com

**Weiser Homestead reenactments,**
May through September
www.conradweiserhomestead.org

### Lancaster and North

For more information:
Pennsylvania Dutch Convention
and Visitors Bureau
501 Greenfield Road, Lancaster
800-PA-DUTCH [800-723-8824]
www.padutchcountry.com

#### DINING
**Franklin House**[4]
101 North Market Street, Schaefferstown
(717) 949-2122

**Checkers**[13]
300 West James Street, Lancaster
(717) 509-1069 | www.checkersbistro.com
• Cheerful, casual bar and café with American menu.

**Strasburg Country Store and Creamery**[27]
1 West Main Street, Strasburg
(717) 687-0766
• Voted the region's best ice cream parlor, with sandwiches and penny candy.

**Historic Revere Tavern**[28]
3063 Lincoln Highway, Paradise
(800) 429-7383 | www.reveretavern.com
• This 1740s stage tavern was briefly owned by President James Buchanan.

**Prudhomme's Lost Cajun Kitchen**[29]
50 Lancaster Avenue, Columbia
(717) 684-1706 | www.lostcajunkitchen.com
• Rustic family-friendly pub.

#### LODGING
**Hotel Hershey**[40]
100 Hotel Road, Hershey
(717) 533-2171 | www.hotelhershey.com
• Elegant resort overlooking Chocolate Town.

**Lancaster Arts Hotel**[14]
300 Harrisburg Avenue, Lancaster
(866) 720-2787 | www.lancasterartshotel.com
• Boutique hotel in a historic tobacco warehouse near Franklin and Marshall College.

**Cornwall Inn**[6]
50 Burd Coleman Road, Cornwall
(866) 605-6563 | www.cornwallinnpa.com
• This spacious B&B is the former company store of the Cornwall Iron Works. Adjacent to Lebanon Valley Rail Trail.

### York County

For more information:
York County Convention and Visitors Bureau
149 West Market Street, York
(888) 858-9675 | www.yorkpa.org

#### DINING
**John Wright Store and Restaurant**[31]
North Front Street, Wrightsville
(717) 252-2519 | www.jwright.com
• Café serving breakfast and lunch daily on the riverfront.

**White Rose Bar & Grill**[37]
48 North Beaver Street, York
(717) 848-5369
www.whiterosebarandgrill.com
• Downtown bistro with outdoor dining.

#### LODGING
**Yorktowne Hotel**[36]
48 East Market Street, York
(800) 233-9324 | www.yorktowne.com
• Member, Historic Hotels of America.

# Agriculture: Pennsylvania's Enduring Industry

There is often a crowd of curious onlookers when an Amish farmer, standing on a hay-filled wagon, skillfully guides his team of 5 heavy horses across a field. It is a scene from Pennsylvania's rich farm past that brings millions of visitors to Lancaster County. This picture perfect vista, however, masks an important fact. The seemingly anachronistic Amish are among the most successful farmers in the country. They are the active symbols of an industry that has been at the center of Pennsylvania life since Native Americans raised their annual crops of corn, squash, and beans.

When General John Forbes and his redcoats crossed Lancaster County in 1758, they marveled at Pennsylvania's productive farm culture. They rode through the rows of neat German farms, so distinct with sturdy barns and houses built to last and fields rotating through oat, wheat, and clover crops. They met drovers guiding cattle, pigs, strings of up to 30 horses, and flocks of geese to market. They passed a steady stream of canvas-topped red and blue wagons and lines of packhorses carrying supplies to a hungry army. Further west, they saw frontier log communities that were clearing forests and breaking ground for new farms. Abundant agriculture, blessed with good soil, temperate weather and flowing water, fueled success for both the Forbes Campaign and the Commonwealth of Pennsylvania.

The Pennsylvania Historical and Museum Commission (PHMC) traces the Keystone State's rich farm history with several museums and living history farms along the Forbes Trail. Lancaster's Landis Valley is in the east, the State Museum is in Harrisburg, and the Somerset Historical Center and Ambridge's Old Economy Village are in the west. Old farming traditions are kept alive by hobbyists at annual festivals. The Blue Mountain Antique Gas and Steam Engine Association annually puts the old whirling, hissing and popping machines through their paces at Jacktown Grove in Bangor, north of Easton. The September Stahlstown Flax Scutching Festival, near the Donegal Turnpike exit, has been demonstrating the lost and labor intensive process, turning flax into linen by hand, for over a century.

A drive on Pennsylvania's country roads reveals that farming is far from a lost tradition. The number of farms peaked at over 200,000 in 1910 but today, there are still 59,000 families farming 7.7 million acres in the state. With ever increasing efficiency, an agricultural community that has been tilling the Pennsylvania soil for over three centuries now exports $1.5 billion of its $4 billion annual cash output, much of it through Philadelphia's port to the world. One of Pennsylvania's original businesses, agriculture pours $45 billion into the state economy each year and has spawned major corporations like Hershey, Hanover, and Heinz.

Modern agriculture is best explored at fairs, farm shows and markets. America's oldest fair at York, dating to 1765, has expanded to ten full days every September. Pennsylvania's almost century old January Farm Show, the country's largest indoor exposition, promising everything agricultural including 10,000 apple dumplings from local fruit growers, attracts half a million visitors to the 24 acre Farm Show Complex and Expo Center. The Harrisburg Complex and Expo Center features

*Old-fashioned farming in Lancaster County attracts millions of visitors.*

Pennsylvania agriculture throughout the year, hosting the All American Dairy Show and Keystone International Livestock Exposition.

With America's growing interest in buying fresh and buying local, local farmers markets are thriving throughout the state. Hundreds of markets, some, like Philadelphia's Headhouse/Shambles Market and Lancaster's Central Market operating continuously since the days of Ben Franklin, are again making local family farms productive and profitable.

## Agricultural Events
- Farm Show, All American Dairy Show and Keystone International Livestock Exposition
  Pennsylvania Farm Show Complex and Expo Center
  2300 North Cameron Street, Harrisburg
  (717) 787-5373 | www.agriculture.state.pa.us/fscomplex/site/default.asp
- Blue Mountain Antique Gas and Steam Engine Association, Inc. | www.jacktown.com
- Stahlstown Flax Scutching Festival, September
  (724) 593-2119 | http://flaxscutching.org
- York Fair, September
  (717) 848-2596 | www.yorkfair.org

## For More Information
- History and background on agriculture in Amish Country
  Pennsylvania Dutch Convention and Visitors Bureau
  (800) PADUTCH, [800-723-8824]
  www.padutchcountry.com
- Background on modern agriculture in Pennsylvania
  Pennsylvania Department of Agriculture
  (717) 787-4737 | www.agriculture.state.pa.us
- Consumer Guide to Pennsylvania Farmers Markets
  (610) 767-5026 | www.pafarm.com
- **Farm Museums** administered by the Pennsylvania Historical and Museum Commission
  (717) 787-3362 | www.phmc.state.pa.us

## Farmers Markets
- **Historic Shambles/Headhouse Farmers Market** in Philadelphia
  (215) 575-0444
  www.foodtrust.org/php/headhouse/
- **Lancaster Central Market**, the oldest farmers market in the U.S.
  (717) 291-4723 | www.fandm.edu/departments/tdf/MarketSite/FSet.html

## Living History Farms
- **Colonial Pennsylvania Plantation**
  Ridley Creek State Park, Media
  (616) 566-1725 | www.colonialplantation.org
- **Quiet Valley Living Historical Farm**
  1000 Turkey Hill Road, Stroudsburg
  (570) 992-6161 | www.quietvalley.org

*The contours of this farm in the Allegheny Mountains cover the remains of a fortified camp on the 1758 Forbes Road.*

Colonel Henry Bouquet arrives in a busy frontier Carlisle that resembles the Wild West. He has a big job ahead, organizing the Pennsylvania provincial troops and wagonloads of supplies for the army's march west.

# Carlisle
## May 24, 1758

# On the Edge of the Frontier

General Forbes and his staff reached the modest village of Carlisle on the evening of July 4, 1758. Nestled in the fertile Cumberland Valley between Yellow Breeches and Conodoquinet Creeks, Carlisle was the front line for European settlers moving west. Trotting at dusk between the town's log cabins and stone houses, their windows glowing with hearth fires, Forbes headed for the makeshift stockade protecting the town from attack. He was finally at a base camp for his unfolding campaign, the beginning of a pioneering road that would bear his name.

The party had traveled almost twenty miles since crossing the Susquehanna River. The river was Pennsylvania's great divide: wide, rock-strewn and shallow, even fordable, in places during dry summers. Almost cutting the colony in two, this waterway, a main source of the Chesapeake Bay, was the boundary between two different worlds. To the east were the settled parts, rich in agriculture and growing communities. To the west were the wild mountains and forests, home only to Native Americans and a few hardy Europeans. The Susquehanna was a formidable obstacle for all travelers. A handful of river ferry operators were the only lifeline between east and west.

## Crossing the Susquehanna

Eighteenth century ferries were noted for their simplicity. Wide-beamed, shallow-draft boats, rafts or flats lashed to canoes were poled or rowed from side to side, sometimes hooked to a line if the current was strong. Men and their mounts, domestic animals, bales, barrels, boxes and wagons were the usual freight. Wind, high water and ice stymied anyone in a hurry.

In 1758, there were two well-known ferries on the lower Susquehanna. Wright's Ferry linked Lancaster and York while Harris' Ferry, upriver, was the window to the frontier. After 1733, Yorkshire-born Indian trader John Harris and his son, John, Jr., ran a popular ferry near the mouth of Paxton Creek. It became a magnet for traders and immigrants and a spur of the Great Wagon Road that headed southwest across the Potomac River to the Valley of Virginia. A growing settlement at the ferry would become Pennsylvania's capital, Harrisburg, in 1812.

The British army, rolling, riding, and marching from all directions, clogged the frontier ferry on its way to Carlisle. Storms and angry water on the river delayed the crossings. When General Forbes crossed "upon rafts and flats," he was amazed at the expanse of the Susquehanna, 1900 yards across by his count. More than a month earlier, Colonel Bouquet struggled with high water. He reported that it took nearly three days to ferry thirty wagons across, with much trouble and danger. Faced with the need to get hundreds of wagons from shore to shore, Bouquet thought that "a couple of rafts would also be needed to carry over the wagons, but we have neither time nor workmen to build them."

Still suffering with his flux, General Forbes set up headquarters in Carlisle. The frontier town was a rough place but at least it was a community. Everything beyond was Indian trails, woods, rivers, swamps, rocks, and steep slopes with an occasional clearing.

Forbes wrote to Colonel Bouquet on July 6, complaining that "I did not find things quite so well as I could have wished particularly the Wagons, which have fallen into the greatest confusion." Having spent most of June in the saddle overseeing road building, Bouquet now was setting up a fortified camp one hundred miles ahead, deep in the mountain forests at Raystown.

*Spring downpours make the wide and rocky Susquehanna River a major impediment to redcoats moving men, horses, wagons and artillery across the Harris Ferry to a base camp at Carlisle.*

## The Last Towns of Note

Before the recent troubles, Carlisle had been growing at a rapid rate. Europeans had been in the Cumberland Valley for a generation. In 1751, Irish immigrant John Armstrong surveyed a plat for a new court town called Carlisle. Cumberland County, carved out of Lancaster County in the same year, was the mother county for what became most of western Pennsylvania. Settlers wasted no time flooding across the Susquehanna into lush valleys of the Conodoquinet and Conococheague Creeks.

Settlers who moved west of the Susquehanna endured isolation and backbreaking labors. Limitless land, however, was a reward unknown in Europe. The blend of risk and opportunity was ready-made for a tough and hungry mix of Celts: Irish, Anglo-Irish, Scots, Scots-Irish, and Welsh. The Scots-Irish were independent, "frequently rude and lawless, excitable and hotheaded, implacable to enemies."

Carlisle quickly became a Scots-Irish community. Among the hundred or so structures, a log courthouse and a few brick and several stone and frame houses of "genteel taste" stood out among the rows of "small trifling" log cabins. The town also had a substantial collection of inns and taverns. Hard-drinking patrons brought trouble to establishments like the Sign of the Indian Queen and the Spread Eagle. Tavern keeper George Hook was chased to Carlisle from York in 1758 for "keeping a disorderly house." Store and tavern owner Elizabeth Ross was beaten for not paying her bills. No wonder General Forbes, often frustrated by the colonials, called them "an extreme collection of broken inn-keepers, horse jockeys and traders."

Whatever their vices, the Scots-Irish brought their strict Presbyterian faith. Carlisle's Presbyterian founders saw no need to separate church and state. Some uneasy German Moravians, traveling south through "Carl Isles" in 1753, "set up our tent four miles beyond so as not to be too near the Irish Presbyterians." While Lancaster had placed its impressive courthouse at the very center of town life and its churches elsewhere, John Armstrong and his fellow faithful dragged stones to the village square for a permanent church while their courthouse was still in a temporary log building.

### George Croghan, Frontiersman

George Croghan was a knave. He was called "as vile a wretch as could be pick'd up." Colonel Henry Bouquet was wary of this "intriguing, disaffected person." It was "highly necessary to keep a watchful eye upon [him]."

The Pennsylvania frontier was a perfect setting for Mr. Croghan (pronounced Crone), an Irish immigrant who began patenting property near Harris Ferry in 1742. He never stopped speculating for millions of frontier acres. Croghan was also a tireless Indian trader with posts wherever Native Americans wanted to trade furs for his wares. He was a master of the deal, always on the edge of financial ruin.

George Croghan was a brave and steady companion. He built forts and chased enemy raiders in the forest. He led Indian scouts for both Braddock and Forbes. He took his deal-making skills to Indian councils and became the Iroquois agent in Pennsylvania. Edward Shippen observed, "if he could not bring [Indians} in [for a conference], no man on the continent could do it."

Croghan courted frontier dangers and opportunities for four decades. Among his hard drinking companions, he could "push about the [liquor] Glass copiously and briskly." He once got a black eye trading blows with Teedyuscung in a drunken brawl. He received a hatchet blow during an Indian attack, later claiming, "the hatchet would not enter, so you may see a thick skull is of service on some occasions." Opportunist or upright settler, George Croghan left an indelible mark on early Pennsylvania.

*General Forbes designates Carlisle the rendezvous for the Pennsylvania forces that will form the largest single contingent in his army.*

## La Petite Guerre

The Woodland Indians were unmatched in what Europeans called light infantry tactics or irregular warfare. George Washington once admitted, "I cannot conceive the best white man to be equal to them [Indians] in the woods." Pennsylvanian James Smith, an Indian captive for several years, had great respect for Indian warriors. "British officers call the Indians undisciplined savages [but they] have all the essentials of discipline. They are under good command, and punctual in obeying orders; they can act in concert…when they go into battle they are not loaded or encumbered with many clothe."

The French called irregular warfare *La Petite Guerre*, the hit and run little war on the edges of major battles. George Washington criticized the redcoats for adapting too slowly to the forest tactics they had never faced in the flat, open lands of Europe. European armies, however, were long time veterans of *La Petite Guerre*, using bands of irregular troops or partisans to harass enemy armies on the march. In America, Indians had perfected forest warfare to a high art and French Canadians learned how to effectively use Indian warriors and their tactics.

Although the British lightened the loads and uniforms of redcoats and trained special units in forest tactics, they struggled to enlist Indian allies as scouts and light infantry.

## Years of Terror

In July of 1755, the citizens of Carlisle suddenly were "under great apprehension." Within days of hearing the bad news of Braddock's defeat, nine Carlisle men subscribed to a Night Watch for mutual security. John Armstrong soon joined the defense and suggested a long chain of blockhouses, admitting that "this part of the world [is] in a drooping melancholy condition." By November, Carlisle had a small stockade surrounding William Blyth's tavern north of the town square.

The first attack came in October, near the Forks of the Susquehanna. After two days of killing at Penn's Creek settlements, the attackers, led by the Delaware Pisquetomen, disappeared carrying fifteen scalps and tugging ten women and children into captivity. A month later, raiding parties painted black for war, destroyed a German family with eight children under age fourteen at Tulpehocken. The forays continued as fleeing settlers, who had lived near Indian neighbors for decades, were "in the worst fear and terror."

Pennsylvania sprang into action in early 1756. As recruits were trained, the colony built and manned more than twenty forts stretching over 100 miles with four guarding the western flanks of Cumberland County. A lonely outpost at the Forks of the Susquehanna (now Sunbury) became Fort Augusta, the largest and best constructed of the Pennsylvania-built forts.

*Paddling through a vast river and lake network in Indian canoes and French bateaux, reinforcements come and go with the seasons to protect the remote outpost at Fort Duquesne.*

*Beginning his July peace mission deep into Indian Country, Christian Frederick Post faces regular dangers riding through wild mountains. "We went down a very steep hill, and our horses slipped so, that I expected, every moment, they would fall heels over head."*

## Some Good News with the Bad

The French and Indian assault continued, especially in the western settlements. The square stockades in the mountains housed small garrisons that patrolled the nearby forests. These rangers found out how dangerous the duty was in late July, 1756. More than fifty French and Indians, led by a notorious Delaware leader called Captain Jacobs, captured and burned Fort Granville (now Lewistown). They killed its commander Lieutenant Edward Armstrong, the younger brother of John. Collecting scalps and dragging away thirty prisoners, the attackers broke the colonial line of defense. In a year, hundreds of frontier settlers had been killed, captured and forced from their cabins.

With fortunes at a low ebb, Lieutenant Colonel John Armstrong and his Pennsylvania troops decided in late August to strike at western Indian country. The target was Kittanning, a Delaware village on the Allegheny River that was the source of many raids. Armstrong and 300 men marched for nine days across unknown terrain. They used the Frankstown Path, "a very bad road, abounding with morasses and broken hills." On September 8, the attackers took many casualties and netted few captives, but they burned the Kittanning village and killed Captain Jacobs.

The wounded Colonel Armstrong was awarded a sword, a belt and cash for Indian scalps. He was later rewarded again with a grant of land at Kittanning that he named "Victory." Philadelphians, pleased to hear any good news, struck a medal to honor the new found heroes.

## John Armstrong "First Citizen of Carlisle"

John Armstrong was on the opposite side of the ledger from George Croghan. Both were ambitious immigrants, but while Irishman Croghan ranged near and far seeking his fortune, the Scots-Irish Armstrong invested 50 years developing the new town of Carlisle.

As a colonial surveyor, Armstrong launched an influential career. He surveyed much of Cumberland County and had a large network of clients. By 1758, he was a Carlisle leader and Presbyterian elder, winning respect for his honesty and intellect. It was his three years of brave military service, however, that made him a legend. As the hero of the Kittanning raid, Armstrong became a pillar of the defense against French and Indian attacks.

The citizen soldier spent the next three decades continuing an active public life. He was an early supporter of rebellion against English rule, a major general of Pennsylvania militia during the year of Valley Forge and a member of the Continental Congress during the United States' formative years. He was a good friend of George Washington and left behind a lively correspondence with the Founding Fathers. In Carlisle, he is best remembered as one of the founders of Dickinson College. John Armstrong's career illustrates how a generation of striving, capable Pennsylvania immigrants energized the American experience.

## A Dangerous Peace Mission Begins

Two years almost to the day after peace talks began in Easton, eastern Delaware leader Teedyuscung was again meeting with Pennsylvania Governor Denny, this time in Philadelphia. Colonial officials were seriously considering the Delaware leader's request for return of the land lost in the 1737 Walking Purchase. A flock of Quaker-led carpenters were building new houses for the Delaware on the upper reaches of the Susquehanna. This July 1758 Philadelphia meeting, however, became a tipping point for Teedyuscung's fortunes.

The Quakers were still searching for peace. Israel Pemberton had won General Forbes' confidence. The General told Pemberton; "no person [is] more zealous to bring [Indian negotiations] to a speedy and happy conclusion than you are." Turning their attentions away from the often unreliable Teedyuscung, the Quakers were now looking to Pisquetomen, the western Delaware leader who was in Philadelphia with a delegation talking peace. Governor Denny saw the new opportunities and decided to send a little known envoy named Christian Frederick Post, guided by Pisquetomen, to Indian villages in the far west.

## A Mutual Defense Pact

Thus began one of the most unusual partnerships in diplomatic history. Pisquetomen was a sixty-year-old man who had lived along the Susquehanna River until his people were forced west by the Walking Purchase. He was tough talking, often assertive, even abusive. He led the attack on Penns Creek in 1755 and

left a warning to settlers, two tomahawks buried in a half-burned body. Yet, he and his brothers, Tamaqua (the Beaver) and Shingas, were looking to the English, now marching towards the Forks of the Ohio, for an end to a cruel war. It was a risky business, passing through frontier settlements, because the Indians' reputation preceded them. The "Irish people, knowing some of the Indians, in a rash manner exclaimed against them, and we had some difficulty to get them off clear."

Christian Frederick Post faced the same dangers in Indian country. He would go through villages where the people "surrounded me with drawn knives. Their faces were quite distorted with rage, and they went so far as to say, I should not live long." Throughout these frontier trials, the forty-eight-year-old Post, a furniture joiner by trade, remained a self-possessed missionary sure in his Moravian faith. Born in Prussia, he came to America in 1742, preached to the Indians in New York and Connecticut, married a baptized Indian woman and returned to Europe in 1751. The well-traveled Post was now back in Pennsylvania, determined to continue his mission to the Delawares whom he considered "his own flesh and blood." When this quiet, gentle man met Pisquetomen, he decided, with no diplomatic experience, to take on a dangerous mission of great importance. Post and the old Indian sachem would protect each other with a mutual defense pact.

On July 15, 1758, Post received his orders from the governor and began a journal. He rode with his Indian guides to Pennsylvania Fort Allen, north of Bethlehem. There Teedyuscung, seeing his influence waning, tried to talk the envoys out of the trip. When he said that he feared for Post's safety, the missionary said he "was resolved to go forward, taking my life in my hand, as one ready to part with it for [the Indians'] good."

The travelers headed west as Post observed many plantations deserted and laid waste, and prayed for the restoration of "peace and prosperity to the distressed." Reaching Fort Augusta, they were outfitted for the trip and "set out with good courage." Crossing the Susquehanna, they rode into the big woods, slept in heavy rain and spent much of the first day of August finding precious horses

*Privacy is non-existent for enlisted soldiers and their families who share tents and prepare their own meals in 4-6 man "messes."*

that had run away. The next day, they found "two poles, painted red, to which [the Indians] tie their prisoners when they stop at night." Post was upset by the "disagreeable and melancholy sight, to see the means they use to distress others."

## The Troubles Continue

In spite of the Kittanning raid, attacks remained a frightening fact of life. The Reverend Thomas Barton, a newly-arrived Anglo-Irish Anglican missionary, observed that "Carlisle is the only remains of that once populous country; They have a garrison of about 100 men; but how long they will be able to defend themselves is very uncertain."

Carlisle's attempts at building a strong fort were fitful at best. James Burd, Edward Shippen's capable son-in-law, was more successful. A stockade at nearby Shippensburg, named Fort Morris to honor the governor, was erected in 1755. The Carlisle fort was finally begun in March of 1756. In spite of regular alarms, a Pennsylvania officer complained that "the people of this town cannot be prevailed on to do any thing for their own safety." Philadelphia sent provincial weapons and supplies but the fort remained unfinished and garrison troops were housed outside the fort. After a snowy 1756-1757 winter, the Reverend Barton feared that "the approaching spring will make us all tremble."

Experienced help arrived when Colonel John Stanwix and five companies of the Royal Americans marched into Carlisle during May of 1757. Six more companies joined the force in September. The redcoats immediately went to work throwing up a large entrenched camp with dirt breastworks on the northeast edge of town. Colonel Stanwix noted the toll two years of war had taken "at this beggarly place where one half of the few houses are uncovered and deserted." The colonel, a veteran royal officer nearly seventy years of age, was sent to pave the way for another expedition against the French. His decisive but gracious authority was just what less experienced provincial officers like John Armstrong needed.

## A New Breed of Military Leader

On the eve of the Forbes campaign, Pennsylvania reorganized its regiment into three battalions. The three young commanders, John Armstrong, James Burd, and Hugh Mercer were models for a new brand of frontier leader. Armstrong and Mercer were born in Ireland and Burd in Scotland. They were hardy, capable, and eager for New World opportunities. They were community leaders who sought fortunes in land speculation, agriculture, industry, and Indian trade. They married into established families and labored to pass on substantial estates to their heirs.

Carlisle was the epicenter for this new breed building a new society. Early settlers John Harris, father and son, opened the door with their Susquehanna ferry. Scots-Irish and German immigrants to the back country crossed the river to take advantage of that opening. During the crisis, several saw their military careers as a community responsibility, a chance for adventure and an opportunity to attract notice for their selfless deeds. These tough, experienced backwoodsmen were a matchless resource for General Forbes and Colonel Bouquet.

## Base Camp at Carlisle

Everything was coming together at Carlisle. Pennsylvania was finally providing the needed arms, supplies and manpower. Battalions of Pennsylvania troops, still gathering recruits, passed through the town on their way west in June. All of the Highlanders escorting the siege artillery reached Carlisle by July 11. Shaking their heads at colonial attempts to build forts, British engineers, led by Captain Harry Gordon, another veteran of Braddock's defeat, were hard at work on the still unfinished Carlisle Fort.

Almost a ghost town the year before, Carlisle was alive with ranks of soldiers drilling, couriers and cavalry dashing about on their horses, snarls of wagons with teamsters cursing at their teams, drovers steering their beef cattle down the dirt streets, rows of tents, cook fires, clothes lines with flapping laundry, stacks of forage harvested from local fields, immense piles of boxes and barrels and, now, scores of horses straining to pull large, bronze cannons into town. The British invasion force was taking shape.

In the midst of the commotion, a very human story, rarely told in 18th century armies, was playing out in the Carlisle jail. Veteran camp follower Martha May, a laundress and nurse married to a redcoat for twenty-two years, had incurred

### Following the Army

The colorful elements of Forbes' army that began to gather in Carlisle in late May 1758 included more than just soldiers and warriors. Most military camps and garrisons in Europe and the American colonies were indeed little communities that included numerous women and children. Forbes' growing army was no exception.

In the 1750s, the British army typically authorized a ratio of five to ten women for each 100 men in a regiment. These women, who were usually soldiers' legal or common law wives, and sometimes siblings, drew army rations in exchange for serving as laundresses and nurses. The officially recognized women of a regiment were usually joined on the fringes of every military encampment by scores of unofficial camp followers. Together, they formed a teeming and sometimes disorderly crowd. In addition to taking in laundry, many army women supported their families by acting as sutlers—selling foodstuffs, clothing, and especially alcohol to the troops.

Rowdy behavior was certainly a common occurrence when soldiers, alcohol, and camp followers mixed. But it is a mistake to think of army women (as has been common through history) in merely a smirking, condescending way. "I have been a wife 22 years," a camp woman named Martha May informed Bouquet in a letter written in Carlisle on June 4, 1758, "and have traveled with my husband every place or country the company marched to and have worked very hard ever since I was in the army." Stubbornly determined to keep their families together through every hardship, women like Martha May shared the triumphs and tragedies that lay ahead in the 1758 campaign.

Colonel Bouquet's wrath and was literate enough to plead for her freedom. "I hope yr Honour will be so Good as to Pardon this…time that I may go with my Poor Husband, one time more to carry him and my good Officers water in ye Hottest Battle as I have done before." Her fate is unknown. She showed up for a moment in the June, 1758 record books and disappeared.

*Camp followers like Martha May, a 22 year army veteran, wash laundry, help with cooking and care for the sick and wounded.*

## 18th Century Dining, Army-Style

British and American provincial soldiers serving in North America during the French and Indian War ideally received a weekly ration of 7 pounds of bread or flour, 7 pounds of beef or 3½ pounds of pork (either fresh or preserved in salt brine), 6 pints of dried peas, ½ pint of rice, and 6 ounces of butter. This ration was usually supplemented by small quantities of rum or whiskey, generally about a 1/4 pint per day. Depending on supply, soldiers might receive various substitutes, including mutton, fresh game, or salted fish, oatmeal, beans, or other foodstuffs. During sea voyages, and sometimes on campaign, soldiers received a type of hard, unleavened bread known as biscuit—the "hardtack" of the American Civil War.

Each soldier carried his own provisions over his shoulder in a square cloth pouch known as a haversack, and groups of four to six men formed a "mess" to share cooking utensils and responsibilities. A mess, which occupied a single tent in the regiment's encampment, was generally issued a light kettle of tinned iron and a hatchet for cutting firewood. With this basic fare and simple cooking apparatus, soldiers endured a nearly unrelenting diet of boiled meat and starches, although seasonal gardening (and plundering!) contributed fresh vegetables and fruits at certain times.

By contrast, British and American provincial officers generally enjoyed a much more varied and nutritious diet than the men under their command. Merchants known as sutlers accompanied Forbes' army on campaign, offering for sale prepared meals and a variety of foodstuffs including sugar, raisins and dates, American and imported cheeses, chocolate, coffee, tea, pepper, mustard, wine and cider vinegars, salad oil, and butter, as well as various dried and cured meats. In an era when the drinking of water was often looked on with suspicion, sutlers offered Madeira and other wines, rum, whiskey, and various kinds of alcoholic punch.

Not surprisingly, an officer typically dined in greater comfort than his soldiers. When Colonel George Washington returned to Virginia after the 1758 campaign, for example, his camp equipment included 3 tablecloths, a teakettle, cups and saucers (some with pieces broken out of them after the hard campaign), tea and tablespoons, 13 plates and 2 pewter dishes, forks and spoons, spices, and a copper cooking kettle. Indeed, archeologists have uncovered thousands of fragments of wine glasses, liquor bottles, and fine ceramic plates, cups, and saucers at sites along the Forbes Road.

*Officers bring their own servants, food, furniture, and cookware, enjoying fine wine, spirits, even delicacies like chocolate, cheese, and raisins.*

## Searching for a Better Route West

For his part, General Forbes was sorting out "the greatest degree of confusion" over the wagons, "for in this place everything was mixed, so we neither knew what we had or what we wanted." He criticized Sir John St. Clair, now in Carlisle, whom he said "had [not] taken the smallest pains, or had made the least inquiry how to set those matters to rights." Forbes had another bone to pick with Sir John. Trying to find the best route to the Forks of the Ohio, he wrote to William Pitt in London, "I am in hopes of finding a better way over the Allegheny Mountains than that from Fort Cumberland which General Braddock took, if so I shall shorten my March 40 miles." Sir John originally recommended Raystown as the army base camp. Now, he was advocating Fort Cumberland and a new supply road from Fort Frederick to Cumberland in Maryland. Forbes "spoke very roundly" to Sir John and sent him to Raystown to scout a road west across Allegheny Mountain. By the end of July, the General was still in Carlisle, again "extremely reduced and low in spirits with the flux, and other afflictions."

Colonel Bouquet was at Raystown carrying most of the load of field command. He had left Carlisle on June 8, riding southwest on the route cut by James Burd to support General Braddock in 1755. Skirting the first range of the Allegheny Mountains, he passed the stone and log village of Shippensburg and the small stockade called Fort Morris. Water and forage were still abundant for the men and their animals along this rolling Cumberland Valley route. By June 10, Bouquet rode around Parnell's Knob, a local landmark, and entered the gates of Fort Loudoun. He was briefed on the steep trail ahead, climbing through deep woods to the top of Tuscarora Mountain.

*Soldiers in the ranks endure a monotonous and unhealthy diet relieved only by daily drams of liquor.*

# Perfecting the Common Life through Education

The Society of Friends brought educational milestones to Pennsylvania in the 1680s. The Quaker commitment to individual excellence and spiritual depth still guides their many schools throughout the country. In the 18th century, two famous Pennsylvanians were determined to put education on the public agenda. The astute and public-minded Ben Franklin was convinced that "good education of youth is the surest foundation of happiness." His efforts in Philadelphia helped launch the Ivy League **University of Pennsylvania** (1740). Dr. Benjamin Rush believed that "one general and uniform system of education will render the mass of people more homogenous," creating a "uniform and peaceable government." Rush, another revolutionary thinker John Dickinson, and French and Indian War hero John Armstrong saw to it that a college, the first chartered in the new United States, was created as a "bulwark of liberty" in Carlisle, Pennsylvania.

Dating back to 1783, **Dickinson College** is thriving today as a landmark along the Forbes Trail. The respected school, however, is only one among scores of colleges and universities on the Trail. The strong tradition of good education has continued unabated since the earliest days of our republic. Religious and ethnic groups have led the way: Quakers at **Haverford** (1833) and **Swarthmore** (1864), Baptists at **Bucknell** (1846) and **Temple** (1884), Presbyterians at **Washington and Jefferson** (1781), Catholics at **Villanova** (1842) and **Duquesne** (1878), Germans at **Gettysburg** (1832), Moravians at **Bethlehem** (1742) and the Church of the Brethren at **Juniata** (1876). These institutions have consistently molded young people into productive citizens and integrated ethnic groups into the American melting pot.

A trip across Pennsylvania on the Forbes Trail proves that the dreams of Franklin and Rush have come true. In Philadelphia, one of the oldest medical schools in the country, **Thomas Jefferson University** (1824), has granted more than 26,000 medical degrees. The health care trail winds through the state to Pittsburgh with its innovative 19 teaching hospitals in the **University of Pittsburgh Medical Center**. Philadelphia's Quaker-inspired **Bryn Mawr** (1885) begins a statewide chain of pioneering first class colleges for women that stretches to **Wilson** (1869) in Chambersburg and **Chatham** (1869) in Pittsburgh.

In the farm country of Lancaster, **Franklin College** (1787), created to bring Germans into the English mainstream, began with a gift from Ben Franklin. By the 1850s, financial challenges brought on a merger with a small Reformed Church college in Mercersburg and **Franklin and Marshall** (1853) was born. Mercersburg, the original site of Marshall College, launched **Mercersburg Academy** in 1893. One of Pennsylvania's premier preparatory schools, the Academy numbers actor James Stewart among its famous alumni. Besides Dickinson College, Carlisle boasts the **U.S. Army War College** (1903), a think-tank that teaches army officers the responsibilities of strategic leadership. The college opened its doors in Washington, moved to Fort Leavenworth and finally came to Carlisle Barracks, one of America's oldest military posts, in 1951.

**Shippensburg** (1857), next on the trail, began as a normal school training teachers. Today,

the university is one of 14 schools throughout Pennsylvania that are members of a State System of Higher Education serving over 100,000 students. **Penn State** (1855), once a small agricultural school tucked in the remote mountains, has grown into a giant university with a world reach. The Forbes Trail carried educational traditions with it over the Allegheny Mountains. In 1787, while still a humble village, Pittsburgh founded the Pittsburgh Academy (now the **University of Pittsburgh**), the first college in the country west of the Alleghenies. Just down the street from Pitt's great Cathedral of Learning, steel magnate Andrew Carnegie created Carnegie Technical Schools in 1900. The school became **Carnegie Mellon University** in 1967, a global research institution searching for "real solutions to society's problems."

*pg. 74, left to right, Juniata College (1876), established by the Church of the Brethren in the Allegheny Mountains, has always been dedicated to coeducational learning; Carlisle's Dickinson College (1783) was the first founded as the United States won its independence.*

*pg. 75, clockwise from lower left, Visitors to Philadelphia can share a bench with University of Pennsylvania Founder Benjamin Franklin; the pioneering University of Pittsburgh (1787) is noted for its 42 story Cathedral of Learning completed in 1937; Founding Father Dr. Benjamin Rush was an early proponent of Pennsylvania and American higher education; Chambersburg's Wilson College (1869) was a ground-breaking school for women created after the Civil War; Lancaster's Franklin and Marshall College (1787) was started with a donation from Benjamin Franklin.*

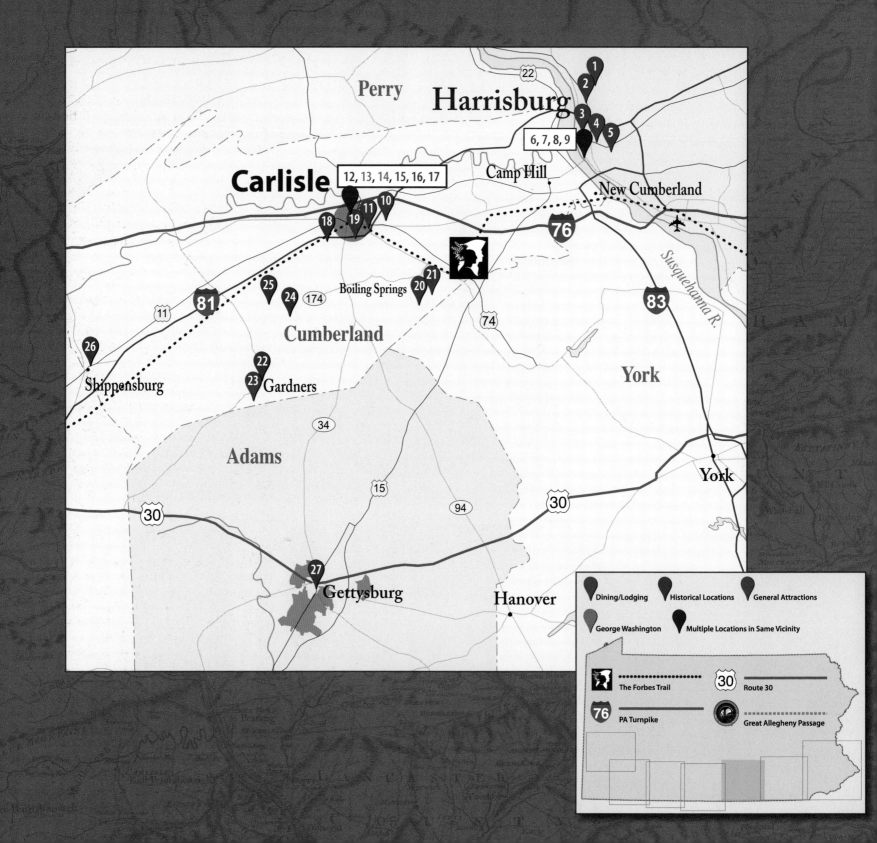

# Carlisle Regional Map

## Visiting Carlisle

At the intersection of High Street and Hanover in Carlisle, buildings strike a patriotic note, clad in red brick and white limestone against bright blue skies. To call this square a traditional meeting place is an understatement. Five Indian paths converged here before Europeans crossed the Susquehanna, founding the city in 1751. Carlisle became a frontier outpost, a county seat, and briefly, a Civil War battleground. Its original street grid has remained unchanged over nearly three centuries of history. Proud and preservation-minded, the town of 19,000 boasts a remarkable number of historic sites around the square, and excellent wayside markers illustrate the town's vivid history.

*Carlisle's Courthouse rises over a historic town square.*

# See 1758 Today

Over 500 people lived in Carlisle in 1758, the majority of them Presbyterian. Carlisle's oldest churches face each other across a town square laid out by John Armstrong, working for the Penn family. When Benjamin Franklin journeyed to Carlisle to negotiate with Indians at a 1753 conference, the participants may have met at the year-old **St. John's Episcopal Church**[12] (1 North Hanover Street; 717-243-4220; www.stjohnscarlisle.org). The handsome current structure dates from 1826. Set aside by the Penns for an Anglican church, it has operated continuously on this site since its founding. The Scots-Irish settlers built their **First Presbyterian Church**[13] on the opposite corner (2 A North Hanover Street; 717-243-4612; www.firstprescarlisle.com). Now the oldest public building in Carlisle, the sturdy stone church from the late 1760s suggests the strength of the congregation. The southeast corner of the square was reserved for a public market. While the new Cumberland County Courthouse now commands the site, a weekly farmers market is still held downtown. Just south of the square, a comfortable coffee shop claims the site of the inn that hosted Franklin during his 1753 visit.

Carlisle has been an army town ever since locals began building a fort near the square in 1755. A Pennsylvania militia led by Colonel John Armstrong, 300 strong, mustered here to attack western Indians in 1756. Though Armstrong returned a hero, the frontier Indian struggles continued. Eight years later, settlers held as Indian captives were returned to the town square. A wayside marker describes the dramatic arrival.

Armstrong is buried in the **old graveyard** on East South Street, along with other veterans of the American Revolution. One is Mary Hays McCauley, better known as Molly Pitcher. The stone house of William Armstrong, John's brother, stands at 109-111 East Pomfret Street. Carlisle continued to play important roles in the American Revolution and beyond. Other wayside markers detail the 1783 founding of **Dickinson College**, emancipation riots, and more. The **Cumberland County Historical Society**[15] features a museum with topical exhibits, a research library, and directions for self-guided walking tours (21 North Pitt Street; 717-249-7610; www.historicalsociety.com).

Among the Society's displays are artifacts from the **Carlisle Indian Industrial School**, located at the Army's Carlisle Barracks. Over 10,000 indigenous children attended this boarding school, on the site of today's U.S. Army War College, between 1879 and 1918. Intended to assimilate American Indians into mainstream culture, the school left a mixed legacy among students separated from their tribes and families. Its most famous graduate was Olympic athlete Jim Thorpe.

*from left, Carlisle's 18th century cemetery includes a monument to Molly Pitcher; children from western tribes attended the Indian Industrial School founded here in 1879; St. John's Episcopal Church commands the town square.*

# George Washington Was Here

George Washington's visit here as president lasted a full week from October 4-11, 1794. A state historic marker by First Presbyterian Church commemorates the occasion. Deeply concerned about the growing threat of the Whiskey Rebellion to the west, he paused here en route to Bedford to muster troops to quell the unrest. He was a guest at the **Ephraim Blaine House**[14] (4 North Hanover Street). Blaine was building several elegant brick homes along Hanover Street, and gave one to each of his sons. The rear portion of the house, made from limestone, is a generation older; the building was Semple's Tavern, a popular Revolutionary-era ordinary. Recently restored, the home is now a law office.

Though Washington worshipped at the Anglican Christ Church while in Philadelphia, he attended services at the First Presbyterian Church in Carlisle. He reviewed militia from Pennsylvania and New Jersey at the corner of High and West Streets before they marched to Bedford.

*Washington's 1794 stops on Hanover Street included the First Presbyterian Church (left) and the Ephraim Blaine House.*

# History: The Roots of the U.S. Army

As an army post for 250 years, it is fitting that Carlisle should honor military history. The Carlisle Barracks on the northeast edge of town occupies the site of a rough fortified camp created by Colonel John Stanwix in 1757. The **U.S. Army War College**, headquartered at the Barracks, trains U.S. senior officers and foreign military leaders. While the campus limits visitors with strict security, the **Army Heritage and Education Center**[19] next door welcomes the public (950 Soldiers Drive; 717- 245-3971; www.USAHEC. org). Celebrating the stories of individual soldiers and the engagements in which they served, it includes an indoor heritage center, open weekdays, and an outdoor trail, open daily. The center has amassed the largest collection of Civil War photography in the world. Other artifacts from a vast collection may spotlight a World War II soldier's diary or technological breakthroughs. The outdoor trail, accented by a massive Huey helicopter perched alongside I-81, includes eleven exhibits in an interactive outdoor museum. Along the path are interpretations of U.S. military campaigns, from the French and Indian War to the redoubts of the Battle of Yorktown and the simple farm fences that became deadly barriers at Antietam. Visitors can scramble through soldiers' quarters from Civil War-era winter cabins to World War I trenches.

*pg. 80, top, Chambersburg natives, the cannoneers and drivers of Battery A, 1st Pennsylvania Light Artillery (the Keystone Battery), are lined up with their horses, guns, and limbers ready to engage the enemy; bottom left to right, the old Carlisle Courthouse was a target of Confederate cannon fire before Gettysburg; one of the United States military locomotives that revolutionized warfare was named for Superintendent of Union Railroads General Herman Haupt, once an engineering professor at Gettysburg College.*
*pg. 81, left to right, Men of Company K, 1st Pennsylvania Reserve Infantry, were defending their hometown when they fought at the Battle of Gettysburg; three veteran Confederate soldiers, captured at Gettysburg, marched all over southern Pennsylvania with General Lee's army before the battle.*

## The Roads to Gettysburg

During the last week in June, 1863, an invading Confederate army was spread out all over southern Pennsylvania. Throughout Cumberland, Franklin, Adams, and York counties, towns close to the Maryland border endured rebel raids in the run-up to the Battle of Gettysburg. Rebel cavalry and infantry roamed the Cumberland Valley, seeking food, forage and additional supplies, as a fourteen-mile-long wagon train lumbered along the Old Forbes Trail from Shippensburg to Carlisle. Cumberland County marked the army's northernmost advance. From Camp Hill, Confederate Cavalry General Albert Jenkins eyed Harrisburg's defenses before turning south towards Gettysburg. After camping a few days in Chambersburg, to the west, General Robert E. Lee ordered the bulk of his army to Gettysburg along today's Route 30. Confederate raiders would return to burn Chambersburg a year later.

Relics of those 1863 skirmishes remain. One well-preserved location is the old courthouse in Carlisle. A sandstone column on the Hanover Street façade was hit by cannon fire from rebel cavalry under General Fitzhugh Lee, who knew the city well. Lee had been an Army cavalry instructor at Carlisle Barracks before the war. Marked "July 1, 1863," the damaged pillar still stands. On Sunday, June 28, General Jubal Early's infantry rode into York, demanding a ransom from the city. Union troops withdrew to Wrightsville and crossed to the Columbia side of the Susquehanna, burning the bridge behind them. Unable to cross the Susquehanna, the rebels turned around and marched back towards Gettysburg. Rebel forces attacked Hanover Junction, attempting to seize control of rail lines, on June 29. The next day, a determined northern force of 3,500 Yankees thwarted General J.E.B. Stuart's troopers in a battle fought in the streets of Hanover. A sidewalk marker shows where a brand new Union general, George Custer, tethered his horse at the city square.

By the time 165,000 soldiers converged on Gettysburg on July 1, southern Pennsylvania had already become a battlefield. Explore the region's saga on the state's **Civil War Trails** (www.pacivilwartrails.com) and consider a stop at the **National Civil War Museum**[5] in Harrisburg's Reservoir Park (One Lincoln Circle; 717-260-1861; www.nationalcivilwarmuseum. org). Opened in 2001, the museum dramatizes military and civilian stories from both sides of the conflict with artifacts and compelling videos.

Over two million people visit **Gettysburg** each year. A spacious new **Museum and Visitors Center**[27], relocated to a site behind the battle lines, improves the interpretation of the famous site with exhibits, visitor services, a comprehensive bookstore, and an orientation video (1195 Baltimore Pike, Gettysburg; 866-889-1243; www.gettysburgfoundation.org). The massive cyclorama, Paul Philippoteaux's vivid oil painting of Pickett's Charge, has been restored for display here. In partnership with the National Park Service, the **Gettysburg Foundation** preserves and restores both the battlefield and its artifacts. Existing downtown buildings, like the train station where Lincoln arrived to deliver the Gettysburg address in November 1863, and the David Wills Home, where he revised his remarks, are also open to the public.

# Family Fun

On the eastern bank of the Susquehanna, 30 minutes from Carlisle, Pennsylvania's capital city offers attractions on land and water. A summer playground in the middle of the river, Harrisburg's **City Island**[9] is a short walk from the Capitol over the pedestrian Walnut Street bridge (www.harrisburgpa.gov/parksRec/cityIsland). From pro sports to pontoon boats, it covers the waterfront. The Harrisburg Senators, part of the AA Eastern League, play baseball here. A 24-foot climbing wall dubbed the Climbnasium and an 18-hole mini-golf course are open seasonally. Boardwalk-style food concessions and arcades line the recreation trail on the island's city side, where the *Pride of the Susquehanna*, an old-fashioned red-and-white paddleboat, docks. A scale-model steam train and horse-drawn carriages loop around the perimeter of the island, and a swimming beach, kayaks and bike rentals are available.

At the **State Museum of Pennsylvania**[6], even pre-schoolers are welcome (300 North Street; 717-787-4980; www.statemuseumpa.org). The free museum adjacent to the Capitol recounts 310 million years of Commonwealth history, including fossils and dinosaur footprints, a top-floor planetarium, fine arts and pop culture exhibits, and Radius, a museum shop with handmade Pennsylvania crafts. The ground-floor **Curiosity Connection** (separate admission fee) gears its hands-on exhibits to children aged two to five, with models of life-sized farm animals, a crawl-through forest, and a hands-on assembly line. Older children will enjoy tours of the Capitol (see "Uniquely Central Pennsylvania" on page 86). To combine a trip to the Capitol, State Museum, and City Island, consider parking in the City Island lot.

To the west, see how auto enthusiasts put the "car" in Carlisle. Events at the **Carlisle Fairgrounds** from spring through fall include auto auctions and specialty shows that attract a half-million visitors a year. For the full schedule, visit www.carsatcarlisle.com.

*pg. 82, Military reenactors from three centuries celebrate Army Heritage Day with visitors at the U.S. Army Heritage and Education Center.*
*pg. 83, Paddleboat tours of the Harrisburg waterfront depart from City Island; pint-sized exhibits at the State Museum (top and right) engage even the youngest visitors.*

# Great Houses and Gardens

Local historians estimate over 50 existing **tavern houses** remain in Cumberland County from the 18th and early 19th centuries. Farmers and drovers taking goods to market preferred **Walnut Bottom Road** because it was toll-free. By 1825, there were fifteen busy taverns to serve them on the twenty-mile stretch between Carlisle and Shippensburg. One, the **Two Mile House**[18] (1189 Walnut Bottom Road, Carlisle; 717-243-3437) is now owned by the Cumberland County Historical Society. Others are private homes that can be seen along the road, now rural Route 465.

Six miles from Carlisle, at 2408 Walnut Bottom Road, stands the Cumberland Hall Tavern, which dates from 1788. A two-story brick structure at number 2675 was Weakley's, built in 1790 and praised in the early 1800s by travel writer John Melish. At number 1879, the stucco two-story inn once known as The Plough and Sheaf of Wheat is still owned by descendants of the 1803 owner, Benjamin Smith.

Along Route 11, the Mount Rock Tavern was several decades old when missionary and diplomat Christian Frederick Post passed by in 1758. A brick house now stands on the site, its old stone milepost showing 14 miles to Shippensburg. The **Widow Piper's Tavern**[26], built of sturdy stone, still commands the corner of East King Street and Queen Street in Shippensburg. The tavern held two Cumberland County court sessions in 1750 and 1751. Today, the restored building is home to the Shippensburg Civic Club. Find detailed itineraries at www.visitcumberlandvalley.com.

The region's best gardens can be found on the eastern shore of the Susquehanna. North of Harrisburg, the 810-acre **Felicita Resort**[1] offers a stunning series of themed gardens (2201 Fishing Creek Valley Road; 888-321-3713; www.felicitaresort.com). Developed since 1971 are a sweeping Italian Renaissance garden accented with fountains, reflecting pools, pergolas and formal plantings; an English perennial garden; and 30 acres of nature trails. Others include a Monet water lily pond and a Japanese garden. Some gardens are open to guests, while others require an admission fee. The resort includes a golf course.

An old city park has been reclaimed as a nature preserve at Harrisburg's **Wildwood Lake**[2] (100 Wildwood Way; 717-221-0292; www.wildwoodlake.org). Trails, boardwalks and bike paths surround the 150-acre lake, and a nature center offers interpretive programs.

*Well-preserved 18th century buildings are a hallmark of Cumberland County, from Widow's Piper's Tavern (left) in Shippensburg to private houses (center) and taverns. The Two Mile House (right) is open to the public.*

# Great Outdoors

The Appalachian Trail passes through the Cumberland Valley at **Pine Grove Furnace State Park**[22] (1100 Pine Grove Road, Gardners; 717-486-7174; www.dcnr.state. pa.us/stateParks/parks/pinegrovefurnace.aspx). Pine Grove Furnace is the midpoint of the 2,175-mile national trail. The park maintains a unique hostel at the 1827 home of ironmaster Peter Ege, which provides inexpensive dormitory-style accommodations for individuals and families. The Buck Ridge Trail links Pine Grove Furnace State Park with the **Kings Gap Environmental Education Center**[24] in Kings Gap State Park (500 Kings Gap Road; 717-486-5031; www.dcnr.state.pa.us/stateparks/Parks/kingsgap.aspx), which offers programs year-round. Sixteen miles of trails here range from short to strenuous. Climb to the top of the Ridge Overlook Trail for a scenic panorama, or lead youngsters on a woodland ecology trail with signage about local plant life. The **Kings Gap General Store**[25] (1155 Pine Road; 717-486-5855) in nearby Montsera is a quaint stop for snacks or antiques.

The wily brown trout of the **LeTort Spring Run** and **Yellow Breeches Creek** have lured fishermen since the 18th century, and fly-fishing still draws international anglers to the Cumberland Valley. Several limestone spring creeks run through the bottom of the valley at a constant temperature of fifty degrees. Many sections are now private fishing preserves, and anglers practice catch and release. Five miles south of Carlisle, the village of Boiling Springs offers a municipal park where enthusiasts can cast a line into the Yellow Breeches—so named, legend says, for the stained trousers of British redcoats who waded in the stream. Nineteenth-century homes cluster around the spring-fed lake at the village center, across the road from the **Boiling Springs Tavern**[20], serving guests since 1832 (1 East First Street; 717-258-3614; www.boilingspringstavern. net). The neighboring **Yellow Breeches Outfitters**[21] (2 First Street; 717-258-6752; www.yellowbreeches.com) offers angling gear, flies, books, and plenty of expert advice.

*The area's streams and level roads attract both cyclists (right) and anglers, who find gear at Yellow Breeches Outfitters in Boiling Springs (left); Appalachian Trail hikers can rest at the Ironmaster's Mansion, now a hostel in Pine Grove Furnace State Park (below).*

## Uniquely Central Pennsylvania

President Theodore Roosevelt famously called the **Pennsylvania Capitol**[7] "the handsomest building I ever saw" when he opened it in 1906 (Third and Walnut Streets; 800-868-7672; www. legis.state.pa.us). With a broad flight of steps cascading towards the Susquehanna and a massive domed rotunda, it shares the grand style and era of the U.S. Capitol. Inside, tours depart from the grand staircase copied from the Paris Opera House. Gleaming mosaics adorn the 272-foot dome overhead, while the terracotta floor tiles include handcrafted designs by Henry Mercer's Moravian Tileworks. The Senate and House chambers are far more ornate than their federal counterparts. Pennsylvania artists Violet Oakley, Edwin Austin Abbey and William Brantley Van Ingen contributed the magnificent murals, paintings and stained glass.

The capitol's newer east wing houses a skylit cafeteria and an interactive **Welcome Center** with a light historical touch (it explains that the state dog is a Great Dane because William Penn owned one). "Making a Bill" is an entertaining Rube Goldberg-style contraption that explains the legislative process.

*Joseph M. Huston designed the Pennsylvania Capitol in grand Beaux-Arts style.*

## Did You Know?

What's a whoopie pie? This sandwich of sweet cake and cream filling might be called a gob elsewhere. In central Pennsylvania, it's called a favorite. Chocolate, vanilla or pumpkin, filled with whipped cream or even peanut butter, it's a farmers market specialty.

# Plan a Visit

## Annual Regional Events

**Pennsylvania Farm Show,** January
www.agriculture.state.pa.us

**Army Heritage Day,** May
www.USAHEC.org

**Carlisle Summerfair,** July
www.carlislesummerfair.com

**Shippensburg Corn Festival,** August
www.cornfestival.net

*Jacob's Resting Place*

## Carlisle

For more information:
Cumberland Valley Visitors Bureau
401 East Louther Street, Suite 209, Carlisle
(888) 513-5130 | www.visitcumberlandvalley.com

### DINING
**Piatto**[17]
22 West Pomfret Street, Carlisle
(717) 249-9580 | www.piatto.com
- Italian regional cuisine in an old Victorian house. BYOB.

**Boiling Springs Tavern**[20]
1 East First Street, Boiling Springs
(717) 258-3614
www.boilingspringstavern.net
- Serving food and drink in the village since 1832.

### LODGING
**Carlisle House**[16]
148 South Hanover Street, Carlisle
(717) 249-0350 | www.thecarlislehouse.com
- Ten suites and rooms in the center of the historic district.

**Jacob's Resting Place**[11]
1007 Harrisburg Pike, Carlisle
(888) 731-1790
www.jacobsrestingplace.com
- An 18th century tavern restored as an elegant B&B. The original Forbes Trail ran through this property along the LeTort Spring Run.

**Pheasant Field Bed and Breakfast**[10]
150 Hickorytown Road, Carlisle
(717) 258-0717 | www.pheasantfield.com
- This 200-year-old country farmhouse offers wheelchair-accessible rooms. Room and board for horses available in the "horse hotel."

**Pine Furnace State Park
Ironmaster's Mansion**[23]
1212 Pine Grove Road, Gardners
(717) 486-7575
www.dcnr.state.pa.us/stateParks/parks/pinegrovefurnace.aspx
- American Youth Hostel for individuals and families. Private cabins also available.

## Harrisburg

For more information:
Hershey Harrisburg Regional Visitors Bureau
112 Market Street 4th Floor, Harrisburg
(877) 727-8573 | www.hersheyharrisburg.org

### DINING
**The Fire House Restaurant**[8]
606 North Second Street, Harrisburg
(717) 234-6064
www.thefirehouserestaurant.com
- Two blocks from the Capitol, this casual pub serves microbrews from an old red hydrant.

**Broad Street Market**[4]
1233 North Third Street, Harrisburg
(717) 236-7923 | www.broadstreetmarket.org
- Wednesday through Saturday, the 1860s-era market provides fresh produce, baked goods, candies and preserves.

### LODGING
**Felicita Resort**[1]
2201 Fishing Creek Valley Road, Harrisburg
(888) 321-3713 | www.felicitaresort.com
- Elegant resort and gardens ten miles north of the Capitol.

**The Milestone Inn**[3]
2701 North Front Street, Harrisburg
(717) 233-2775 | www.milestoneinn.com
- An elegant B&B four miles north of the Capitol along the river.

# An Angler's Paradise

Eighteenth century writers frequently remarked on Pennsylvania's fine waterways and rich fisheries. Just a few years before General Forbes arrived in the city, German traveler Gottlieb Mittelberger noted that the tidal waters of the Delaware and Schuylkill Rivers around Philadelphia abounded in "multitudes of fish" each spring. Anglers targeted many varieties of game fish, including Perch and Striped Bass (or Rockfish), but the most dramatic event of the season was the annual run of American Shad which returned from the sea to spawn in freshwater rivers each spring.

Among Pennsylvania's many historical firsts, Philadelphia's **Schuylkill Fishing Company**, founded in 1732, is the first and oldest angling club in America. The club's original headquarters was located near the present site of the Philadelphia Museum of Art. Today, visitors can learn about ongoing efforts to restore the American Shad run in the Schuylkill River during the annual **Urban Shad Watch**, held each year on Earth Day at the Fairmount Water Works Interpretive Center.

Passing westward from Philadelphia toward the Allegheny Mountains, General Forbes' journey carried him through the rich farmland of Lancaster and Cumberland Counties. The abundant limestone deposits that make the region's soils so fertile also create one of the most significant concentrations of spring creeks in North America. Fed by cool water that flows through limestone caverns before emerging aboveground, the spring creeks of southeastern Pennsylvania were renowned as trout fisheries even in the 18th century. Gin clear and rich in dissolved minerals, the limestone waters that are so beneficial for trout and the aquatic insects on which they feed are a precious resource. The 13,000-member **Pennsylvania Council of Trout Unlimited** is a conservation organization dedicated to preserving and restoring the commonwealth's coldwater streams and fisheries. Visiting anglers should not miss the **Pennsylvania Fly Fishing Museum Association**'s annual Heritage Day, held each June at Allenberry Resort near Carlisle.

The Allegheny, Monongahela, and Ohio Rivers that frame the historic Point at Pittsburgh offered tremendous fishing opportunities for military garrisons and inhabitants during the 18th century. Indian trader James Kenny, who kept a diary during several years' residence in the fledgling town of Pittsburgh immediately following the Forbes campaign, measured a four foot long Pike and thirty pound Buffalo fish in August 1759. After more than a century of industrial pollution, a remarkable decades-long effort to clean up the Three Rivers has succeeded admirably. Many game fish species have been restored to their historic range in western Pennsylvania, and fishermen are now a regular sight in boats and on the banks of Pittsburgh's rivers.

**For More Information:**

**Fairmount Water Works Interpretive Center**
640 Waterworks Drive, Philadelphia
(215) 685-0722
www.fairmountwaterworks.org

**Pennsylvania Council of Trout Unlimited**
www.patrout.org

**Pennsylvania Fly Fishing Museum Association**
1240 North Mountain Road, Harrisburg
(717) 541-062
www.paflyfishing.org

*bottom, A fly fisherman moves into position on the internationally famous Yellow Breeches Creek near Boiling Springs. Anglers travel enormous distances each year to pursue the wily trout of central Pennsylvania's limestone streams.*

*right, Many British officers are devoted practitioners of "country sports" like shooting, fox hunting, and fishing. This young subaltern forgets the rigors of the Forbes campaign during a few precious hours of trout fishing.*

# *Fort Loudoun*

## June 14, 1758

New to Indian diplomacy, Colonel Henry Bouquet offers gifts and implores over 100 Cherokee and Catawba warriors not to desert the British cause.

# Fort Loudoun at Center Stage

On June 14, 1758, Colonel Henry Bouquet was at Fort Loudoun for the second time in a week. He was back for an important meeting with Cherokee allies camped around the fort. The all but indefensible stockade was set in a soggy meadow near the banks of Conococheague Creek's west branch. Army chaplain the Reverend Thomas Barton called it a poor piece of work. It would hardly have impressed its namesake, the Earl of Loudoun, former British commander in America.

Parnell's Knob stood prominently nearby, guarding the trail winding up the forested slopes. The long ridges spread west like waves: Kittatinny, Broad, Cove, Tuscarora, Shade, Blacklog, Sideling, and Rays. Hundreds of soldiers were now cutting, scraping and shoveling a usable path through those mountains. Road building would be the main British mission for the next several months. Colonel Bouquet was in a hurry. It was his job to get an army to the Forks of the Ohio before winter. The next camp at Raystown (later Bedford) was more than fifty miles to the west. Daily letters between General Forbes, still in Philadelphia, and Bouquet, three days of hard riding away, detailed the thousands of troops, hundreds of horses, and scores of wagons converging on Fort Loudoun.

## Hugh Mercer: a Fugitive Becomes a Patriot

A desperate twenty-one-year-old Scottish physician fled to America. Dr. Hugh Mercer had chosen the losing side during the 1745 rebellion against King George. With a price on his head, he sought a quiet life on the Pennsylvania frontier. For almost a decade, Mercer was a godsend to local settlers, practicing medicine in Mercersburg, the community that bears his name.

Adventure and danger, however, would not leave Hugh Mercer alone. When war engulfed the Cumberland Valley in 1755, he joined the militia chasing French and Indians. A captain at the 1756 Kittanning Raid, he was wounded, abandoned, and survived, eating plums and a raw rattlesnake as he walked and crawled for over 100 miles through uncharted country. In 1758, he commanded one of the three Pennsylvania battalions that accompanied General Forbes. The General chose Mercer to stay behind with 200 men and defend the Forks of the Ohio after the British victory.

Colonel Mercer's friendship with Colonel George Washington and other Virginians lured him to Fredericksburg where he again found peace and prosperity. He opened an apothecary shop, married, and became an important local doctor and community leader. Revolution again called him to action in 1775. A year later, Mercer was a Continental Army general serving with Washington during some of the darkest days of the American Revolution. Killed at the Battle of Princeton, his bravery and sacrifice made him a colonial hero.

*Sentry duty can sometimes be terrifying in provincial forts, but most of the time it is lonely, uncomfortable and monotonous.*

## Pennsylvania's Frontier Forts

In July, 1755, Anglo-Irish minister Thomas Barton was alarmed that Pennsylvania was poorly prepared for war. Among his frontier congregation, Barton observed: "not a man in ten is able to purchase a gun, not a house in twenty has a door with either a lock or bolt to it." In fact, the only fortification standing in 1755 was a crumbling artillery battery on the shore of the Delaware River below Philadelphia.

As raiding parties attacked the backcountry, frontier settlers and provincial leaders scrambled to build forts. With few experienced military leaders, most forts were stockade walls, lines of vertical tree trunks, erected around existing buildings. The enemy fired down from nearby hills into the poorly-sited enclosures. Thatched roofs or wooden shingles were easy targets for attackers with torches. Little wonder that many frontier posts were destroyed or abandoned during attacks.

The Reverend Barton played an active role in Pennsylvania's frontier defenses. His journey west in 1758 carried him past several of the provincial forts. Shippensburg's Fort Morris, he noted, "was a trifling piece of work. It does not appear that a Vauban [Sebastien le Prestre de Vauban (1633-1707) the French military engineer] had any hand in laying it out." Barton was even less impressed by Fort Loudoun, "a poor piece of work, irregularly built, and badly situated at the bottom of a hill subject to damps and noxious vapors. It has something like bastions supported by props, which if the enemy should cut away, down tumbles men and all."

*On his self-appointed inspection tour of provincial forts, the Reverend Thomas Barton finds that the stockades are "poor pieces of work."*

## Colonel Bouquet's Demanding Schedule

On June 12, Bouquet rode twenty miles south into Maryland to meet with Maryland Governor Horatio Sharpe, Quartermaster Sir John St. Clair, and a Virginia colonel named Washington. Returning to Pennsylvania with St. Clair who was riding on to Carlisle, Bouquet reported to Forbes that the Virginia troops would march from Winchester, Virginia to Fort Cumberland at the end of June. With the old Braddock Road still being considered for the march to Fort Duquesne, Governor Sharpe proposed that 500 men could cut a 42-mile Maryland road (today's I-68) between Forts Cumberland and Frederick, 12 miles south of Fort Loudoun, in three weeks.

Colonel Bouquet rushed back to Fort Loudoun to persuade Cherokee and Catawba warriors, camped nearby and close to abandoning the slow moving campaign, to march west with the army. In a June 14 letter to General Forbes, Bouquet mentioned another problem that was a nightmare for everyone: "As if we did not have enough trouble with them [the Indians], the smallpox lent a hand, and there is one of them very sick here."

The troops marching in by the hundreds made Fort Loudoun a beehive of activity. For the previous two years, the humble provincial fort, irregularly built and badly situated, had been the loneliest place in Pennsylvania.

## War and Suffering along Conococheague Creek

Amidst the serene patterns of prosperous farms, it is hard to imagine a time when the Cumberland Valley was wild and remote. Before paved highways, fenced properties, even communities, there were solitary log houses in small clearings. Travel was possible only along a few Indian paths and creeks. Despite the isolation, settlers felt a sense of an untamed world for the taking.

Hardy Scots-Irish, Welsh and German families were carving out lives here in the 1750s. A few of the toughest had crossed the first mountain ridges and moved into another valley beyond called the Great Cove (McConnellsburg). With Braddock's 1755 defeat, fierce raids descended on the Great Cove and Conococheague Creek. The settlers in these nooks and crannies of land were the most vulnerable, choosing to tempt fate on the lonely edges of the frontier.

*During three years of terror, most of the settlers west of the Susquehanna River have been killed, captured or chased from their burned out cabins.*

## The Horrible Situation of this Beautiful Country

Three years of nearly ceaseless conflict had left Pennsylvania's backcountry settlements in shambles. Highland soldier Robert Kirkwood later recalled the appearance of the countryside along the army's 1758 route.

"Nothing could be more shocking," he penned in his memoirs almost twenty years later, "than to view the horrible situation of this beautiful country." Passing over the same ground in 1762, twenty-year-old Moravian missionary John Heckewelder later recalled: "In every direction, the blackened ruins of houses and barns, and the remnants of chimneys met our eyes."

Many of the soldiers of the Pennsylvania Regiment had been frontier settlers themselves before the French and Indian attacks had turned them into refugees. By fall 1756, Cumberland County leaders estimated that 100 remained of 3,000 men of military age living there a year earlier. Only the poorly supplied garrisons, laid out from the Delaware Water Gap north of Philadelphia to the Conococheague settlement, prevented Pennsylvania's frontier from collapsing in 1757.

The Forbes Expedition and diplomacy with the Ohio Indian nations reduced the number of raids in 1758, but the western settlements remained vulnerable. In early April, raiders marched boldly through Cumberland County and captured most of Thomas Jemison's family, including his young daughter Mary, near present-day Gettysburg. More than sixty years later, Mary shared the story of her life as an adopted American Indian with author James Seaver. His *Narrative of the Life of Mrs. Mary Jemison* remains one of the best known captivity narratives in American literature.

## A Terror beyond Description

The French and Indian attacks were sudden, random, terrifying, and effective. Imagine an ordinary day, feeding your livestock, chopping wood or plowing. A scalp halloo, the shrill cry from a warrior painted black for war and hidden nearby, breaks the silence. A footrace to the cabin or a rifle, anything that will give hope, ensues. A few minutes of desperation, always feared but never expected, could yield a burning cabin, tortured and mutilated bodies and young haltered captives being led away, spared for an uncertain fate.

During November 1755, half of the 93 settlers were lost in the Great Cove. For more than two years, the attacks continued and the casualty list grew. By the spring of 1758, eighty percent of the local population was gone: killed, captured or chased out of the neighborhood. It was almost impossible to find a farm that had escaped the torch. The few families that did not flee the attacks organized citizen patrols and set up a defensive line of stockaded safe houses.

Katherine Bard, captured in 1758 and later retrieved by her husband, watched her infant child tomahawked and scalped and was almost beaten to death running a gauntlet with her two sons. The terrible stress of such ordeals produced Indian haters but also sympathizers. Prisoner exchange was a major issue for settlers when wars ended. Some captives, however, refused to go home. Fifteen-year-old Mary Jemison, taken in 1758, marched into captivity accompanied by the scalps of her murdered family. Married twice to Indian leaders, she had many children and died at age ninety-one, much celebrated as the "White Woman of Genesee, New York."

At the foot of the mountains, the home guard used McDowell's Mill as a fort but faced repeated attacks. In 1756, provincial officer John Armstrong advised the Pennsylvania governor that "McDowell's is a necessary post, but the present fort [is] not defensible." On a visit in November, Armstrong selected a spot near Parnell's Knob. "I'm making the best preparation in my power to forward this new fort." Fort Loudoun was a lonely outpost for another year but Pennsylvania set the stage for an important stop on the Forbes Road.

*For captives taken during raids on frontier settlements, their ordeals are just beginning.*

## American Indian Allies from the South

General Forbes expected many Indians from the south to join his 1758 expedition. Southern Indian nations were enemies of the Ohio Valley and Great Lakes tribes who had sided with the French. By the end of 1757, hundreds of Cherokee, Catawba, Nottoway, and other warriors were in Pennsylvania and proved to be a potent defense against incursions from Fort Duquesne.

During the winter of 1757-58, the British promised arms, equipment and gifts to warriors who accompanied General Forbes. By April, more than six hundred Cherokee and Catawba warriors were in Winchester, Virginia, expecting an army ready to march west. The warriors were frustrated that no troops were ready. They became angry when the goods they had been promised for risking their lives as British allies had not been prepared or even purchased.

These tensions came to a head on Saturday, May 20, 1758. Believing the British had lied to them, forty Cherokee warriors threatened to seize trade goods at Fort Loudoun and depart for home. General Forbes sent redcoats from Philadelphia with some artillery, hoping that "the seeing of our Cannon and the Highlanders" would persuade the warriors to remain. Colonel Henry Bouquet met with 130 Cherokees and Catawbas at Fort Loudoun in June. He observed that "I was amazed to see so much of true understanding, dignity and strength of argument in their propositions." Assuring the warriors that the promised goods would be awaiting their return to Fort Loudoun, Bouquet told Forbes that the Indians were determined "to conquer or perish with us."

## An Unlikely Diplomat Courts the Cherokees

When the Forbes Campaign finally materialized in the spring of 1758, Cherokees and Catawbas, southern Indian warriors, were at Fort Loudoun. Their raiding parties and scouts had been in Pennsylvania for over a year. Rumors that they were enemy raiders preceded the Cherokee allies as they entered Pennsylvania to aid the British efforts. A jumpy Fort Loudoun garrison almost attacked them when they camped nearby. A year-long diplomatic dance began as dozens of war parties ranged throughout the region. Courted with promises of generous gifts, the southern Indians quickly ran out of patience waiting for the promised British offensive.

*American Indian women are skilled artists whose beautifully worked sashes, straps, and moccasins are highly prized as souvenirs by Europeans who visit America.*

General Forbes thought "the Cherokees of such consequence that I have done everything in my power to provide them in their necessaries." With a rumored 700 warriors ready to march, the General was pessimistic. "They are capable of being led away upon any caprice or whim that seizes them. The Cherokees are no longer to be kept with us neither by promises or presents. We have no mortal of consequence to manage them."

Upset with the assigned Indian agents, Forbes sent his cousin, James Glen, to assist with negotiations. Glen, former governor of South Carolina and a friend of the Cherokees, was visiting Forbes. The General was also commending Virginia Colonel William Byrd who had personally traveled to South Carolina and talked Cherokees into marching north to join the fight. It was Colonel Bouquet, however, who, for the moment carried British hopes for the alliance.

As the Colonel arrived in June with Highlanders and cannons, the Indians at Fort Loudoun were close to abandoning the alliance. Bouquet, a novice diplomat, reached out, wampum in hand, with rousing speeches to the skeptical Indians. After two days of intrigues, dinners, and public meetings, Bouquet reported to Forbes that "the 200 [Indians] we can count on would be preferable to 500 rogues who do nothing but filch our presents without rendering any service. I foresee good results in regard to the promises they have made."

*Hundreds of Cherokee and Catawba warriors use frontier posts like Fort Littleton as bases for raids against Fort Duquesne. To prevent "friendly fire" from nervous redcoats or provincials, General Forbes directs his Indian allies to tie yellow cloth around their guns.*

## Peace Envoys in the Back Country

A month after Colonel Bouquet's June council with the Cherokees, Christian Frederick Post and the Delaware Pisquetomen set out to bring an offer of peace to the western Indians. They spent a week crossing mountains and rivers in deep woods, running into French Fort Venango where Post "prayed the Lord to blind them [the French] that I might pass unknown." Some surprised French did see Post but the party moved on unmolested.

The hungry travelers finally reached Kuskuskies (New Castle), a sprawling set of four Delaware villages with sixty houses and 200 able warriors. Post sent Pisquetomen ahead with wampum to announce the arrival of the peace mission. The Moravian missionary followed, bravely marching into the enemy camp with his offer of peace. He was warmly welcomed by the Delaware sachem Tamaqua (Beaver) and delivered his message to sixty young men, asking that it be sent to all their towns.

Indian messengers, insisting that Post bring his message to the eight nations then at Fort Duquesne, arrived with large wampum belts. They were accompanied by French soldiers out to discredit the envoy. Post had nothing but his wits to protect him but the Delawares rallied to his defense. The Delaware sachems told him, "Brother, we have but one great fire. When we have called all the nations, we will hear the good news you have brought." The lonely diplomat started for Fort Duquesne with forty horsemen and runners. On August 24, 1758, Post was standing across the river from the French fort, surrounded by over a hundred leaders and warriors. Tamaqua introduced him, proclaiming "Here is our English brother, who has brought great news."

## Taking on the Allegheny Mountains

Few Europeans had seen anything as frightening and mysterious as the mountain forest ahead. The army saw this vast sea of trees as dark, dismal and dreary. They were certain that evil spirits lurked behind the giant trees. On one trip long before, the exhausted traveler Conrad Weiser sat down under a tree to die. Talked into going on, he felt as if he had escaped from Hell.

Colonel Bouquet launched his combined force into the teeth of this formidable obstacle on June 2, 1758. He followed on June 16, "compelled to go groping into an unknown country." Climbing 600 feet straight up Tuscarora Mountain through Cowans Gap and riding on to provincial Fort Littleton on the on the toe of Cove Mountain, he next climbed the well-engineered, nine steep switchbacks over almost 2,000 foot high Sideling Hill. The Colonel traversed more switchbacks going down the sheer side of Rays Hill and reached the Juniata River Camp, a river crossing three-and-a-half days by wagon from Fort Loudoun, on June 21.

Still feeling his way forward, Bouquet moved a portable city over this mountain trail one 1500 pound wagon load at a time. In a detailed note to General Forbes, he argued a case for replacing wagons with pack horses. He had passed broken, abandoned wagons on the trail. The capable wagon master, Pennsylvania Captain Robert Callender, an Indian trader called by Bouquet "the most suitable man in America for the task," was doing his best. Almost half of the old farm wagons, however, needed extensive repair after the trip only as far as Fort Littleton. Bouquet argued that pack horses with 200-pound loads needed smaller trails, were faster, and caused less trouble.

*In order to construct a military road capable of carrying wagons and artillery across the steep mountain ridges of central Pennsylvania, soldiers laboriously dig and pry, cut and drag. For most, the shovel and axe are far more familiar than the musket and bayonet.*

*The Forbes Road is littered with wagons, broken on the rough mountain trails. Strings of packhorses carry smaller loads, but many, including Colonel Bouquet, think they are cheaper and more efficient.*

## Pushing the Road to Raystown

Everyone was worried about the Juniata River Crossing. Armies fording rivers were vulnerable to ambush. Colonel Bouquet assigned newly-arrived Engineer Captain Harry Gordon to his first important task on the Forbes Road. Gordon laid out a stockade for 100 men to cover the three-and-a-half foot deep ford. Bouquet had decided that a substantial fort was not worth the labor.

Colonel James Burd and 200 men pushed the road ahead and began to lay out a major base camp at Raystown as Colonel Bouquet rode to meet them. Listening to experienced colonial officers like George Washington, he was already adapting to this wild country. He was thinking of "making Indians part of our provincial soldiers. Remove their coats and breeches, give them moccasins and blankets; cut off their hair and daub them with paint and intermingle them with the real Indians. The impression would be useful to us."

Finally settled at the next fortified camp on June 27, Bouquet sent instructions to Colonel Washington, with his troops about 28 miles south at Fort Cumberland, to begin cutting the road "to open communication between us." No enemies had appeared, but the Colonel reminded Washington to cover the men with strong flanking parties.

The British continued to be almost blind to French intentions. Bouquet related the story of a Virginia soldier scouting near Fort Duquesne with some Cherokees. He was bitten by a rattlesnake. "The Indians gave him a root which he was to chew, swallowing his saliva and washing the wound. His legs swelled so much they [the Indians] abandoned him. He continued to chew the roots and is almost cured." Unfortunately, the lucky soldier had a good story but no information about the French.

General Forbes, just leaving Philadelphia at the end of June, consoled Colonel Bouquet who was carrying so much of the burden of command. "I make no question of many hindrances that you meet with, from the care of the roads, to the smallest minutiae, for my part I have my own share but [in French] as the wine is poured, it must be drunk."

## The Journal of Chaplain Thomas Barton

A 25-year-old Anglo-Irish minister, Thomas Barton, came to America to save souls. The Church of England missionary was tasked with creating new congregations along the Pennsylvania frontier. He hoped to become a "happy instrument to subject some nations of savages [Indians], poor ignorant creatures, to the Kingdom of God."

Only months after his arrival in 1755, the Reverend Barton found himself in the middle of a "time of public calamity and distress with the greater part of five counties depopulated and laid to waste." He sought out General Forbes in 1758 and soon traveled to Raystown as a chaplain-at-large. With limited duties and access to military leaders, this keen observer soon became one of the best chroniclers of the Forbes Campaign.

Nothing escaped the Reverend Barton's attentions. His daily entries are the mix of tedium, humor, hardship and violence that describe soldiers' lives.

August 30, "a warm dispute between a major and a captain…was happily ended by flinging a few bottles and glasses." September 14, "many of our provincial officers got drunk this night , broke their shins in returning home and were upon crutches through the camp next day." September 25, "guards upon hearing the cackling of wild-geese at night, ran into camp, and declared that they had heard the voice of Indians all around them." Throughout his three months at Fort Bedford, the Chaplain was optimistic; "Everything promises success and it is generally believed that Fort Duquesne will fall an easy conquest."

*The Reverend Thomas Barton is not impressed by the scanty cover that Fort Loudoun's ill-fitting stockade posts provide.*

The towering, endless forest shuts out the sun and is often described as dismal and dreary. Filled with steep slopes, briars and quagmires, it is also a frightening place where a traveler is often unaware of a man hiding a few feet away.

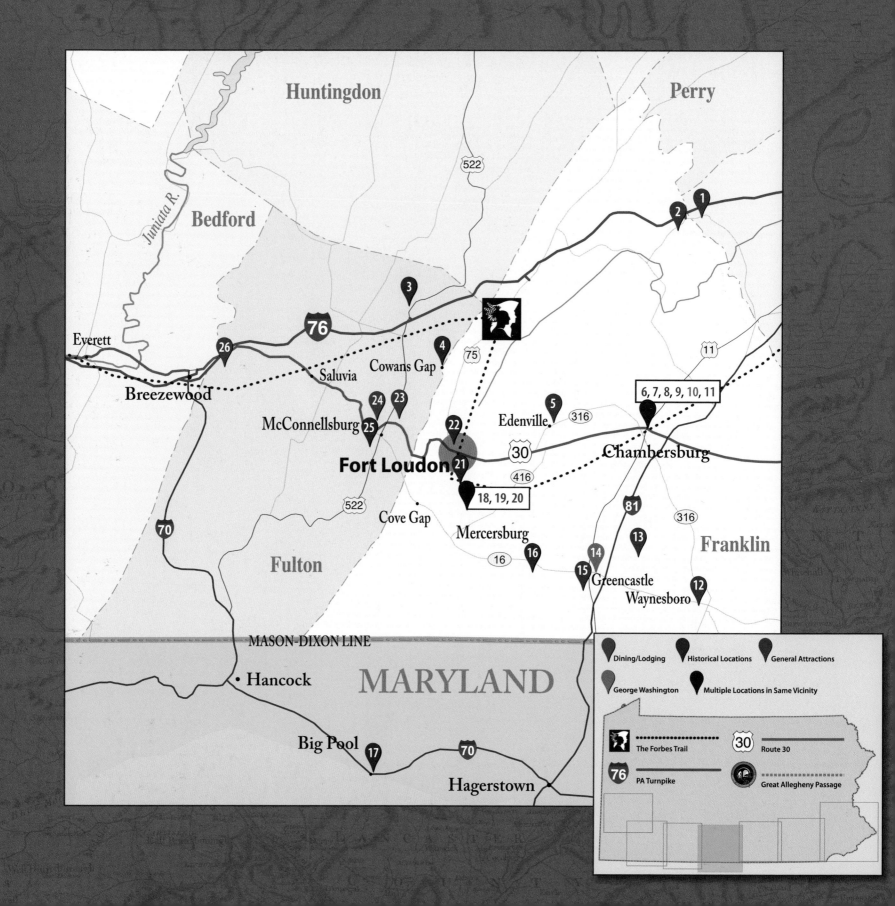

# Fort Loudon Regional Map

Huntingdon

Perry

Bedford

Juniata R.

522

2 1

Everett

76

26

3

Saluvia

Cowans Gap

4

75

11

Breezewood

McConnellsburg

24 23

25

Edenville

5

316

22

6, 7, 8, 9, 10, 11

**Fort Loudon**

21

30

Chambersburg

522

416

Cove Gap

18, 19, 20

70

Fulton

Mercersburg

16

16

13

Franklin

81

14

15

Greencastle

12

Waynesboro

MASON-DIXON LINE

MARYLAND

Hancock

Big Pool

17

70

Hagerstown

Dining/Lodging    Historical Locations    General Attractions

George Washington    Multiple Locations in Same Vicinity

The Forbes Trail    30 Route 30

76 PA Turnpike    Great Allegheny Passage

## Visiting Fort Loudoun

The level landscape of the western Cumberland Valley, braced by the looming Tuscarora Ridge to the west, preserves the spacious skies and rich soil that first attracted European settlers. In the mid 18th century, Welsh, Scots-Irish and German families surged into the valley, despite fierce French and Indian attacks. Seven generations have farmed here along Conococheague Creek. With an Indian name meaning "a long, long way indeed," the creek meanders 80 miles from its source atop South Mountain to meet the Potomac in Maryland.

*Cowans Gap State Park, Fort Loudoun.*

# See 1758 Today

An effort to preserve the region's frontier heritage is underway at the **Conococheague Institute**[16], headquartered at a homestead that dates from 1752 (12995 Bain Road, Mercersburg; 717-328-3467; www.geocities.com/welshrunpa). The Institute has preserved three homesteads to interpret the cultures that blended here. Rock Hill Farm was first settled by Welsh Quaker John Davis and occupied after 1794 by the Presbyterian Chambers family. Davis' home, built of sturdy chestnut logs, was improved by the Chambers with glass windows, a second floor, and white stucco: it is furnished with period pieces including a Hepplewhite table. The Negley farmhouse, dating from 1810, incorporates the traditional three-room German design, with a double entry (one for family, one for guests). A third corner-post log home, moved to the southern edge of the site, serves as a visitors center. Across the western branch of the Conococheague lie the crooked headstones of a small community cemetery, which may be the resting place of unnamed victims of the Indian attacks that plagued the settlement in the 1750s.

Protected by a conservancy, the surrounding farmland offers a peaceful vista. But Rock Hill Farm illustrates the desperate measures taken by the Davises and others to protect their families from attack. Private forts in the region greatly outnumbered provincial or British forts. Essentially fortified homes, private forts like the one that stood on the Davis farm provided settlers a fighting chance in an era when hundreds lost their lives in Indian raids. Local tribes kidnapped dozens of women and children along the Conococheague. The Institute collects and publishes the dramatic stories penned by survivors such as James Smith and Jean McCord Lowry. Though most of the 18th century log cabins are gone, a half-dozen historical markers note the sites of 1750s private forts in southern Franklin County. At **Fort Chambers** on Falling Spring, in the center of Chambersburg, Benjamin Chambers reinforced the roof of his cabin with lead against attacks; his grave is two blocks east, at **Falling Spring Presbyterian Church cemetery**[7]. Southwest of Chambersburg, markers for **Fort McDowell**[21] and **Fort Waddell** stand along Route 416, and a sign for **Reverend Steele's Fort** lies along Route 16 east of Mercersburg. The site of **Fort McCord** north of Chambersburg is marked along Route 4008, near Edenville.

The Conococheague Institute has mapped a tour of fifteen frontier history sites from Seneca campgrounds to forts and churches within a thirty-mile radius. Uncrowded roads make the route ideal for cycling as well as driving.

Along Route 522 near McConnellsburg, look for a state historical marker at **Big Spring Cemetery**[25], where victims of the 1755 Great Cove massacre were buried. Along the same road, a marker at the town of **Fort Littleton**[3] notes the site of that provincial fort.

**Fort Loudoun**[22] has been recreated off Brooklyn Road near its original location. The simple timber enclosure, sited on a branch of the Conococheague Creek, is minimally interpreted. A better glimpse of the rigors faced by Forbes' soldiers can be found at the 2,100-foot summit to the west. From Fort Loudoun, follow Route 75 north, tracing the army's march to the top of the Tuscarora Ridge. The magnificent climb culminates at **Cowans Gap State Park**[4] (6235 Aughwick Road, Fort Loudoun; 717-485-3948; www.dcnr.state.pa.us/StateParks/parks/cowansgap.aspx).

*pg. 103, clockwise from lower left, A sculpture in downtown Chambersburg honors the three generations of the founding Chambers family; the Conococheague Institute interprets and preserves historic structures like the Pennsylvania-German Martin-Negley House; early settlers built private forts throughout southwestern Franklin County; isolated Fort Loudoun sits along a tributary of the Conococheague.*

FORT LYTTELTON

Begun in 1755 by George Croghan, named by Governor Morris after Sir George Lyttelton, then the Chancellor of the Exchequer. Garrisoned variously by Provincial and regular troops, as well as local volunteers in 1763. By 1764 it was reported in ruins.

PENNSYLVANIA HISTORICAL AND MUSEUM COMMISSION

*For centuries, commanders in European and American armies have named forts after political and military leaders and heroes. General John Forbes came to America with a list of commanders, friends and patrons to provide names for the new forts built during the 1758 campaign. Pennsylvania leaders followed that tradition when they built Fort Loudoun and Fort Littleton. Provincials named Fort Loudoun after John Campbell, the 4th Earl of Loudoun in Scotland. Loudoun (above) was the commander of the British armies in North America from 1756-1758. Forbes came to America in 1757 as an aide to his friend and patron. Arrogant and luckless, Loudoun was replaced by General James Abercromby in 1758 after several reverses against the French and Indians. Another Fort Loudoun, also built in 1756, was on the far Cherokee frontier in present-day Tennessee. Fort Lyttelton (now Fort Littleton) was named for Sir George Lyttelton, chancellor of the British Exchequer, in 1755.*

# PRIVATE FORTS, MILITIAS AND HUGH MERCER

## FOUNDING FAMILY MEMORIAL STATUE "THE HOMECOMING"

### The Sculptor

## George Washington Was Here

Before bringing his Virginia regiment to Bedford in September 1758, George Washington rode north from Winchester for a military meeting here. While the date of the meeting—June 12, 1758—is certain, the location is recorded only as "Conococheague." Washington's meeting with Colonel Bouquet, Maryland Governor Horatio Sharpe, and Deputy Quartermaster General Sir John St. Clair may have taken place near where the creek enters the Potomac at Williamsport, Maryland. Twelve

miles west lies **Fort Frederick**[17], the massive stone-walled fortification built at Sharpe's order in 1756. Two of the fort's barracks have been restored as an interpretive center with a short film on the war and the fort (11100 Fort Frederick Road, Big Pool, MD; 301-842-2155; www.dnr.state.md.us/publiclands/western/fortfrederick.html).

Washington broke his October 1794 journey west to Bedford at several points in Franklin County. In **Greencastle**[14], the president stopped at the town square, the home and tavern of Robert McCullough. On October 12, the president and his staff dined with

Benjamin Chambers and lodged at **Morrow's Tavern**[10] at 37 South Main Street in Chambersburg. Look for the state site marker just off the Diamond (Memorial Square).

*Split-rail fences edge the grounds of Maryland's Fort Frederick, the region's strongest 18th century fortification.*

## Maryland Forts

General Braddock used a stockade, built on the Maryland frontier where Wills Creek joins the Potomac River, as the base camp for his march west in 1755. Named Cumberland in honor of the British Duke, the stockade survived French and Indian frontier threats and remained an important base of operations throughout the war. When the Reverend Thomas Barton visited, he called the fort "so ill put up that General Braddock declared he could make a better [fort] with rotten-apples."

The other Maryland fort, called Frederick to honor the last Lord Baltimore, was another matter altogether. After Braddock's defeat, Governor Sharpe took advantage of the fear of attack and extracted funds out of a frugal Maryland Assembly. Sharpe picked a spot along the Potomac River 40 miles east of Fort Cumberland. While other commanders were erecting log forts, the Maryland governor built a unique stone fortress.

Fort Frederick almost became a major player during the historic 1758 events. In June, General Forbes and Colonel Bouquet considered building a new road, between Forts Frederick and Cumberland, as their main route toward the Forks of the Ohio. However, they soon decided to go directly west through Pennsylvania, leaving Fort Frederick as a store house for the campaign. The stone fort later housed refugees from Pontiac's Rebellion in 1763, British and Hessian prisoners during the Revolution, Civil War soldiers, even cows for a local farmer. The restored walls survive today as a monument to Governor Sharpe's ability and commitment.

# History:
# A Civil War Crossroads

As farmers prospered in the Cumberland Valley, they moved to towns with better markets for their goods. The valley was the ideal route for a rail line that became a strategic prize during the Civil War.

The busy Cumberland Valley Railroad operated between Harrisburg and Hagerstown from 1837 until 1952; in 1908, it carried 1.6 million passengers. The depot in Chambersburg, just 17 miles from the Mason-Dixon Line, drew Confederate invasions three times during the Civil War. Confederate cavalry cut telegraph lines, destroyed warehouses, and wrecked rail yards in 1862, and more than 60,000 troops occupied the town in 1863, just prior to the Battle of Gettysburg. Finally, on July 30, 1864, Confederate troops set the city ablaze. Unable to pay the tribute demanded by Confederate General Jubal Early, the town lost over 500 downtown structures, leaving a third of its residents homeless.

**Chambersburg's Heritage Center**[9] recounts the county's rich history in a fine exhibit at the southeast corner of Chambersburg's Memorial Square, a National Historic District (100 Lincoln Way East; 717-264-7101; www.chambersburg.org). The handsome 1915 marble bank building was designed by the architectural firm of Furness Evans & Company. Now the home of the local Chamber of Commerce, its first floor offers a concise overview of three centuries. The Center explores frontier settlement, architecture, the Underground Railroad, the Civil War, and transportation history, and offers an excellent series of themed driving tours. A thoughtfully designed children's corner at the Center offers games and dress-ups.

**Mercersburg**, founded in the 1750s along the west branch of the Conococheague southwest of Chambersburg, was named to honor colonial leader Hugh Mercer. The site of several Civil War incidents, the town square includes two extant houses that were the childhood homes of President James Buchanan and his niece, Harriet Lane. Lane served as bachelor Buchanan's White House hostess from 1857 to 1861, earning the title "First Lady."

Buchanan's family moved from a nearby cabin near **Cove Gap** (now a state park named for the 15th president) to the home at 15 North Main, now a pub and restaurant, in 1796. They followed another famous Mercersburg native who apprenticed as a carpenter on this site.

Patrick Gass, a young local Indian fighter, was a member of the Lewis and Clark Expedition from 1803 to 1806. He achieved instant celebrity by writing the first published accounts of the acclaimed journey. He later volunteered for service in the Union Army at age 87. He died in Ohio in 1870 at age 99.

Today's peaceful Main Street includes several 19th century inns, shops and restaurants and invites a stroll.

*clockwise from lower left, The ornate bank vault in the town's Heritage Center opens to visitors; a locomotive sculpted from ice echoes Chambersburg's history as a train depot; a gilt Benjamin Franklin tops the county courthouse on the central Diamond.*

# Family Fun

Children too young to read maps can still enjoy finding their way along Route 30, thanks to the fanciful exhibits called the Roadside Museum. Erected by the **Lincoln Highway Heritage Corridor**, the museum is actually a series of murals, wayside markers, hand-painted gas pumps and photo spots that give a lighthearted interpretation of local history from Adams to Westmoreland County (724-238-9030; www.lhhc.org).

In **St. Thomas**, look for a tribute to hometown baseball great Nellie Fox, portrayed on the 1920s gas pump outside the New Oak Forest Restaurant. The Fifties all-star of the Pittsburgh Pirates was later a popular sports announcer. Listen to a country song honoring the highway at Chambersburg's Diamond, or pose as a stylish Thirties traveler at the nearby photo stop. On the side of the Green Leaf gift shop in **McConnellsburg**, view a mural of a Tin Lizzie climbing to the **Mountain House**[23]. The inn is still open, at the crest of the Tuscarora Ridge on Route 30.

*Music, photo stops and art, including the mural and gas pumps below, tell the story of the Lincoln Highway through Pennsylvania. The route is also one of the state's Artisan Trails; shops selling handcrafted wares display this keystone sign. Ed Brechbill offers artisanal cheeses at Whispering Brook Cheese Haus.*

**Gypsie**[8], on the northwest corner of Chambersburg town square, is one of a dozen Route 30 shops that feature the work of local artists (21 North Main Street; 717-263-0203). The weavers, jewelers, quilters, woodworkers and other artisans whose work is sold in the stores were juried into the state-sponsored project. Each piece is unique and handcrafted. Keystone-shaped **Handmade along the Highway** signs indicate participating merchants; for a full list of shops and artists, call (724) 238-9030 or visit www.handmadealongthehighway.org.

Chambersburg is a great destination for shoppers with a sweet tooth. In addition to a dozen small boutiques, bakeries and a restored 1920s era theater, Main Street offers the **Olympia Candy Kitchen**[11], a century-old store still owned by the Pananes family (43 South Main Street; 717-263-3282; www.olympiacandy.net). Filled candies, seasonal specialties and fudge are homemade and fresh. Walk down the alley to **Olympia Ice Cream**, where the fudge is served hot.

Franklin County's dairy herds make it a center for delicious farm-made cheeses. In fact, the village of Cheesetown was named, locals say, for a cheesemaker who hung her products from the front porch. Amish and Mennonite families pitch in to make artisanal varieties from cow, sheep and goat's milk, selling the results at farmers markets throughout the region. Several also sell their wares right on the farm. Near Chambersburg, visit the Brechbills at the **Whispering Brook Cheese Haus**[5] (8875 Edensville-Cheesetown Road, Chambersburg; 717-369-2355). At **Pipe Dreams Fromage**[15], Bradley Parker raises goats for French-style specialties (2589 Shanks Church Road, Greencastle; 717-597-1877; appointment only). Also try **Otterbein Acres**[2] (10071 Otterbein Church Road, Newburg; 717-423-6689; closed Sunday) and **Keswick Creamery**[1] (185 Quigley Road, Newburg; 717-423-6758; www.keswickcreamerycheese.com). Shop hours vary, and some close during winter.

# Great Houses and Gardens

An old metal rooster has special significance at **Renfrew**[12], including a house museum, a restored German farmstead and public park in Waynesboro (1010 East Main Street; 717-762-4723; www.renfrewmuseum.org). Local 19th century potter John Bell, whose distinctive stoneware creations are prized by folk art collectors, crafted the rooster weather vane that now stands in the museum's visitor center.

At the picturesque bank barn near the mansion, Renfrew has assembled the world's largest collection of Bell Family pottery and redware. Authentic examples of this quintessential Pennsylvania folk art now command five-figure prices, but reproductions are commissioned annually by Renfrew to support the museum.

In addition to Bell, Renfrew's pottery exhibit includes work by other well-known local potters, including his sons Upton and John W. Bell, Jacob Heart of Chambersburg, and Henry Rudolph of Shippensburg.

Farmed by Daniel Royer two hundred years ago, the Renfrew property now includes the nearby Fahnestock homestead and outbuildings. The mansion house, open seasonally, retains its 19th century furnishings and overlooks a branch of Antietam Creek. The last owner named the 107-acre estate for Sarah and Jane Renfrew. The sisters are thought to have been victims of a pre-Revolutionary Indian massacre on the frontier. Renfrew welcomes visitors to walk the creekside paths and fly fish in the stream.

The tail feathers of Bell's rooster, which crowned his workshop at West Main and Potomac Streets in Waynesboro, are dented by gunfire. Local lore says the shooters were the Confederate soldiers who passed through town and used the weather vane for target practice.

Canna lilies and geraniums are the stars of the casual country garden at the **Cordell Farm**[13] south of Chambersburg (8979 Grindstone Hill Road, Chambersburg; 717-597-7415). Merle and Beulah Cordell cultivate an acre of summer blooms each year, and thousands of visitors come to admire the results. Stop by anytime: look for the sign that says "welcome to tour garden" by the road.

*From left: Antique hunters frequent Gypsie in downtown Chambersburg; in Waynesboro, the Renfrew Museum's collection of glazed redware includes work by local potter John Bell, who crafted the rooster weather vane to top his studio.*

# Great Outdoors

Within earshot of the Pennsylvania Turnpike, cyclists can pedal an empty, eight-mile stretch of asphalt rolling through—and under—the Alleghenies in Fulton County. Thanks to a local conservancy, a chunk of the nation's first superhighway has become the **Pike to Bike Trail**[26] (814-784-5000; www.piketobike.org).

The section became an appendix to the state's main east-west artery in 1968, when the turnpike was rerouted through bigger four-lane tunnels. The Southern Alleghenies Conservancy reclaimed the route between the old ones, Sideling Hill and Rays Hill. The easy, level trail winds through **Buchanan State Forest**, with a thrill at either end: the two old tunnels, a constant 55 degrees, are completely unlit. The Sideling Hill tunnel to the east is 1.3 miles long. The Rays Hill tunnel to the west is a three-quarter mile passage. While future access from the Sideling Hill service plaza of the turnpike is planned, trailheads are open west of McConnellsburg off Route 30 in Saluvia and at Route 30 and Tannery Road in Breezewood. **Grouseland Tours** guides bike tours on the trail, as well as mountain biking expeditions on private lands in the area (467 Robinsonville Road, Clearville; 814-784-5000; www.grouselandtours.com).

Serious hikers will welcome the challenge along the **Tuscarora Trail** in Cowans Gap State Park in Fort Loudoun. A spur of the Appalachian Trail, this path climbs to an elevation of 2,100 feet and provides views east over the Cumberland Valley and west to the Juniata Crossings. The primitive path that was the **Forbes Road** follows the berm of Stumpy Lane and Aughwick Road through the park, but is not recommended for recreational users. To view the ridge from a lower elevation on the eastern side, walk along the paved road called Forbes Road Trail or choose the popular Lakeside Trail on the perimeter of the 42-acre lake. The park offers ten miles of hiking trails of varying difficulty, swimming from a sandy beach, cabins, and ice skating and ice fishing in season.

*Pack a bike light for the dark tunnels of the Pike to Bike trail; Cowans Gap State Park offers winter ice fishing and ice skating.*

## Uniquely Cumberland Valley

As prosperous Conococheague farmers built their barns, they hired brick masons to create patterns using the ventilation holes on the sides. Known as brick-end barns, several examples of the designs survive along Route 16 between Greencastle and Mercersburg. One, at Greencastle's **Stover Farm**, is now an environmental center for the Greencastle-Antrim School District. Another famous example is the **Donkey Barn** (left), four miles west near Mercersburg. The farmer who commissioned the brickwork wanted to be portrayed on a great steed, the story goes; however, when he reneged on payment, the craftsman went ahead, getting revenge by portraying the farmer astride a donkey—and wearing a dunce cap.

*Dillsburg, Cumberland County*

## Did You Know?

"Allegheny Uprising," set at Fort Loudoun, was one of the forgotten film dramas of a great movie year, 1939. John Wayne portrayed Captain James Smith, who organized a group of settlers protesting British trade with the Indians. Based on the actual 1765 uprising by Smith and the Black Boys, it co-starred Claire Trevor and George Sanders.

*Right: A peaceful garden welcomes guests at Mercersburg's Steiger House.*

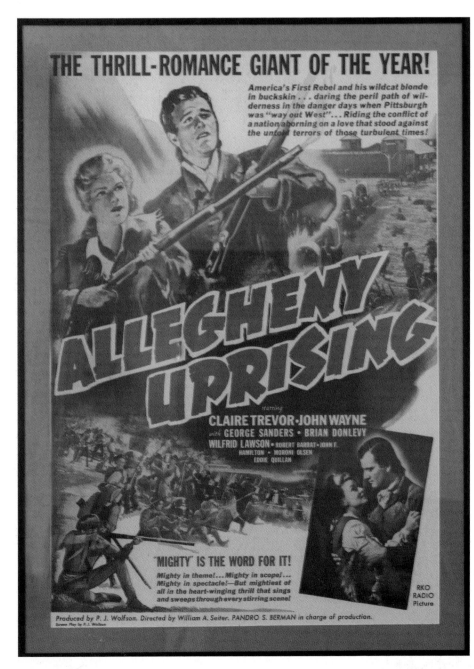

# Plan a Visit

## Annual Regional Events

**Chambersfest**, July
www.chambersburg.biz

**Fort Frederick, Maryland:**
www.dnr.state.md.us/publiclands/western/
fortfrederick.html

- **Market Fair and Rifle Frolic**, April

- **Grand Encampment**
  (French and Indian War reenactment), May

- **Colonial Children's Days**, June

## Franklin & Fulton Counties

For more information:
Explore Franklin County
14 North Main Street, Chambersburg
(866) 646-8060
www.explorefranklincountypa.com

Fulton County Chamber of Commerce
201 Lincoln Way West, Suite 101,
McConnellsburg
(717) 485-4064
www.fultoncountypa.com

### DINING
**James Buchanan Hotel and Pub**[19]
15 North Main Street, Mercersburg
(717) 328-3008
www.jamesbuchananhotel.com
- Fine New Orleans-style menu served in
  the president's boyhood home. Lunch
  and dinner.

**Byron's Dining Room**[18]
405 South Main Street, Mercersburg
(717) 328-5231 | www.mercersburginn.com
- Upscale American menu Thursday
  through Sunday at the Mercersburg Inn.

**The Boar's Head**[24]
207 Lincoln Way East, McConnellsburg
(717) 485-0099
- Southern style barbecue in a casual
  family cafe.

**Mountain House**[23]
18734 Lincoln Highway, McConnellsburg
(717) 485-3887
- A timeworn old roadhouse at the
  Tuscarora Summit, with great views from
  the patio.

### LODGING
**The Mercersburg Inn**[18]
405 South Main Street, Mercersburg
(717) 328-5231 | www.mercersburginn.com
- The former home of the Byron family,
  circa 1910, features lavish Greek Revival
  details and a view of Mercersburg
  Academy.

**Steiger House**[20]
33 North Main Street, Mercersburg
(877) 385-2989 | www.steigerhouse.com
- An 1830s-era bed and breakfast with
  gardens in the center of town.

**Craig Victorian Bed and Breakfast**[6]
756 Philadelphia Avenue, Chambersburg
(717) 263-3371 | www.craigvictorian.com
- Dates from the 1880s. On a quiet
  residential street in the north end of town
  near Wilson College campus.

# Penn's Woods

As General Forbes made his steady and inexorable march west toward the Forks of the Ohio during 1758, the vast woods that lay before him must have been ample proof of the appropriateness of Pennsylvania's name: literally, the combination of the founder's name, William Penn, with the Latin for woods, *silva*. Plentiful water, coupled with the right soil and a moderate climate, had produced some 27 million acres of forest. Dense, wild and forbidding, the woods and the resources they nourished seemed endless. Natural forces, like wind and fire, huge herds of grazing wildlife, and fires set by Native Americans to clear underbrush for better hunting had established open areas and grasslands. But even so, forest probably still covered nearly 95 percent of the land.

General Forbes would have seen conifers, most notably eastern white pines and hemlocks, and a wide variety of deciduous trees. The leaves of American chestnuts, oaks and hickory turned brilliant as the summer of 1758 turned to fall. The trees were plentiful, and their seeds, needles and leaves supported a virtual smorgasbord for Forbes' moving army: white-tailed deer, black bear, elk, turkeys, ruffed grouse, red and gray squirrels, snowshoe hares, and cottontail rabbits. Passenger pigeons, now gone from our skies, were so numerous that they could completely block the sunlight as they flew over the trees in their foraging and migratory patterns.

General Forbes would have found eastern white pines (*pinus strobes*), the tallest tree native to eastern North America, in habitats as yet untouched by Europeans, growing to heights of more than 200 feet. Lightweight, with a durable and straight-grained wood, the then-dominant white pine was soon lumbered, its straight, long branches and trunks perfectly suited for the masts of sailing ships.

The eastern hemlock (*tsuga canadensis*), now Pennsylvania's official state tree, has a bark rich in tannic acid, and was used by Native Americans and colonist alike to tan hides. Slow growing and resilient, the hemlock George Washington planted at Mount Vernon in 1785 is still providing summertime shade. Beautiful stands of old growth hemlocks can be found in the Allegheny National Forest.

Probably the greatest change to the forests since the Forbes expedition was the complete eradication of the American chestnut (*castanea dentata*), once the most dominant tree in Pennsylvania's forests. Forbes and his army would have encountered chestnuts that averaged 100 feet in height, some with trunks measuring more than 10 feet in diameter. Early settlers relied heavily on chestnuts. They produced tannin from the bark, harvested the nuts, and milled lumber suitable for everything from furniture to fences to caskets.

In the early 1900s a fungus bark disease became epidemic, and in less than one human generation the American chestnut was gone. Before the blight, one in every four hardwood tree in the Appalachians was an American chestnut. The tree's strength in numbers was no match for the invisible fungus for which it had no natural defense. By the 1950s, four billion trees were dead.

The perceived vastness of Pennsylvania's forests was almost its undoing. From the time of early European settlements, demand simply continued to grow for lumber, charcoal and other wood products. Coupled with extensive and unregulated clearing to create agricultural land, the 27 million acres of woods General Forbes found in 1758 was reduced to only 9.1 million acres by 1895. Statistical abstracts tell a chilling tale: in 1700, Pennsylvania's population was 11,450, consuming an annual average of 4,580,000 pieces of wood; by 1800, the population had reached 602,000, but the amount of annual wood consumption had grown to 156,520,000 pieces.

William Penn was likely Pennsylvania's first political leader to promote conservation, urging that one acre of trees be left for every five acres of cleared land. His plea was uniformly ignored. It was not until 1895 that J.T. Rothrock succeeded in establishing formal forest management policies for the state. By creating the first forestry commission, Dr. Rothrock created the mechanism for Pennsylvania to buy land for preservation, train foresters, institute effective fire protection systems, and establish tree nurseries. Thanks to Pennsylvania's continued commitment to forest preservation, it is still possible to experience a sense of the vast, forbidding and beautiful woods that Forbes and his army once traversed.

*pg. 112, Thanks to modern preservation efforts in state and national forests, millions of acres of Penn's Woods are still alive and well for visitors to the Allegheny Mountains in western Pennsylvania.*
*pg. 113, A red-tailed hawk enjoys the solitude deep in western Pennsylvania's mountain forest (below); some remnants of old growth forest still stand in remotes parts of the Allegheny Mountains (right).*

# Bedford

**Raystown**
**September 15, 1758**

General John Forbes may be ailing but his long-awaited arrival at the Raystown Camp (Bedford) is a welcome sight for his assembled troops.

# General Forbes' Long Journey

Fall was approaching and the redcoats' Pennsylvania campaign was running out of time. By September 15, 1758, thousands were at Raystown Camp (later called Fort Bedford), with forested ridges looming all around. The isolated valley was, for the moment, one of the largest inland cities in America. Most of the credit for moving the battalions of men and mountains of equipment and supplies into this back country lay with Colonel Bouquet. Fort Duquesne, however, was still another 100 miles to the west and fall would soon turn into winter.

It took General Forbes months to catch up with his army. The General's cursed flux would not go away. His recent trouble started while he was in Philadelphia suffering with a severe colic. He seemed to get better in Carlisle, but by early August, he was still in Carlisle struggling with "a most violent and tormenting distemper [that] has left me as weak as a new born infant."

The General finally felt well enough to ride to Shippensburg on August 15. The journey, however, "raised my flux again and pains intolerable." Considering giving up his command, he suddenly improved and decided to soldier on. Unable to mount a horse or bear the roughness of a wagon, he ordered his doctor and servants to concoct "a horse litter, a hurdle carried betwixt two horses." Forbes was carried into the Fort Loudoun stockade on September 6. He reported to Secretary William Pitt, "I hope the animating spirits of being able to do the smallest service for King and Country, will leave nothing undone on my part."

*General Forbes reviews thousands of his redcoat and provincial soldiers in the sprawling tent camps at Raystown.*

## Duty in the Face of Misery and Distress

General Forbes, in spite of his infirmities, had set in motion a campaign that would wait for no one. During the two months that he was struggling to reach the camp at Raystown, his headquarters coped with the mounting turmoil stirred up by a marching army. Intelligence of the French was so lacking that General Forbes lamented, "We are, like people in the dark, perhaps going headlong to destruction."

Finally, during the second week in September, Forbes was in his litter, rocking and jostling west with the last of his troops. The column plunged into thick forest and threaded its way up Tuscarora and Cove Mountains, passing burned-out settlers' cabins on a trail strewn with broken wagons. Leaving the overnight security of Fort Littleton, one of the Pennsylvania stockades, the party "was shaken up on that abominable road from Littleton," facing many windings and turnings up Sideling Hill. Stopping for water at the free-flowing Jerry's Spring and descending the steep slope of Ray's Hill, the redcoats were at the newly-fortified Juniata River crossing. They continued west through the gap in Tussey Mountain and rested at the meadows around Snake Spring. From there, it was another twelve miles of relatively good road, passing through the narrows of Evitt's Mountain and again fording the meandering Juniata.

Now close to fifty miles out from Fort Loudoun, the General's arrival caused quite a stir. The Reverend Thomas Barton watched Forbes come in. "[He was] carried in a sort of sedan-litter between two horses and guarded by [a] troop of light horse and 100 Highlanders. He was in a low state, yet a great satisfaction and pleasure appeared in his countenance upon finding himself in Raystown. The roads were crowded with people to see him, whom he saluted with a smile as he passed along. The troops seem to [be] inspired with fresh spirits upon the General's arrival."

## An Instant City at Raystown

About 800 Pennsylvanians and Virginians began building what became Fort Bedford on June 28. The Virginians wanted pay for ax and shovel work so the on-site commander Colonel Bouquet, worried about funds, settled on a third of a pint of rum or whiskey per day for labor. Bouquet also reported that the Indian allies were behaving very well, hunting and scouting for the British and wearing yellow ribbons as allies. Within weeks, he was calling the Catawbas scoundrels for deserting him. The Colonel, however, soon had the growing camp in a tight military routine. Over the next two months, Raystown became a city of thousands with scores of log and plank buildings, hundreds of tents, bake ovens and earthworks spread over three-quarters of a mile on the banks of the Juniata River.

Fort Bedford, the work of engineer Harry Gordon, was an irregular, 400 foot square pentagon. The stockade, enclosed in an earthen moat, was tucked on the Juniata's rocky bluffs with a protected covert-way providing access to the river's water. Saws were cutting planks day and night for large storehouses and hospitals near the fort. Just west, along with eleven ovens baking heavy loaves of bread, there were cabins for an unruly set of sutlers and traders following the army. Among hundreds of details, Colonel Bouquet was worried about deserters slipping quietly into the vast forest. He found a man who offered his services to hang a few.

## The Rhythms of Camp Life

During two summer months in 1758, the Anglican chaplain Thomas Barton lived and worked at Raystown. With fervor for the spiritual well-being of this rough community, the chaplain recorded the pulse of events in his vivid journal; the moody mountain weather, the comings and goings of officers, troops, work parties, wagons and packhorses, Indian attacks on the edges of the camp, dangerous scouting trips into enemy country, deaths and baptisms of soldiers and their children, sermons sometimes to thousands, drill using Indian tactics in a meadow near the camps, and the brutal realities of military discipline.

On July 31, an Irish butcher named Michael Scully, with very large though clumsy limbs, came running into camp in bloody condition. Scully was searching for lost horses when three Indians tried to capture then shoot him. One attacked him and "with a sword and tomahawk strove to kill him." He "gave him [the Indian] several thumps with the butt of his gun which he thinks near finished him." Another Indian attacked and wounded him. He knocked this attacker down and "hearing a rustling in the bushes he was obliged to run," escaping his pursuers.

On August 19, with hundreds in the hospital, the garrison buried a Virginia soldier. He was "launched into a little hole out of a blanket and there left naked." When Barton complained, a sergeant said he had orders to return with the blanket. "I [Barton] got some small bushes thrown over him, till I performed the service."

Chaplain Thomas Barton watches the execution of deserter John Doyle, "a shocking spectacle to all around him and a striking example to his fellow soldiers."

## "Discipline is the Soul of an Army" George Washington, 1757

With a harsh code of military discipline, 18th century European armies prescribed daunting punishments for a wide variety of offenses. After trial by a military court of officers drawn from the army, British soldiers who deserted their regiments or displayed cowardice during battle could receive sentences of up to several thousand lashes or death by shooting or hanging. A regimental court martial could condemn prisoners to several hundred lashes for less serious offenses, including immoralities, misbehavior, or disobedience of orders. Although many provincial corps, particularly those from New England, traditionally used less onerous punishments, all were subject to the strict British Rules and Articles of War during joint expeditions with the redcoats.

Provincials in Forbes' army were no strangers to the gibbet and the lash. Hoping to end a rash of desertions after Braddock's Defeat in 1755, Colonel George Washington erected a forty-foot gallows at Fort Loudoun in Winchester, Virginia. Regimental courts martial regularly sentenced provincial soldiers to corporal punishment every bit as harsh as that in the British army.

The first major public display of military punishment during the Forbes Expedition occurred in September, after most of the army had gathered at Raystown. Diarist Thomas Barton noted the solemn mood as five soldiers from Pennsylvania, Maryland, Virginia, and North Carolina prepared for execution by firing squad the following morning. "Visited the prisoners in the evening," Barton wrote, "who I found in tears under terrible apprehensions of approaching death." Forbes pardoned all but Pennsylvanian John Doyle the following morning, condemning the deserter to serve as an example before the assembled army.

## The Virginians Enter the Mix

Eight hundred Virginia troops had joined the main column at Fort Loudoun, but the majority had marched from Winchester to Fort Cumberland in late June. They were awaiting orders but expected to march west on the Braddock route after the rest of the army joined them. The Braddock Road, from Cumberland to the Forks of the Ohio, was Virginia's chosen path to settlement and expansion.

Colonel Bouquet, settling in at Raystown on July 11, was relieved to hear that General Forbes had rejected a new road and route from Fort Frederick to Cumberland. "The change of route at such an advanced season seemed to me a hazardous measure. All the letters from Virginia are filled with nothing but the ease of going by Braddock's Road. This is a matter of colonial politics between one province and another, in which we have no part."

The Virginians committed two infantry regiments, light cavalry and many wagonloads of supplies to the expedition. One regimental commander, Colonel William Byrd, was courting the Cherokees for the British cause. The other regimental commander, Colonel George Washington, had rejoined his troops to cap his short military career with a glorious victory over the French. He and his comrades wanted Virginia to share the benefits of that victory.

## George Washington Throws Down the Gauntlet

On July 24, Colonel Bouquet politely asked Colonel Washington, "I would be glad to know if it would be agreeable to you to march that way [west over Laurel Hill]," adding, "he [the General] has several times expressed to me how much he depends on you." Washington answered quickly. "I shall most cheerfully proceed to work on any road, but since you desire me to speak, every person

Officers like Colonel George Washington, here dressed in the blue and red of his Virginia troops, often carry small muskets called fusils into battle.

## British Scouts and Rangers

The British army in colonial America has a reputation for ignorance and arrogance in their war against the French and Indians. The truth is, redcoat commanders had European experience with irregular warfare, using hit and run tactics against infantry columns. Before his 1755 defeat, the ill-fated General Edward Braddock was seeking Indian scouts and protecting his columns from surprise attack. By 1757, New England officer Robert Rogers had drafted a 28-rule manual, "running and firing in the Indian manner," and was raising a hand-picked company of "Rogers' Rangers." Other specially-trained rangers were soon using Rogers' tactics in New York, fighting alongside their Indian allies with forest green uniforms and lighter equipment.

Although the 1758 Pennsylvania campaign had no official ranger units, General Forbes and Colonel Bouquet were versed in irregular warfare. Their frustrations with Indian allies led them to colonials with hard-earned frontier experience. Colonel Washington's suggestion to dress his troops with Indian trappings, even paint, was taken seriously. Although good intelligence on the French was often scarce, colonial officers were regularly leading available Indians on dangerous scouting trips, some to the gates of Fort Duquesne.

The Reverend Thomas Barton, impressed with the army's drill practice at Fort Bedford on August 13, left us a detailed description of its maneuvers. After marching in column, then "forming a line of battle with great ease and expedition," the men kept up a running fire for some time, finally making "a sham pursuit with shrieks and halloos in the Indian way."

who has knowledge of that country [reports] that a road comparable to General Braddock's cannot be made." For the next week, the post riders on the new road between Raystown and Cumberland carried painfully formal messages filled with passionate opinions.

Colonel Bouquet proposed a July 29 meeting halfway between Raystown and Cumberland where "we shall I hope be able to determine what is most eligible, and save the General trouble." The meeting accomplished very little, for Washington returned to Fort Cumberland and poured out his arguments. "The more attention I give, the more I am confirmed in the reasons for taking the old road. I ask if we have time to make a road from Raystown? Certainly not-surmounting the vast difficulties to be encountered, in making it over such monstrous mountains covered with woods and rocks, would require so much time as to blast our well grounded hopes."

Washington wrote Virginia officials, arguing against a new road that "forebode our manifest ruin." Then he confided in General Forbes' aide, his friend Major Francis Halkett. Washington's message to Halkett was all but hysterical. "If Colonel Bouquet succeeds in this point with the General-all is lost-all is lost by heavens-our enterprise ruined." General Forbes soon saw the letter, calling Washington's arguments a "scheme that I think was a shame for any officer to be concerned in," later commenting that "his [Washington's] behavior about the roads, was no ways like a soldier."

Colonel Bouquet delivered the General's verdict on August 3. "I received express orders to begin to open the road from this place across the Allegheny Mountains." Washington was properly humble. "The General's orders, when once given, be a law to me." He slipped in, however, a last comment on the matter. "If I unfortunately am right [about the roads]; my conduct will acquit me of having discharged my duty on this important occasion."

## Pushing the Road

Washington did have a point. The British had fierce challenges that he kept repeating, "the height of the hills-the steepness of them-the unevenness of the ground—the shortness of the season." With favorable reports from his scouts, General Forbes picked the shorter route with none of the river crossings vulnerable to ambush.

The redcoat army faced two giant ridges, Allegheny and Laurel, with another, Chestnut, beyond. The first was the 1,300 mile long Allegheny Front, one continuous, unbroken range of high table land. In late July, scouts Colonel James Burd and a capable young engineer, Ensign Charles Rohr, found an almost 2,000 foot climb through thick forest. It looked impossible for a large army until Ensign Rohr found a gap that still bears his name. A daunting three quarters of a mile, 600 foot climb through Rohr's Gap held the key to getting over the mountain. General Forbes praised "Mr. Rohr [who] was of more service than all the rest of that class [of engineers] put together." With the road decision made, seven hundred men were soon digging, filling and tamping the narrow wagon trail.

Colonel Bouquet was juggling men between building the Bedford fort and trail-blazing the military road. He was protecting, supplying, and feeding a growing army base plagued with disease. He was mending broken supply lines and regularly drilling the raw colonial soldiers. While promising to "take upon myself as much of the burden as I can," Bouquet also exhorted his sick General. "If prayers count for anything, you will soon be in a condition to join us."

Quartermaster Sir John St. Clair was back at the front. At the General's stern command, he joined the party building the road over the mountains. Sir John, the model for misdirected energy, built redoubts and picked routes without engineers, all the while issuing orders to everyone. "The work to be done on this road is immense. If I have not two hundred men more, I do not know when it will be finished. Pick axes, crows and shovels is what is most needed, likewise more whiskey. Send me my down quilt, the weather is cold." His high-handed antics soon brought more trouble. When Virginia Lieutenant Colonel Adam Stephen took exception, Sir John placed him under arrest for mutiny.

Real Indian allies are scarce, so the British are making "Indians part of our Virginia soldiers. It is difficult for the enemy to distinguish them and the impression is useful to us."

## The Virginia Regiment

Colonel George Washington's Virginia Regiment was the longest-serving provincial unit in General Forbes' army. It was originally raised in early 1754 for an expedition that led unexpectedly to the outbreak of the French and Indian War. Eager to become a British officer as his beloved elder half-brother Lawrence had been, Washington reorganized his corps, modeling it on the British regiments that he observed during the 1755 Braddock Expedition. From the fall of 1755, the young Virginia colonel labored tirelessly to distinguish his regiment from the often ill-disciplined soldiers of other colonies. After a 1758 review in Winchester, Virginia, Deputy Quartermaster Sir John St. Clair informed Forbes that Washington's "regiment does honor to its colonel."

The corps was designated the 1st Virginia Regiment in 1758 when a second regiment was raised and led by the wealthy planter William Byrd III. Like Pennsylvania recruits, about half of the Virginia provincial soldiers were immigrants, mostly from the British Isles while the rest were native born. Seven out of ten were young men who worked as laborers, tradesmen, or farmers.

Many Virginia soldiers spent the summer of 1758 in a campaign uniform inspired by troubles with the Cherokee and other southern warriors. As these valuable scouts began leaving for home in increasing numbers, Colonel Bouquet suggested that Forbes "make Indians a part of our provincial soldiers." By replacing the provincials' uniforms with typical warriors' dress, Bouquet hoped to deceive the French into thinking that hundreds of southern Indian warriors still accompanied Forbes' army. When some Virginians equipped in this fashion arrived at Fort Bedford in early July, Bouquet complimented Washington, noting "their dress should be our pattern in this expedition."

## The Silent Enemy

Diseases and infections were the most dangerous enemies soldiers faced in the 18th century. Although spotty record keeping and loss of Forbes Expedition manuscripts make exact figures impossible, far more soldiers and camp followers suffered and died from sickness than by the hand of French soldiers or enemy Indians. With little understanding of disease and infection, 18th century army doctors often hastened the death of their patients with bloodletting and medicines like alcohol, opium, and arsenic. At best, military hospitals helped slow or stop the spread of disease by separating patients from camps and garrisons.

Military encampments were among the most densely populated places in North America. Poor sanitation and unprotected sources of water led to outbreaks of disease. One of the first tasks that Colonel Henry Bouquet set for his troops at Raystown was construction of the army's General Hospital, a massive structure measuring 160 by 30 feet, the largest building constructed during the 1758 expedition. Here, army surgeons or surgeon's mates and female camp followers acting as nurses cared for sick and recovering soldiers. Two months later, Thomas Barton noted in his journal that "near 400 persons are now in the hospital, sick of fluxes, diarrheas, agues, fevers, smallpox, and etc." Many patients died. Those who recovered were often left susceptible to further illness.

The soldiers who remained in remote garrisons, far from sources of fresh provisions, suffered the most. After spending the winter of 1758-59 in garrison at Fort Ligonier, Pennsylvania Captain Thomas Lloyd informed his commander, "I am extremely sorry to tell you, what now remains of your unfortunate battalion is hardly worth writing about. The graveyard has most of them."

*The real danger of frightening looking medical tools is their use under unsanitary conditions.*

*Soldiers ripped apart by large musket balls face a harrowing, uncertain recovery in primitive field hospitals. Sickness and disease are formidable enemies in military camps.*

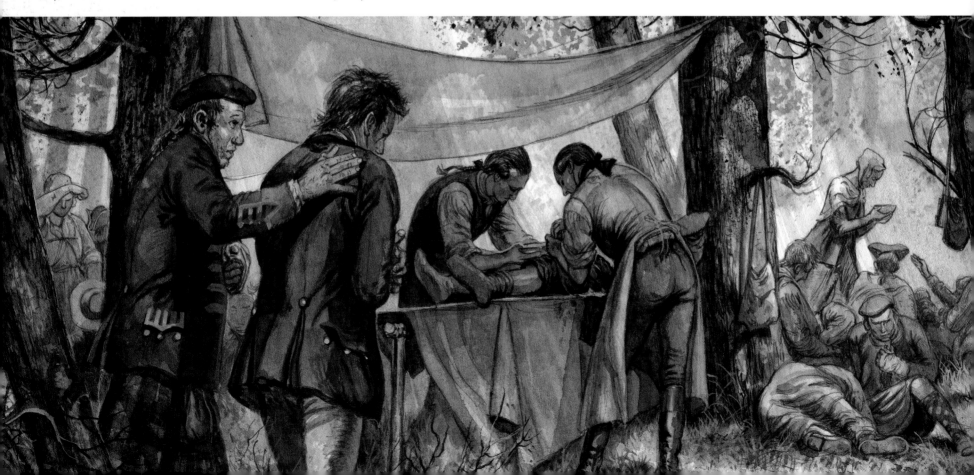

## Peace Talks in the Shadow of the Enemy

Christian Frederick Post was alone and talking peace right under the noses of the French. On that August 26, he was standing in front of three hundred Indians and French officers in the shadow of a recently reinforced Fort Duquesne.

The French wanted to silence Post, but he had seventy Delaware Indian protectors. The envoy, sticking close to the security of the council fire, "spoke in the middle of them with a free conscience, and perceived by the look of the French, they were not pleased with what I said." After a long impassioned speech punctuated with wampum, Post finished by proffering a large peace belt. "By this belt I take you by the hand, and lead you at a distance from the French, for your own safety, that your legs may not be stained with blood." Soon after, Shamokin Daniel, one of Post's trusted Delaware travelling companions, was courted by the French at their fort and suddenly became an enemy exclaiming, "the English are fools, and so are you [his fellow Indians]!" On the trip back to the Kuskuskies villages with the Delawares, Daniel shouted at Post. "Damn you, why do not you and the French fight on the sea? You come here only to cheat the poor Indians, and take their land from them."

Despite Indian detractors and bounties for his scalp, Post was on the trail east in early September, carrying a peace belt sent by all the Delaware sachems. Pisquetomen was still protecting him as a nervous, hungry, often wet Post plunged through swamps, thorns and over steep, rocky hills with hostile war parties shadowing him. Finally at Fort Augusta on September 22, Post sent Pisquetomen on to Easton and headed south to report to General Forbes at Raystown. He confided to his journal, "There is not a prouder, or more high minded people than the Indians. The white people are, in their eyes, nothing at all. They [the Indians] say, through their conjuring craft, they can do what they please, and nothing can withstand them."

*With hostile French soldiers nearby, envoy Christian Frederick Post stays near the safety of the council fire as he shows hundreds of Ohio Indians the British Belt of Peace.*

## The British Endure a Self-Inflicted Reverse

On August 23, large work crews were still carving a path through the mountain country. Colonel Bouquet ordered Colonel James Burd to march west with 1,500 men: Burd's Pennsylvania battalion, other small colonial detachments, the four Royal American Companies, some artillery, eighty wagons, and Major James Grant leading five companies of Highlanders. Five Virginia companies were waiting for them in the mountains. Bouquet ordered Burd to use "all hands to be employed in entrenching" a new camp at Loyalhanna.

Two weeks later, Bouquet rode the fifty miles to the new post. He reported to General Forbes that the new roads were abominable, but the Loyalhanna advanced post was very strong. Threatened by Indian raids and ignorant about the enemy, the Colonel mentioned he was letting Major James Grant pick a large party to march to Fort Duquesne and "check the boldness of the Indian rabble." The Highlander Grant, with little confidence in colonial troops, was a favorite with officers. Bouquet told Colonel Burd to "consult Major Grant, whose experience and perfect knowledge of the service you may rely entirely upon."

By the dawn of September 14, Grant and 750 men, amazingly undetected, were at the gates of Fort Duquesne. The redcoat major ordered a pre-dawn foray, an advance guard, wearing white shirts over their uniforms to find each other in the darkness. His aim was to lure the enemy out of the fort and into the jaws of his main force.

Indians suddenly attacked from all directions, turning the British reconnaissance into a smaller version of Braddock's defeat. Ensign Rohr, brought along to inspect the French fort, was killed. Major Grant and 270 of his troops were lost. French casualties were 16. One Highland private was "pursued by four Indians, shot through my clothes and wounded in the leg with buckshot." Revealing the unpredictability of woods fighting, Robert Kirkwood "was immediately taken, but the Indian who laid hold of me would not allow the rest to scalp me, in short he befriended me greatly." A brave last ditch stand led by Major Andrew Lewis sacrificed 58 Virginians but saved the column from being cut to pieces. Lewis, who had replaced the arrested Lieutenant Colonel Stephen, was captured along with a disconsolate Major Grant, who surrendered while meekly sitting on a log in the midst of the mayhem. One Virginia company escaped by feigning surrender then blasting the Indians as they approached, "an expedient contrary to all the established laws of arms." The terrified survivors fled through fifty miles of forest to the safety of the Loyalhanna Post.

## No Less Surprise than Real Concern

An express rider brought the melancholy news to Raystown on September 19. General Forbes, just arrived, was displeased and disappointed. He was displeased with Colonel Bouquet: "Our road almost completed; our provisions all upon wheels, and all this without loss on our side. Thus the breaking in upon our hitherto so fair and flattering hopes of success." He saved his disappointment for Major Grant, who would soon be blaming colonials for his disaster. The Major "ran headlong to grasp public applause, forgetting the inevitable mischief he was bringing upon me and the rest of us." And Forbes mourned the loss of engineer Rohr, "of more service than all the rest of that class put together."

As fall arrived, a sick and exhausted Forbes conceded that "to describe the many, many impediments that I meet with this wilderness would take a volume." When the envoy Christian Frederick Post arrived, bringing some promising news from Indian country, Forbes quickly drafted a message to the Easton Indian Council, urging diplomats to abandon "foolish trifles. Strengthen ourselves and diminish our enemy's influence with the Indians."

*Like General Braddock before him, Major James Grant finds out that nothing can be more devastating to an army in the woods than a surprise attack.*

Cutting through the "fine rich" Cumberland Valley between Evitts and Wills Mountains, U.S. 220 is a picturesque route that links Bedford and Cumberland, Maryland. In 1758, Colonel Washington and Virginia troops carved out a road through the valley so that soldiers and supplies could join the main British column building the new Forbes Road west through the Laurel Highlands.

# The Indispensable George Washington

George Washington was on an important mission when he rode into Philadelphia in 1775. The 43-year-old Virginia planter had visited the city almost two decades earlier. Seeking a commission in the King's army, he had been snubbed by the British commander in North America. Now he was back, again in uniform, to seek quite a different commission. The Continental Congress, trying to guide a homegrown rebellion, selected the French and Indian War hero to lead its new ill-trained and ill-equipped army. Washington confided to his colleague Patrick Henry, "From the day I enter the command of the American armies, I date my fall and the ruin of my reputation."

Thus began the last two legendary decades of George Washington's career. The all but impossible, uphill challenges that he faced were ready made for his ambition to rise above what he called the common run. During the many years of crisis, intrigue, defeat, and, finally, surprising victory, the roads kept leading to Philadelphia, the war capital of the new nation. Literally living out of a suitcase for almost nine years, the American commander faced some of his greatest tests in and around the City of Brotherly Love.

The last half of 1776 brought defeat and retreat for Americans, from New York across New Jersey to Pennsylvania. Washington and his ragged army then launched a Christmas attack across the icy Delaware River and made history with two much-needed victories at Trenton and Princeton. The General was so important to his men marching into battle that, when they passed him sitting bravely on his horse, they touched him to bolster their own resolve. The fall of 1777 brought more defeats as the British army won the Battle of Brandywine, captured Philadelphia, and forced the Continental Army into the trying winter at Valley Forge. Far from vanquished, Washington used winter quarters to train his troops. Private Yankee Doodle became a potent fighting man who, with French help, prevailed at Yorktown in 1781.

After refusing a role as dictator and retiring to his Mount Vernon plantation, General Washington, now a famous hero, returned to Philadelphia during another crisis for the young United States. He chaired a contentious constitutional convention during the hot summer of 1787 and used his fame and reputation to help sell a new government to the nation. He was again the unanimous choice to lead, this time as the first president. Washington began his administration in New York, but moved to Philadelphia in 1790 where he lived and worked in the shadow of Independence Hall, the Pennsylvania State House that played such a major role in colonial America.

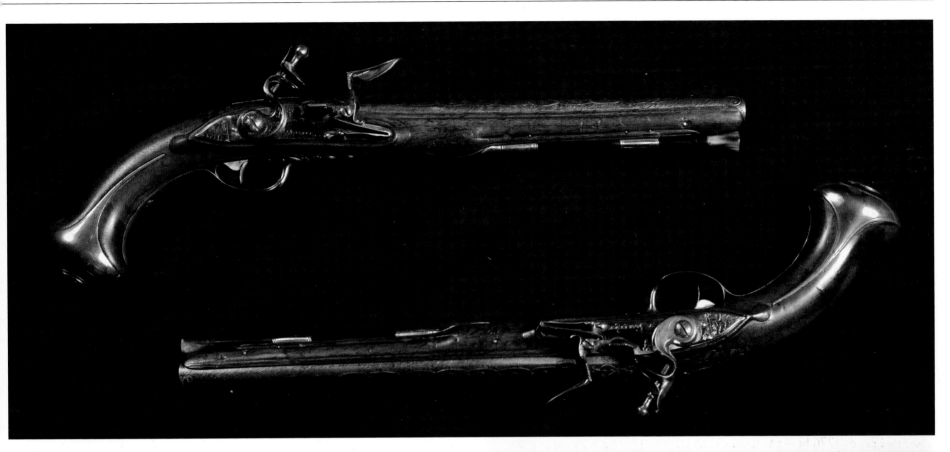

George Washington was a Virginian who spent much of his lifetime of service in Pennsylvania. The roads and trails of the Keystone State ushered in and closed out the great man's career, so indispensable to the country's founding generation. In 1753, the young diplomat rode through the wintry wilds of western Pennsylvania searching for the French. Forty years later, he returned, riding on the Forbes Road to quell the Whiskey Rebellion and guarantee a national union.

*pg. 124, Artist Charles Willson Peale was commissioned by the State of Maryland to paint General George Washington, attended by his loyal French ally, the Marquis de Lafayette, and chief of staff Colonel Tench Tilghman. The giant portrait, still displayed in the Annapolis State House, commemorates the decisive 1781 victory at Yorktown.*
*pg. 125, above, A pair of pistols, now on display at Fort Ligonier, has a special pedigree. A gift from the Marquis de Lafayette to General George Washington during the American Revolution, the pair was presented to General Andrew Jackson after his victories in the War of 1812; after painting George Washington many times over more than three decades, artist Charles Willson Peale had the president sit for a last portrait in 1795. So many Peale family members attended the sitting that painter Charles Stuart was heard to remark that poor Mr. Washington was being "Pealed all round."*

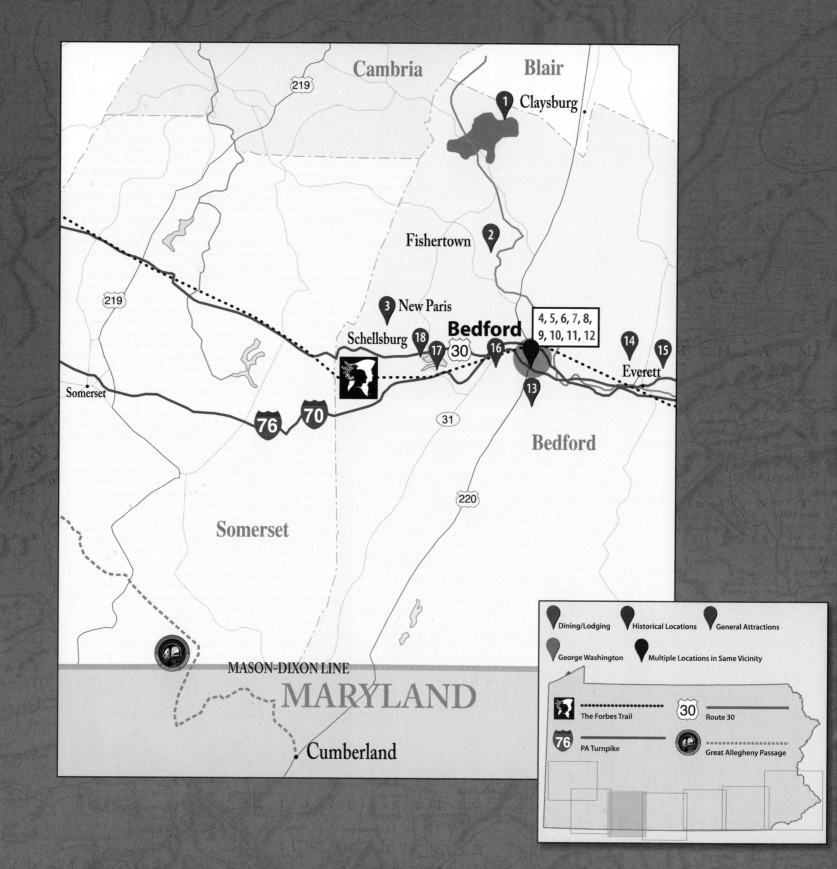

# Bedford Regional Map

Cambria     Blair

1 Claysburg

2 Fishertown

3 New Paris

Schellsburg

18 17 30 16 **Bedford**   4, 5, 6, 7, 8, 9, 10, 11, 12

14 Everett 15

13

Bedford

Somerset

31

220

Somerset

MASON-DIXON LINE

**MARYLAND**

Cumberland

219

219

76 70

**Legend:**

Dining/Lodging    Historical Locations    General Attractions

George Washington    Multiple Locations in Same Vicinity

The Forbes Trail    30 Route 30

76 PA Turnpike    Great Allegheny Passage

## Visiting Bedford

The year 1758 was a high water mark for Bedford. The 6,000 troops camped at the Raystown fort that autumn made it, briefly, one of Pennsylvania's largest cities. The hospitals, storehouses, and ovens serving the huge encampment have given way to orderly, tree-lined residential streets, showcasing American architectural styles from Federal to Victorian. Now a peaceful county seat with 3,000 residents, Bedford sits at the top of the long valley from Cumberland, Maryland. The current-day crossroads of Route 30 and Route 220, Bedford is where Forbes' decision to strike west across the mountains, instead of following the route of the 1755 Braddock expedition through Maryland, made American transportation history.

*Old Bedford Village is a living museum of frontier life.*

## See 1758 Today

First settled in 1750, Bedford's street names retain a distinct British accent. Penn, Juliana and Richard Streets honor the founding father of the Commonwealth and his descendants, and Pitt Street runs through the center of town. A historical marker on Pitt Street notes the site of **John Fraser's Tavern**[9] from that era. A shrewd businessman, Fraser made a career of following Forbes' army along its route. Two blocks from Pitt Street, on the banks of the Raystown branch of the Juniata River, stands a monument to **Fort Bedford**[6]. The town commemorated the bicentennial of the fort in 1958 by building this small blockhouse-style structure (110 Fort Bedford Drive, Bedford; 814-623-8891; www.fortbedfordmuseum.org). A scale model of the complete fort and a small collection of weaponry, Indian artifacts, and household goods are displayed at the museum, which is open seasonally.

Opened as an outdoor museum of early American life, Old Bedford Village[4] has expanded to become a center of military reenactments from a variety of eras (220 Sawblade Road, Bedford; 800-238-4347; www.oldbedfordvillage.com). The thirty-eight original buildings on this unusual site, one mile north of town on Route 220, range from the covered bridge at the entrance to homesteads, print shops and chapels. One common element is the extremely long, straight timber hewn from local forests by settlers. The Gardner Theater, one of the largest log structures ever built, is still used by performers. Craftspeople demonstrate skills from coopering and quilting to basket making. The handmade results are sold at the village shop, and classes are available. The Village hosts a French and Indian War reenactment annually, and Civil War and even Napoleonic War reenactors converge here.

Two famous routes diverge four miles west of Bedford. A historical marker at Routes 30 and 31 marks The Forks, where the Forbes Road turned away from the established Burd Road. It is also the site of the **Jean Bonnet Tavern**[16], easily seen from the Pennsylvania Turnpike (6048 Lincoln Highway, Bedford; 814-623-2250; www.jeanbonnettavern.com). The tavern, which dates to 1762, was licensed to Bonnet as a public house in 1780 and is still open to travelers. The original ground-floor dining room maintains a massive fireplace, and two upper floors are used for a pub and bed and breakfast.

**Shawnee State Park**[17], four miles further west at Routes 30 and 96, was an old Indian camp called Shawnee Cabins when Forbes' troops stopped here (132 State Park Road, Schellsburg; 814-733-4218; www.dcnr.state.pa.us/StateParks/parks/shawnee.aspx). The former bottomland along Shawnee Creek was dammed to create a 450-acre lake, the park's focal point. Among the park's fifteen miles of hiking trails is a section of the original **Forbes Road**. Beginning at the southern lakeshore, the route parallels the creek for a half-mile stretch southeast, crossing the dam and ending at the Colvin Covered Bridge.

*below, Fall foliage enlivens rural Route 30.*
*pg. 129, upper left, General Forbes named the Raystown Camp Fort Bedford in December of 1758, honoring John Russell, the 4th Duke of Bedford (1710-1771), seen here in a portrait copy at the Fort Bedford Museum; in 1758, Bedford was Lord Lieutenant of Ireland and an influential member of the Pitt administration. He remained an active politician and statesman until his death, signing the 1763 Treaty of Paris that ended the French and Indian War; bottom right, local forests provided the timber for homes at Old Bedford Village, where herbs hang on a line to dry.*

## George Washington Was Here

Washington and his Virginia Regiment, some clad as Indian warriors, marched into the Raystown Fort in September, 1758. As he argued at camp for Forbes to follow the Braddock Expedition's route west from Cumberland, he made several trips along the **Cumberland Road**, the predecessor of Route 220.

Washington returned to Bedford as president in 1794. The culmination of his march west from Harrisburg was his arrival at the town's finest home, **Espy House**[7] (123 East Pitt Street, Bedford). The president stayed here on October 19 and 20, 1794. Its first floor has been remodeled as a retail store.

*This period painting by folk artist Frederick Kemmelmeyer depicts President Washington in Maryland, on the day before he arrived in Bedford.*

## History: The Whiskey Rebellion

In 1794, just a few miles from the Espy House, local farmers resurrected an old symbol to signal their outrage at the federal tax levied on their whiskey. Whiskey was the main money crop on the frontier, where one of every six

GENERAL GEORGE WASHINGTON.
Reviewing the W▉stern army at Fort ▉▉mberland the 18th of October 1794.

farmers operated a still. They balked at the new law requiring a seven-cent tax on every gallon made.

The liberty pole, a tall staff flying a red flag as a symbol of dissent, had been used throughout the colonies in the 1770s to protest British rule. Raised in town squares or along roads, they were a rallying point for protestors. In Bedford County, the whiskey rebels revived the custom along the Forbes Road. A marker at the **Jean Bonnet Tavern**[16] notes the placing of a liberty pole there in 1794.

Concerned at the threat to the republic posed by the angry protestors, Washington invoked martial law. He ordered 12,000 troops to confront the rebels, and rode out with a large force from Harrisburg. The march marks one of only two occasions in U.S. history that a sitting president personally commanded an army. The second was James Madison's command of forces defending Washington during the War of 1812.

While the president paused in Bedford, some militias moved further west to confront settlers around Pittsburgh, where the first shots had been fired. The forceful military response quelled the disturbance. In early 1796, 27 Pennsylvanians were fined between four and fifteen shillings for setting up their "seditious" liberty pole. The federal government continued to have trouble collecting the whiskey tax, and it was finally repealed in 1803.

*Route 30's Jean Bonnet Tavern marks the divergence of two roads west.*

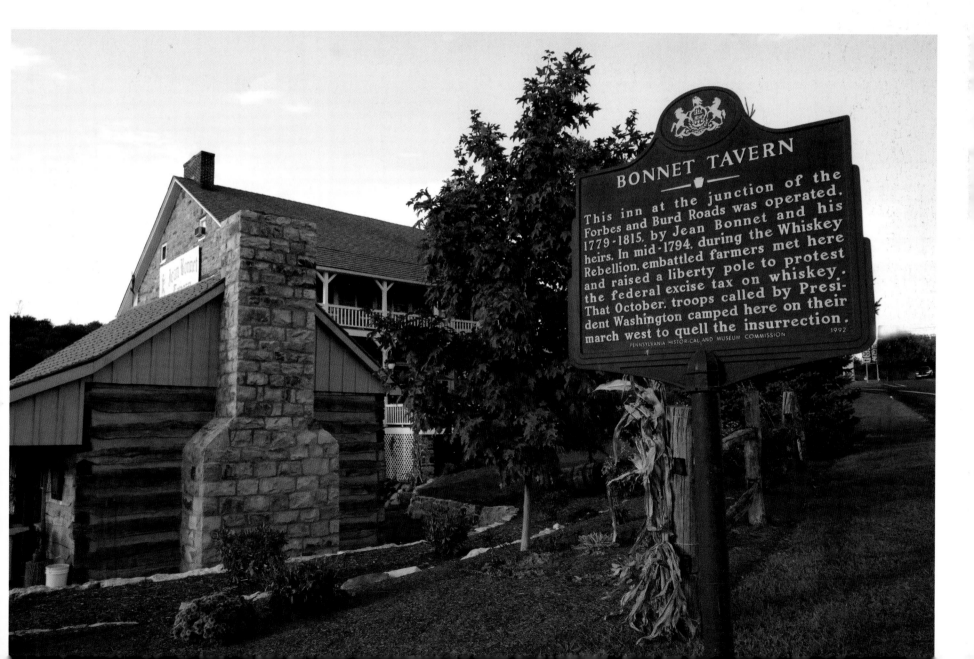

# Family Fun

Whether an enduring mystery or an optical illusion, Bedford County's **Gravity Hill**[3] is an adventure best experienced inside the family car. The "G.H." spray-painted on a silent two-lane road marks the site where cars locked in neutral will slowly roll backwards, uphill. The rural route from Bedford climbs Route 96 toward New Paris, and plunges past cattle pastures, cornfields and orchards. Get the detailed directions from the Bedford County Visitors Bureau (800-765-3331; www. bedfordcounty.net).

Local farms offer a group of unusual animal preserves. From **LaMalot Farm**[15] off Route 30 in Breezewood (430 Crestview Road; 814-735-4736; www.lamalot.com), where a llama herd grazes, continue west past Schellsburg to the **Bison Corral**[18] (2708 Lincoln Highway, Schellsburg; 814-733-2323). The buffalo pastured here may not be native to Pennsylvania, but they are thriving. Near Fishertown, the **Reynoldsdale Fish Hatchery**[2] raises over 300,000 trout for Pennsylvania ponds each year (162 Fish Hatchery Road, New Paris; 814-839-2211). All sites are free and welcome visitors who stay at a safe distance.

*Bedford's fall celebration takes over downtown each October; the herd at Breezewood's LaMalot Farm, right, produces fine wool.*

## Great Houses and Gardens

Indians knew the healing powers of the seven springs near Bedford centuries ago. Later, settlers began to bathe in and drink the waters by the 18th century, and in 1806, physician John Anderson began building a hotel for patients taking a cure. As the resort grew, the original colonnaded hotel expanded along the base of a mountain facing the springs. Today, the restored **Bedford Springs Resort**[13] has the formal grandeur of the mid 19th century, when the elegant hotel was the summer White House for President James Buchanan (2138 Business Route 220, Bedford; 866-623-8176; www.bedfordspringsresort.com).

Shuttered for decades, the newly renovated resort tells its story in a series of vintage photos and antiques in its public rooms, which include four restaurants. Bedford Springs has hosted ten U.S. presidents. A golf course originally designed by Spencer Oldham in 1895 and redesigned in 1923 by Donald Ross is an example of "springs course" architecture. Spring waters are still used in the resort's spas. Twenty-five miles of walking trails on the expansive 2,200-acre property are open to the public.

Bedford's **Memorial Park**, in the center of the historic district, was the town cemetery from 1766 until 1879. Today, it is the town's well-maintained green space. Visitors can stroll its pathways, admire the flowers, and read the well-marked gravestones of two centuries of local residents.

*Left: Bedford Springs Resort, founded in 1806, draws mineral water for its luxurious spa from seven springs on the property. Below: The Chancellor's House, now a bed and breakfast, was built in 1875 for University of Pittsburgh chancellor Dr. John Bowman.*

# Great Outdoors

Rural Bedford County has fourteen **covered bridges**, most of which are in excellent condition and open to drivers. Until recently, they outnumbered its traffic lights. Built in the 19th century, these uniquely American designs protected their floorboards from rot with carefully engineered roofs. The Bedford County Visitors Bureau publishes leisurely tour routes that can be followed by car or bicycle.

The southern Allegheny Mountains challenge cyclists, both on and off their hilly roads. The region is one of Bicycling Magazine's top five **cycling destinations** in the United States. Northern Bedford County is home to the annual Tour de Toona, organized by the Altoona Bicycling Club in 1986 and now the largest pro-am cycling event in North America. For a menu of routes for on-road and mountain biking, visit www.thealleghenies. com. **Blue Knob**[1], Pennsylvania's highest ski resort, is located midway between Altoona and Johnstown (Overland Pass, Claysburg; 800-458-3403; www.blueknob.com). It perches atop the second-highest mountain in the state, at 3,127 feet.

At water level, paddle the pristine **Juniata River Water Trail**[5] (www.fish.state.pa.us/watertrails). The Raystown branch of the Juniata meanders 60 miles through farmland and forests, from the Bedford trailhead to Saxton. Powerboats then begin to use the river as it forms **Raystown Lake**, a major reservoir. Water levels in the Raystown branch vary dramatically from season to season, and kayaks, with a shallow draft, maneuver most easily. The river is generally placid and scenic, and local outfitters offer rental equipment.

*At Juniata Crossings east of Bedford, the river twists through hilly terrain (below left); a tranquil lake and footpaths highlight Shawnee State Park in Schellsburg, at right.*

## Uniquely Bedford

Colonial-era textiles are featured at the **National Museum of the American Coverlet**[10], housed in the 1859 **Bedford Common School** (322 South Juliana Street, Bedford; 814-623-1588; www.coverletmuseum.org). This unusual collection, more a collection of artwork than of bedspreads, includes handwoven folk designs from the 18th and 19th centuries. The figured and geometric patterns, often containing their dates within the weaves, retain their vibrant colors. The museum shop offers replicas of folk patterns on pillows, placemats, and on printed yard goods.

## Did You Know?

As the **Lincoln Highway** boosted traffic through Bedford in the 1920s and 30s, merchants sought big gestures to attract motorists. The efforts, called programmatic architecture, resulted in buildings that resembled the products they sold. The two-story white Coffee Pot perched across from the **Bedford County Fairgrounds**[12] is a classic of the genre, restored and installed here in 2004. In nearby Everett, look for the **Igloo**[14] on Business Route 30. The building resembles a giant scoop of ice cream topped by a two-foot cherry and operates, of course, as a seasonal ice cream stand.

*pg. 136, Bedford's two-story coffee pot is a local landmark (right); the Town of Bedford offers self-guided architectural tours of its historic district as well as weekly guided tours in warm weather (below).*
*pg. 137, The views at Bedford Springs Resort, from a front porch rocker (top) or inside its lobby (bottom), have changed little in two centuries.*

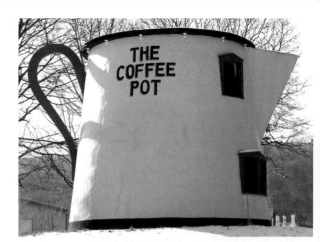

# Plan a Visit

## Annual Regional Events

**British, French and Indian War Reenactment,** usually July | www.oldbedfordvillage.com

**Bedford County Fair,** July
www.bedford-fair.com

**Bedford Fall Foliage Festival,** October
www.bedfordcounty.net

## Bedford

For more information:
Bedford County Visitors Bureau
131 South Juliana Street, Bedford
(800) 765-3331 | www.bedfordcounty.net

### DINING AND LODGING

**Bedford Springs Resort**[13]
2138 Business Route 220, Bedford
(866) 623-8176
www.bedfordspringsresort.com
- Four-star elegance, four dining rooms, golf and more.

**Oralee's Golden Eagle Inn**[8]
131 East Pitt Street, Bedford
(814) 624-0800
www.bedfordgoldeneagle.com
- Restored Federalist-era stagecoach tavern is a B&B, serves lunch and dinner on Bedford's main street, and is convenient to shops and historic sites.

**Jean Bonnet Tavern**[16]
6048 Lincoln Highway, Bedford
(814) 623-2250 | www.jeanbonnettavern.com
- Authentic 1760s inn with ground-floor dining, upstairs tavern with microbrew beers, and guest rooms.

**The Chancellor's House**[11]
341 South Juliana Street, Bedford
(866) 535-8414
www.thechancellorshouse.com
- An 1875 Italianate mansion refurbished as a bed and breakfast.

# Ligonier

**Fort at Loyalhanna**
**October 12, 1758**

A coehorn mortar belches fire inside the new fort at Loyalhanna as British forces probe the rainy night for French and Indian attackers in the nearby woods. The all-day fight is sputtering to a close and the frightened defenders have hardly seen a sign of the elusive enemy.

# "The Post is Strong and in Good Hands"

Pennsylvania Colonel James Burd was standing in an unfinished fort, surrounded by mud, troops, tents, wagons, artillery, and confusion. As evening descended on this rainy October 12, French and Indian attackers were still out in the woods and small mortars called coehorns were belching smoke and fire to keep them there. The fight around the Loyalhanna Post (later Fort Ligonier) was sputtering on but Burd, the redcoats' base commander, was confident the English forces had won the day.

The fortified camp was in wild mountain country halfway between Bedford and Fort Duquesne. It was next to Loyalhanna Creek, which flowed west toward the Forks of the Ohio. General Forbes' army had been there more than a month, working feverishly to protect thousands of soldiers and tons of supplies coming in from the east. The French and Indians were trying to capitalize on their September triumph over Major James Grant's redcoats. They wanted to dislodge the English from their new stronghold and chase them back over the mountains. Colonel Burd was completing a long, exhausting, suspenseful day with optimism. The fort had held its own as the enemy probed for weak spots, hoping to panic the defenders with Indian scalp halloos in the surrounding woods.

Burd dashed off a note to his commander on the other side of Laurel Hill. Colonel Bouquet undoubtedly heard the cannon fire, but an impassable road kept him from coming to Burd's aid. The Pennsylvania colonel was sending 200 men with 100 axes to help Bouquet get over the mountain. He reported, "I have drove them off the field. I don't doubt of a second attack, if they do, I am ready." An anxious Bouquet responded, "I am very easy about you, the Post is strong and in good hands."

## The Rocky Road to Loyalhanna

Colonel Bouquet worried that sharp stones in western Pennsylvania were hard on shoe leather. The rough mountain roads were all stumps, stones, swamps and steep slopes with some streams thrown in. The redcoats, in this landscape soon to be decked out in fall glory, were getting a worm's eye view of the mountains. Nobody could get above the giant, old trees to see much of anything.

Not since the switchbacks on Sideling Hill had the army road-builders faced such a challenge. A grueling 1,800 foot climb up Allegheny Mountain was the gateway to the highlands. A slow 1,000 foot descent followed through the swamp named Edmonds after an Indian trader. Soldiers "corduroyed" the wetlands by laying down planks and poles. It was about fifteen miles to the next ridge through abandoned Indian villages and across Stony and Quemahoning, fast-flowing mountain streams. Thousands of feet, hooves and wheels were tramping and rolling through the rainy weather. Earthen

## Loyalhanna

On September 3, 1758, a column of weary redcoats and provincials slid and stumbled down the steep western slope of Laurel Ridge to Loyalhanna, the spot chosen for a fortified post and staging area for the final march on Fort Duquesne. Working feverishly through heavy rains to fell and pile trees into a rough protective breastwork around their camp, the soldiers could not miss the scattered old log structures that marked an earlier occupation. Loyalhanna (and variants) is an Anglicized version of a Delaware Indian phrase meaning Middle Creek, the name of an abandoned Indian town that became Fort Ligonier.

The town of Loyalhanna had been founded in the 1720s when Indians in eastern Pennsylvania were pressed by colonists to leave their ancestral homelands. Dispossessed by growing colonial populations and unscrupulous land agents backed by the powerful New York Iroquois Confederacy, these native pioneers began to build new homes in the west at places like Loyalhanna. Delawares, Shawnees, and others settling here became known as the Ohio Indians. Most retained strong ties to Pennsylvania traders, but colonists failed to appreciate deep-seated Indian resentment over the loss of their homelands. Native Americans were determined to keep western lands free from European settlements.

Faced in 1755 with a choice between siding with British colonies that wanted their land, or less numerous French who promised vital trade goods, most Ohio Indians fought the British. When British military victories cut the flow of French trade goods and British diplomats reassured Ohio nations their lands would not be taken, Fort Duquesne's commander found support from local warriors disappearing. The October and November French and Indian attacks to forestall Forbes' advance from Fort Ligonier marked the last major military campaign by Delaware Indian warriors until Britain's unfulfilled promises sparked a widespread Indian uprising in 1763-64.

redoubts, thrown up at camps along the way, were a measure of protection against attack. By early September, the Forbes Road reached the forage-rich Clearfields. The next redoubt, Fort Dudgeon, was at the foot of Laurel Hill.

Colonel Burd declared Laurel Hill, another 1,000 foot climb followed by a swift 1,600 foot descent to the Loyalhanna Post, a bad mountain. Colonel Armstrong used the word vile and, later, others chimed in with "terrible mountain." The grades were not as steep and Laurel had better footing than Allegheny Mountain, but slogging through miserable weather, it took several weeks and many scouts to cut a usable trail.

As Royal Engineer Charles Rohr lays out lines for a protective breastwork, Colonel James Burd supervises his advance force of Provincial and regular troops at the abandoned Loyalhanna Indian village. Within a month, thousands of soldiers will erect the stockade that becomes Fort Ligonier.

## "I shall do all in my power to further the service..." —Colonel James Burd

James Burd may have been the most enterprising Scots-Irish immigrant of all. Born near Edinburgh, Scotland in 1726, he came to America in 1747 and soon married into the influential merchant Shippen family. By the 1750s, Burd was managing their extensive Shippensburg properties at the edge of the Allegheny Mountains.

When war came to the frontier, he took his considerable skills into the mountains. Before Braddock's Defeat in 1755, he was hard at work on a support road that laid the path for the Forbes route three years later between Carlisle and Bedford. During the war years, Captain Burd marched north with colonial troops to the Forks of the Susquehanna River (present Sunbury). There he helped build and defend Fort Augusta, the largest and best-designed of the Pennsylvania forts. In command of a battalion in 1758, now Colonel Burd was a trusted member of the British high command and led the troops that built Fort Ligonier.

Unlike several of his French and Indian War comrades, Burd never again saw action on the battlefield. Serving for many years as a Lancaster County justice, he was an early supporter of the rebellion against the British and helped organize Lancaster's military efforts. A dispute with local officials over rank, however, ended his Revolutionary War career by the close of 1776. His son Edward was a major in the Continental Army and became a judge on the Pennsylvania Supreme Court. James Burd's own public service as a county judge continued until his death in 1793 at Tinian, his home that still stands.

Hastily built ovens constructed of green wood and clay allow army bakers to keep up with the enormous demand for the coarse military bread that was a staple of the 18th century soldiers' daily ration.

## Colonel Burd Builds a Fort

At the end of August, Colonel Bouquet faced gridlock as the British tried to leapfrog over the rugged mountains ahead. The army's business kept him in Bedford waiting for General Forbes. Suspicious of provincial officers who he said were not vigilant, Bouquet needed a strong leader at the front. He entrusted Colonel James Burd with two daunting tasks: to push over Laurel Hill and to begin a strong fortification on the other side. Bouquet wanted stealth with no drums beating, no bells on horses, no gun shots, and no fires. There was little room for error close to an enemy that Bouquet wanted "knocked on the head." After years on the Pennsylvania frontier, the 32-year-old Colonel Burd was a steady and experienced hand.

On August 26, Colonel Burd led his force up Allegheny Mountain. Miles of sweating soldiers and teamsters urging on their horses inched up Ensign Rohr's steep gap to a refuge at Fort Dewart redoubt on the summit. Three days later, the column was halted while workers labored to clear the road ahead. Burd's Pennsylvania troops were assigned to assist the 700 workers hacking their way to the foot of Laurel Hill.

The hard toil was "extremely interrupted and discomfited with continual hard rains." Horses, beef cattle, and forage were lacking, wagons were broken, messengers were disappearing on the dangerous trail and officers were bickering. Colonel Burd reported "difficulties in my way that could not

possibly occur to you [Bouquet]." Finally, on September 6, he sent a welcome update from his new camp at the abandoned Loyalhanna Indian village. "The troops here are all employed on the breastwork and hope they will finish tonight." Colonel Bouquet soon rode to the post. The British spearhead was finally scrambling over the Allegheny slopes.

## Fort Ligonier Resurrected

Today's Fort Ligonier reconstruction is a striking window on the challenging days of 1758. The entire post, layers of defense with fields of fire in all directions, again dominates a bluff in the modern community. Colonel Burd and his comrades found a "very fine piece of ground naturally strong being high and having the [Loyalhanna] creek on one side, and a fine spring on the other, just under our works." The retrenchment, a breastwork with gun positions laid out by Ensign Rohr, surrounded much of the tent camp within a few days. With Rohr lost at Grant's defeat, engineer Harry Gordon took over. He erected a fort inside the retrenchment with strong walls, a partially underground magazine protecting ammunition, log storehouses, bastions, gun batteries before the gates, and spiked defenses bristling everywhere. Hearing that Gordon was packing dirt in horizontal log fort walls rather than raising the usual vertical stockade, General Forbes complained he wanted a strong post not a fort fit for a siege. "For God's sake think of both time, money and labor and put a stop to all superfluities!"

Sickness, exhaustion and petty quarrels were taking a toll on the campaign. Colonel John Armstrong, one of the first to take on the Allegheny Highlands, was fighting off the dysentery that plagued almost everyone. Before being ordered east to find more supply wagons, Sir John St. Clair cast a pall over the proceedings. His arrest of Virginia Lieutenant Colonel Adam Stephen for mutiny was a foolish distraction that soon blew over. Pelted with heated messages from both Stephen and St. Clair threatening bloodshed, Colonel Bouquet warned Sir John that "there has been some heat in this affair. You will have a great deal to do to justify such a violent measure against an officer of his rank [Colonel Stephen]."

## British Reconnaissance

Provincial and Indian scouts were probing French defenses and some good intelligence was coming in. Virginia ensign Colby Chew spent two weeks in August scouting French defenses with Indian allies. Only a few weeks later, the ensign was killed near Fort Duquesne during Grant's defeat. Kissity, an Iroquois headman who had served with Colonel Burd, brought a description of Fort Duquesne to the British on August 30. The loyalty of Cherokee scouts, however, appeared to depend on a constant flow of gifts. General Forbes was pinning his last hopes on a party of about 60 warriors coming in with Cherokee leader, Attakullakulla (Little Carpenter).

Major James Grant's September setback proved that Fort Duquesne was still strongly defended. Colonel Bouquet ordered Lieutenant Colonel Stephen, back in action after his short-lived "mutiny," to cover the retreat from Grant's defeat with 300 men. Sending Royal American Ensign Archibald Blane with 32 men, a drummer and a flag of truce to the French fort, Bouquet learned that Major Grant was alive and being sent to Montreal with several other prisoners. For the moment, priorities called for hunkering down in the growing Loyalhanna defenses, keeping the sodden road to Bedford open and urging General Forbes with the rest of the army to the front as soon as possible.

## French Foray

With reinforcements from Illinois Country, the Fort Duquesne garrison went on the offensive in October. General Forbes estimated that less than 600 French and Indians descended on the Loyalhanna outpost. It was a noisy but invisible attack that made war in the woods so terrifying.

October 12 was a moody, showery day with clouds blowing across the nearby peaks. The fight began in late morning with a dozen gun shots and Indian shrieks southwest of the fort. Two parties sent out to surround the intruders were soon in a hornet's nest of musket fire. For the next three hours, 500 British defenders were in a running, confused fight focused on the vulnerable eastern back door of the fort where the Forbes Road came in from Laurel Hill. Pennsylvania and Maryland tent camps became a battleground as two Maryland officers were surprised drinking tea and killed.

Engineer Harry Gordon took charge of the fort guns with extraordinary zeal and the intruders were beaten off. Forays continued through the night but Colonel Burd reported that "I played upon them with [cannon] shells...which soon stopped their savage tones [taunts]." British casualties were about 60, with 12 dead. Colonel Bouquet was not pleased with the result. "The affair appears humiliating to me. [The attackers] keep more than 1500 blockaded, carry off all their horses, and retire undisturbed after burying their dead. This enterprise which should have cost the enemy dearly shows a great deal of contempt for us."

*After a day of hit and run fighting, the British have only a handful of badly wounded prisoners to interrogate about the French and Indian attack, under the watchful eye of a provincial sentry.*

*French and Canadian soldiers are often skilled woods fighters with far more combat experience than their British counterparts.*

## The Garrison of Fort Duquesne

French soldiers and militiamen from scattered parts of New France garrisoned Fort Duquesne for four years at the Forks of the Ohio (1754-1758). The core was several hundred regular soldiers of the *Troupes de la Marine*, men recruited in France to serve in its American colonies. Uniformed in white and blue and armed with muskets, bayonets, and swords, these disciplined troops were the fort's primary defenders. French colonial regulars learned forest warfare and detachments joined raids against British frontier settlements.

Many officers in this corps, including Fort Duquesne's 1758 commander, were native-born Canadians. Captain François-Marie le Marchand de Lignery joined the colonial regular troops as a cadet at 14. He had already served in a dozen military campaigns from the Mississippi Valley to Nova Scotia when war broke out in 1754. He was in the force of *Troupes de la Marine* that helped destroy General Braddock's army in 1755 and became Fort Duquesne's commander the following spring.

Most of Captain de Lignery's garrison was a seasonably fluctuating body of militiamen from Canada and settlements at Detroit and Illinois Country around present-day St Louis. Military-age men in New France were required to turn out for unpaid service. These militiamen constructed fortifications and transported supplies across vast distances. Unused to military discipline, they were ineffective during sieges and open field battles, but excelled at *la petite guerre*, or irregular warfare. Militiamen commonly dressed like Indian allies whose tactics they emulated. In major skirmishes near Fort Duquesne and Loyalhanna in1758, they inflicted considerable casualties on the British. Few of Forbes' redcoats ever caught a glimpse of their enemies. A veteran French commander later observed, "our men were always spread out and hidden behind trees."

## The Great Council at Easton

With British fortunes still in doubt, another Indian council, the third in three years, began at Easton on October 7. It was an impressive council fire, attended by the governors of Pennsylvania and New Jersey, George Croghan, representing Superintendent of Indian Affairs William Johnson, Conrad Weiser, agent for the Penn family, and about 500 Indians from thirteen nations. The Iroquois Confederacy was there in force. Three important leaders and many smaller client nations were pressing the Confederacy's domination of Pennsylvania Indian affairs.

Eastern Delaware leader Teedyuscung faced new challenges. The Iroquois wanted to curb his independence. After signing a treaty assuring Eastern Delawares a permanent home in the upper Susquehanna River Valley, Pennsylvania leaders wanted Delaware claims against colonial encroachment to go away. Quaker Israel Pemberton, a loyal ally, was now willing to make peace with Indian nations at Teedyuscung's expense.

Teedyuscung responded badly to the pressures. Rudely interrupting an Iroquois speaker, the very drunk and belligerent Delaware called the Iroquois fools and crowned himself King of all the world. While negotiations dragged on, Teedyuscung collected himself. At a later session, he addressed the Iroquois as uncles, referring to himself as a "bird on a bough; I look about, and do not know where to go; let me therefore come down upon the ground." Pennsylvania Governor Denny, an impatient diplomat, was another impediment. He swore and stamped his feet at Indian intransigence.

## Pisquetomen Breaks the Impasse

After almost two weeks of largely fruitless meetings, the Delaware Pisquetomen brought in the diplomatic bargain that had been struck with back country Delawares. During the next five days, the wise Conrad Weiser confirmed the wishes of western Indian nations to end the bloodshed while protecting Indian country from intruders. He ceded Pennsylvania lands, obtained by treaty beyond the Allegheny Mountains, back to the Iroquois, removing the immediate danger of colonial settlements.

Governor Denny followed, rekindling the Philadelphia Council Fire, in essence returning to the time when William Penn dealt directly with the Delawares without Iroquois middle men. After formal feasts and gift giving on October 25 and 26, Pisquetomen and his recently-arrived companion Post were again on the road, bearing Treaty of Easton agreements that could end the Indian war. They followed the new Forbes Road west and Post soon decided it was "one of the worst roads that ever was traveled." Pisquetomen, the recent raider of frontier settlements, was recognized and harassed by colonials.

On November 8, the weary travelers rode over Laurel Hill and into the huge encampment at Loyalhanna. With the best news in months in hand, General Forbes wrote letters to the Delawares and Shawnees, stating that "the ancient friendship is renewed with their brethren, and fixed on a firmer foundation than ever." The brave Mr. Post, still traveling alone with Indian companions, continued his western odyssey, carrying Forbes' letters and a treaty proclaiming peace.

## Putting the Final Pieces Together

General Forbes had been carried on his litter into Loyalhanna on November 2. As frost and snow were visiting the mountains, a cabin with a fireplace kept the ailing General warm. The latest leg of the General's torturous journey had lasted more than a week. Most of the rest of the army, Montgomery's Highland companies, Byrd's Virginia battalion and siege guns, marched with him.

Leaving Bedford after heavy rains, the long column passed the Shawnee Cabins

camp and struggled up Rohr's Gap to Fort Dewart. The General, still very much in charge, declared the road frightful. He assigned 100 men to road work on the trail up Allegheny Mountain, "all broke to pieces from down right neglect." Stopping at Stony Creek Camp, he sent ahead 60 cattle and other provisions. Going on to the foot of Laurel Hill, he expected to see Colonel Bouquet, "as I have a great deal of different affairs to talk to you upon."

Forbes had spent a busy month-and-a-half at Bedford, splitting his time between business and medicines. "Fitter for a bed and women's milk than for the active scene," he declared himself alone "in everything down to the trifling detail of camp duty." The General worked relentlessly on his challenges, admitting that "trouble and vexation operates upon me, like the strongest cordial." By mid-October, the much needed wagons and supplies were flowing again. Leaving the Laurel Highlands, Sir John St. Clair quickly rode east to "sweep the whole country indiscriminately of every wagon, cart, or horse he could find." His stunning success won him rare praise from the commander.

The Virginia troops at Fort Cumberland were the last major force to join the army. Colonel Washington conferred with Forbes soon after the General's September arrival at Bedford, making amends for previous misunderstandings and sharing his plans for a protected march in the forest. The Virginians were called to Bedford in late September. Colonel William Byrd, another officer laid low by the flux, was carried from Cumberland in a version of the Forbes litter. Washington, sent with his men to reinforce Loyalhanna on October 14, smugly described the new Forbes Road as "undescribably bad."

## The British Face Tough Choices

The repulse of the French at Loyalhanna on October 12 raised morale among the troops. The army celebrated the victory with a *Feu de joie* (Fire of Joy), a running fire of muskets in camp. General Forbes claimed the wagoners and horse drivers had become brave as lions. By November 3, Forbes had brought his army almost 300 miles west from Philadelphia. He was reviewing more than 5,000 soldiers now in sprawling camps on the western slopes of the Allegheny Mountains.

Settled in his warm cabin, General Forbes faced the negative side of the expedition ledger. Winter weather was closing in. Cherokee leader Little Carpenter and the last of the Cherokee and Catawba warriors disappeared. Forbes, after a year of frustrations, called his erstwhile allies "the most imposing rogues that I have ever had to deal with." The General also admitted that "the enemy's strength is, in spite of all my endeavors, a secret."

Colonel Bouquet was forecasting trouble among the colonial officers. In October, he confined an unruly Pennsylvania captain in a fort redoubt who subsequently had called Bouquet a rascal. A court martial board headed by Colonel Washington acquitted the man but tensions remained high. Now, Bouquet was floating a proposal for a winter expedition against Fort Duquesne, still fifty miles away. Washington vehemently opposed the idea. Bouquet confided to the General, newly arrived at Loyalhanna, "Considering the attitude they [the colonial officers] have toward me, you see how important your arrival is."

*A sick General Forbes, enduring days of bitter, rainy weather on the road, is happy to enjoy a fire in his own hut at the Loyalhanna Camp.*

## Winter Quarters

Armies have always been vexed by winter weather. During the Civil War, a January "Mud March" through freezing rain ended a Union offensive. American soldiers suffered as much from snow and zero temperatures as from the German assault during the Battle of the Bulge. Eighteenth century armies wisely chose to stay in forts or winter camps rather than march and fight in ice and snow.

When British army leaders decided to winter at Fort Ligonier in November of 1758, General Forbes faced tough decisions. He was responsible for thousands of soldiers, most camped out in tents. All food and supplies had to be carried into the far outpost over a frontier lifeline hundreds of miles long. Provincial soldiers who had enlisted only for the 1758 campaign season were due to go home. The French, only fifty miles away, could attack at any time. The General himself was so sick he might not survive a cold winter. The history of Pennsylvania could have been quite different had not Colonel Washington captured a deserter during the misty evening of November 12, 1758.

*Highland soldier's plaid serves as both a garment and, in inclement weather, a handy blanket.*

### The Campaign Stalls

On November 11, General Forbes summoned senior officers to a Council of War. Through the hundreds of miles of marching in hot and cold weather, the days and months of labor on the frontier road, this was the first time the entire high command was together. Besides Forbes, Bouquet, and Highland Colonel Archibald Montgomery, there was Sir John St. Clair, just back from his whirlwind tour finding wagons. The Virginians, Washington and Byrd, were standing with the Pennsylvanians, Armstrong, Burd and Mercer.

The question was straightforward. Should the army continue its advance or batten down the hatches, finding a way to ride out the winter, and hope for a spring offensive? Arguments for advancing were general: driving the French out, stopping Indian attacks, and justifying the enormous costs of the campaign. The many points against were specific: lack of winter clothing, ongoing scarcity of provisions, reduction of troops, ignorance of the enemy

*Colonel Washington risks life and limb to stop his Virginia soldiers from firing on one another in the dark and misty November evening that would haunt him for the rest of his life. Amazing escapes like this build the Colonel's reputation for being bullet-proof.*

strength, holding the enemy fort if it was captured, and facing catastrophe if defeated. "The risks being so obviously greater than the advantages, there is no doubt as to the sole course that prudence dictates."

If his army had to wait for the spring thaw, General Forbes might not survive to lead it. In a moment of resignation, he briefly named the Loyalhanna post "Pittsburgh," honoring the British Secretary of State if the army could not get to the Forks of the Ohio. Hearing of redcoat successes against the French further north, Forbes was reminded that "my cursed wilderness produces nothing but briars and thorns."

### Friendly Fire

November 12, 1758 was not a happy day for the thousands now in the camps at Loyalhanna. At dusk, musket fire erupted west of the fort. Colonel Washington led a detachment of Virginia troops to the sounds of the commotion. Another force of Virginians, commanded by Lieutenant Colonel George Mercer, had orders to try to flank the intruders. Chasing elusive French and Indians in the dying light, cold mists, and deep woods of the Laurel Highlands, the anxious soldiers started firing at shadowy shapes. Three decades later, Washington remembered those moments, running between the firing lines waving his sword, as the most dangerous in his legendary career.

By the time Washington and other officers stopped the carnage, 40 of his troops were killed or missing. The Colonel's two columns had collided and the fog of war had turned comrades into enemies. General Forbes later described what happened. "Two hundred of the enemy came to attack our live cattle and horses. I sent 500 men to give them chase with as many more to surround them, but unfortunately our parties fired upon each other in the dark."

This friendly fire disaster, however, produced an unforeseen turn of events. Three prisoners were nabbed during the confusion by the advancing Virginians. One, a frightened British deserter, under intense questioning, quickly told his captors of the French "weakness, want of Provisions, and desertion of their Indians." With few good options, General Forbes followed his instincts and acted quickly. A force of 2,500 men was mobilized to strike before winter settled in.

*When he can no longer ride a horse, the General is carried over mountain trails in a "sedan-litter." No one knows what the litter looked like, but his important position points to something more imposing than a simple stretcher. With little protection from the bitter cold and damp of November in western Pennsylvania, surgeons and attendants are constantly worried about his declining health. They must frequently administer medicines and liquor to revive his sinking strength.*

## What was wrong with General Forbes?

Even before his appointment to command the 1758 expedition against Fort Duquesne, John Forbes was suffering from a chronic, debilitating illness. "My infirmities are really no joke," he wrote a fellow officer two months before leaving British headquarters in New York City for Philadelphia. Having studied medicine as a young man, Forbes first served as an army surgeon (or primary physician) when he joined the British Army thirty years before, and thus was aware that the rigors of a campaign might well kill him.

Forbes' letters provide a litany of clues about his ailments. In December 1757, he complained that his legs and thighs were broken out, and two months later when the eruptions appeared all over his body, he compared his appearance to that of a "downright Leopard." The change of location from New York to Philadelphia only worsened his condition. After a month in the capital, Forbes remarked that he had been "at deaths door with a severe Cholick," or as he described to another correspondent, "a kind of Cholera Morbus," employing 18th century medical terms for severe abdominal pain and purging known today as gastroenteritis, an inflammation or infection of the stomach and/or intestines by bacteria, viruses, or parasites. These symptoms may also indicate an advanced stage of cancer. By interfering with the body's absorption of vitamins and nutrients, severe gastrointestinal illness may produce skin disorders like those that troubled Forbes.

The general's condition seesawed during the campaign between moments of seeming recovery and frequent relapses that sometimes rendered him virtually incoherent for days. A particularly severe bout came in August, when "a most violent flux, with most excruciating pains" forced Forbes to remain at the ramshackle frontier village of Shippensburg for nearly a month. Unable to ride a horse or bear the jarring of a wagon on the deeply-rutted military road, his doctor and servants contrived "a sort of a sedan-litter" slung between two horses. Forbes traveled nearly five hundred miles in this manner, crossing the Allegheny Mountains in damp and freezing weather that challenged the endurance of healthy soldiers, returning to Philadelphia on January 17, 1759. Two months later, the Philadelphia Gazette carried fifty-one-year-old Brigadier General John Forbes' obituary, noting the cause of death as "a tedious illness."

# Forging George Washington

The twenty-six-year-old Colonel George Washington who led his beloved Virginia Regiment across Laurel Ridge to the British camp at Loyalhanna in late October, 1758, was a very different man than the inexperienced young Major Washington who had first crossed the same mountain (twenty five miles to the south) just five years before. The Forbes expedition marked Washington's final military command before the American Revolution, but it by no means ended the Virginian's interest and involvement in the region. George Washington would become America's Indispensable Man, and western Pennsylvania was one of the most important crucibles to forge his remarkable character.

George Washington's public life began in this region in 1753 with an arduous winter journey across the Allegheny Mountains to deliver a written demand from Virginia's governor that French military forces withdraw from the upper Ohio Valley. The French commander refused to comply, and Washington's bungling efforts to drive the French away the following year culminated in a humiliating defeat at the Battle of Great Meadows (Fort Necessity) on July 3, 1754. The young Virginian, a British politician noted a few years later, managed to "set the world on fire," sparking the global conflict known in North America as the French and Indian War.

Washington returned the following summer as a volunteer aid to British Major General Edward Braddock, who introduced the still inexperienced Virginian to professional military practices that would shape his career in profound ways. Following the disastrous July 9, 1755 Battle of the Monongahela, in which Braddock's force was soundly defeated near Fort Duquesne (present day Pittsburgh), Washington helped to organize the retreat and oversaw Braddock's burial when the mortally wounded general died five days later near the Great Meadows.

On his third journey to western Pennsylvania in 1758, Washington nearly lost his life in a sharp firefight near Fort Ligonier. What began as a confused skirmish with French and Indian raiders on November 12 ended in a friendly fire incident among Virginians that even after the trials of the American Revolution Washington looked back on as the most dangerous moment in his life. After the fall of Fort Duquesne, his marriage to Martha Custis, and (first) retirement to Mount Vernon, Washington eagerly speculated in Ohio Valley lands, eventually claiming thousands of acres in the region, including the site of his 1754 defeat at

the Great Meadows. He returned for a fifth time in 1770 to search for promising tracts of land, and invested heavily in tools and manpower to develop a mill and rental farms on the eve of the American Revolution.

Convinced that the future greatness of the United States, as well as his personal fortune, depended on the control and orderly development of the trans-Allegheny West, Washington promoted numerous schemes to open transportation routes and strengthen economic and political ties between east and west after the American War for Independence. He traveled to western Pennsylvania again in 1784, hoping to secure his lands from squatters who had taken up residence during the Revolution. Ten years later, forty years after the Battle of the Great Meadows, a sixty-two year old President and Commander-in-Chief George Washington realized a lifelong ambition to see the Forks of the Ohio River, the strategic key to controlling the heartland of North America, securely in the control of his countrymen. That year, 1794, saw Washington appear for the last time in military uniform at the head of a federal army at the site of General Forbes' old encampment at Fort Bedford. This force then marched west along the Forbes Road to suppress an insurrection in western Pennsylvania known as the Whiskey Rebellion.

At the same time, another federal army under General Anthony Wayne overcame the last major Ohio Indian resistance to United States control of the Ohio Country. By the time Washington died on December 14, 1799, Pittsburgh, the site of his earliest adventures and the object of his lifelong ambitions, was poised to act as the keystone of America's westward expansion. Scarcely four years later, a wooden keelboat built near the old site of Fort Duquesne pushed off into the Monongahela River, bound for the Rocky Mountains and the Western Sea. On August 31, 1803, Captain Meriwether Lewis of the newly-formed Corps of Discovery began his diary, "Left Pittsburgh this day at 11 ock with a party of 11 hands 7 of which are soldiers, a pilot and three young men on trial they having proposed to go with me throughout the voyage." Washington would have smiled, even with his dental problems.

*pg. 148, George Washington wore a French and Indian War uniform for his first portrait painted by Charles Willson Peale 14 years after the 1758 campaign. In 1787, he recounted his harrowing French and Indian War experiences in hand-written "Remarks" now in the collection of the Fort Ligonier Museum.*
*pg. 149, George Washington helps to organize the solemn retreat from the Battle of the Monongahela, a wrenching experience that revealed the young Virginian's potential as an inspiring military leader.*

# Ligonier Regional Map

Westmoreland

Latrobe

**30**

1

Greensburg

3 2
4 5

New Stanton

**Ligonier**

**30**

**70**

23

6

7

Mount Pleasant

711

119

**76**

**70**

10

219

8
9

12

11

Connellsville

Somerset

Dunbar

14

**Somerset**

381

40

17 15
16

Uniontown

**Fayette**

21

Ohiopyle

281

22

119

20
19 18

13 4

Confluence

*Youghiogheny R.*

## Legend

| | | |
|---|---|---|
| Dining/Lodging | Historical Locations | General Attractions |
| George Washington | Multiple Locations in Same Vicinity | |

The Forbes Trail · · · · · · · · **30** Route 30

**76** PA Turnpike — — — Great Allegheny Passage

W. VA    MARYLAND

## Visiting Ligonier and the Laurel Highlands

The rugged peaks, plunging glens and waterfalls of the Laurel Ridge create a Scottish highland setting in western Pennsylvania. The Laurel Highlands are often called Pittsburgh's playground for its wealth of outdoor activities, but with annual celebrations of their Scots-Irish heritage, Somerset, Westmoreland and Fayette counties keep 18th century history in view. In Somerset, craftsmen work an 18th century farmstead. In Stahsltown, they raise flax for linen. And overlooking the Loyalhanna Creek, the Union Jack still flies proudly at sturdy Fort Ligonier, with a comprehensive collection of 1758 artifacts.

*The Somerset Historical Center overlooks the Laurel Highlands.*

# See 1758 Today

Meet 18th century celebrities in the elegant portrait gallery at **Fort Ligonier**[2] (200 South Market Street, Ligonier; 724-238-9701; www.fortligonier.org). The museum gallery features thirteen original paintings of the British and French monarchs and military commanders of the period, including Lord Ligonier and William Pitt, by period artists Sir Joshua Reynolds, Allan Ramsay, and others. Rembrandt Peale's George Washington depicts the young Virginia officer at age 26, when he was garrisoned at the fort. Two other galleries feature an overview of the French and Indian War locally, dioramas and maps, and artifacts ranging from soldiers' shoes to a 250-year-old apple. The museum also displays several rare items associated with Washington. His 1787 *Remarks*, an 11-page memoir all in Washington's hand, record his recollections of the final days of the Forbes campaign in November 1758. The handwritten essay describes his troop's dramatic "friendly fire" incident in the woods beyond Ligonier. It is the only reference to the event in the President's papers. Near the manuscript, the museum exhibits the pair of saddle pistols that Washington received from the Marquis de Lafayette, which were later owned by President Andrew Jackson.

Washington probably carried these at Valley Forge, Monmouth, Yorktown, and during the Whiskey Rebellion. Several Washington autographs complete the collection.

Eight original acres of Fort Ligonier have been preserved with painstaking restoration and reconstruction. Archeologists have retrieved over 130,000 items from thick clay soil that helped preserve objects. The inner fort, with four bastions and three gates, is 200 feet square: inside is the officers' mess, barracks, quartermaster stores, guardroom, underground magazine, commissary, and officers' quarters. A magnificent reproduction of a brass cannon, aimed west toward Fort Duquesne, shows the meticulous attention to detail in the reconstruction of the fort complex. The site includes a barracks, officer's quarters, a guardroom, and underground magazine; immediately outside the fort is General Forbes' hut. A hospital, a forge and other outbuildings complete the installation. **Fort Ligonier Days** are celebrated the second weekend of October each year with a reenactment of the battle against the French that took place here on October 12, 1758, complete with firings of period weapons.

The **Somerset Historical Center**[10] interprets the region's peaceful agricultural heritage (10649 Somerset Pike, Somerset; 814-445-

6077; www.somersethistoricalcenter.org). From coopering (cask-making) to weaving, craftsmen demonstrate 18th century skills at reconstructed farm homesteads from the 1770s and the 1830s. Annual **Mountain Craft Days**, held the first weekend in September, attract hundreds of artisans.

**Flax scutching**, the laborious process of separating linen fibers from the plant, is a Scots-Irish craft reenacted at both the Historical Center and at an annual September festival in Stahlstown. The Stahlstown event coincides with the **Highland Games** in Ligonier, where kilt-clad athletes, dancers and musicians compete annually.

*pg. 152, left to right, In downtown Ligonier, the British fort overlooks Loyalhanna Creek; the town celebrates the anniversary of the 1758 battle against the French with reenactments and a community parade each October.*
*pg. 153, Fort Ligonier demonstrates the European concept of defense in depth, with rings of obstacles to slow down attackers. The museum has taken on the task of reproducing every major cannon type and piece of equipment, like the Conestoga wagon, that General Forbes had in his siege artillery train.*

The Loyalhanna Camp became "Pittsburgh" in November, 1758, when General Forbes and his commanders briefly decided to go into winter quarters. After victory at the Forks of the Ohio, Forbes renamed Loyalhanna Fort Ligonier in honor of John Ligonier, 1st Earl of Ligonier (1680-1770). Ligonier was a brave and capable French Huguenot who immigrated to England and became a great hero in the British army during the wars in the early 18th century. As supreme commander of the British armies, the 77-year-old field marshal was instrumental in giving John Forbes his 1758 command. His portrait hangs in the Fort Ligonier Museum.

## George Washington Was Here

Washington's years of experience in the southern Pennsylvania woods made him Forbes' pick to lead a strike force west from Ligonier to capture Fort Duquesne. An hour's drive south of Ligonier near Uniontown, three sites along Route 40 interpret the young leader's first adventures in the French and Indian War, in 1754 and 1755.

An exact replica of **Fort Necessity**[19], Washington's 1754 wooden stockade, has been created by the National Park Service in Farmington, Fayette County (One Washington Parkway; 724-329-5512; www.nps.gov/fone).

Advancing north in 1754, Washington learned that the French were nearby. He ordered a party to march through the woods to the French camp during the night of May 27, surrounding the enemy at **Jumonville Glen**[21] (Jumonville Road, Hopwood; 724-329-5512;

open May 1-October 31). Visit the site where the first shots of the French and Indian War were fired by walking down a wooded path to a quiet clearing.

At the Great Meadows, which Washington bravely called "a charming field for an encounter," his troops hastily erected a wooden stockade to deter French retaliation. After a July 3 attack on this "fort of necessity," the French maneuvered Washington into signing the only surrender of his career. Fort Necessity's contemporary interpretive center, a short walk from the stockade, offers a brief film and colorful overview of the shifting alliances among the Indians, the British and the French. Very small children will enjoy the playground's small stockade and Conestoga wagon. The center is near another Washington footnote in the region. When he revisited the region in 1771, he bought property here. As he and other leaders lobbied for a National Road along

this route, Washington bought the land as an investment: his original bill of sale is exhibited at the site. When the National Road became a well-traveled reality several decades later, another owner built a stagecoach tavern on the property. Named the **Mount Washington Tavern**, it is now open seasonally as part of the Fort Necessity property.

The monument that memorializes **General Braddock's Grave**[20] is located along Route 40 one mile northwest of Fort Necessity. Braddock, wounded in the Battle of the Monongahela in 1755, died as his shattered army limped back to Fort Cumberland. Washington supervised his burial here. The retreating troops buried Braddock in the middle of the road and marched over the grave to disguise it.

*Near General Braddock's grave, a trace of the road that he forged from the south still exists. At right, an aerial view of Fort Necessity shows Washington's lonely outpost. Jumonville Glen lies in the dark forest to the upper right.*

# History: 9/11 in Shanksville

The contemporary history of the Laurel Highlands includes the tragedy of September 11, 2001. On that day, a hijacked United airliner en route to Washington, D.C. plunged into a cornfield near **Shanksville**[12], Somerset County. All 44 people aboard Flight 93, including the hijackers, were killed instantly, adding to the toll of more than 3,000 victims who died in attacks on New York and Washington. While a formal monument is being planned, visitors can view the crash site off Skyline Drive from a distance. No trace of the plane or the debris field is visible.

As on the great American battlefields of previous eras, visitors to the scene began to leave personal mementoes almost immediately. Visitors can view the heartfelt messages, photos and other gifts left to commemorate the tragedy. For detailed driving directions to the site and reports on the planned memorial, visit www.nps. gov/flni or call (814) 443-4557. In nearby Somerset, the **Flight 93 Memorial Chapel**[11] is generally open weekends from March through December (1717 Coleman Station Road, Friedens; 814-444-8339).

*Visitors to the crash site of the Flight 93 post remembrances and gifts at a makeshift monument. A formal memorial is planned.*

# Family Fun

The **Youghiogheny River** cuts through the Laurel Highlands, providing gorgeous views, whitewater rafting, and easy float trips. Even young children can enjoy adventures in and around 19,000-acre **Ohiopyle State Park**[15] (Route 381, Ohiopyle; 724-329-8591; www.dcnr.state.pa.us/stateParks/parks/ohiopyle.aspx). They can surprise themselves by steering a kayak, biking an easy ten miles, spelunking in Pennsylvania's largest cave, or riding old-fashioned roller coasters at Idlewild Park.

River outfitters in Ohiopyle specialize in oversized rubber rafts that float in shallow water and bounce off river rocks. The Youghiogheny boasts the busiest stretch of **whitewater rafting** east of the Mississippi in its lower reaches, but amateur rafters, kayakers and canoeists can navigate the Middle Yough, a gentle nine miles between Confluence and Ohiopyle, just as easily.

Go with the flow: outfitters drop rafters at the Ramcat put-in, and the current returns paddlers to Ohiopyle in a few hours.

Guided raft tours are a smart choice on the more dangerous Lower Yough, with its thrilling Class IV rapids. Book these with local outfitters in advance, especially on summer weekends.

Hiking allows visitors to enjoy spectacular views. **Mt. Davis**, Pennsylvania's highest peak, lies just east of the park. Among the park's many scenic waterfalls, the most famous is the thundering Ohiopyle Falls in the heart of the park. Journeying north along the Youghiogheny in 1754, George Washington hoped to find an easy water passage to Pittsburgh. This is the 20-foot torrent that dashed his hopes. Expert kayakers run the Falls each August, in a spectator-friendly competition. At the all-natural **Meadow Run Waterslides**[16], sit down to ride the stream down cool, dark boulders and plunge into deep, rocky pools.

*Bikers and kayakers flock to Ohiopyle, where Cucumber Falls descends from a rock ledge.*

Ohiopyle is friendly to day-trippers, with parking, spacious changing stations, and a handful of friendly cafes. The local outfitters clustered along Yough Street rent bikes as well as river gear.

Rainy days are the perfect time to go underground at **Laurel Caverns**[22] (1094 Skyline Drive, Farmington; 800-515-4150; www. laurelcaverns.com). A twenty-minute trip up Route 40 from Ohiopyle and Fort Necessity, this 430-acre underground park offers easy, two-and-a-half mile family hikes at a chilly fifty-two degrees. Optical illusions and light shows are part of the fun. Open seasonally.

Everyone keeps cool at **Idlewild Park**[1], thanks to the Loyalhanna Creek and a towering forest (2574 Route 30, Ligonier; 724-238-3666; www. idlewild.com). This delightful amusement park, open since 1878, provides plenty of shade and plenty of thrills. Very young children will be charmed by Storybook Forest, which brings nursery-rhyme characters to life. Budding athletes will take advantage of the Jumpin' Jungle, and teens will enjoy the SoakZone water park. Open seasonally.

*Idlewild Park's wooden roller coasters and mazes delight young visitors.*

## Great Houses and Gardens

The iconic **Fallingwater**[14], a sleek home balanced over a waterfall, is the Laurel Highlands' most popular attraction. While the 1935 design is Frank Lloyd Wright's best-known work, several other local homes designed by the architect are open to visitors, too.

Fallingwater docents offer guided group tours of the house; reservations are suggested (1491 Mill Run Road, Mill Run; 724-329-8501; www.fallingwater.org). The furnishings, paint colors and all details except for glowing Tiffany glass lamps were designed personally by Wright for the local Kaufmann family. Visitors can stroll the grounds on their own, dine in the **Fallingwater Café**, and tour exhibits in The Barn. Children under six are not permitted in the house, but adults can take them on the property's outdoor trails or wait with them in a family room at the visitor center. At nearby **Kentuck Knob**[17], a 1953 Wright design, a

*At Frank Lloyd Wright's hexagonal Kentuck Knob (below), a surprising sculpture garden includes "Jute" by Nicola Hicks, and "Apple Core" by Claes Oldenburg.*

low-slung cypress and stone home overlooks the Youghiogheny River gorge (723 Kentuck Road, Chalk Hill; 724-329-1901; www.kentuckknob.com). Built for the Hagan family, it is now owned by Lord Peter Palumbo and open for public visits. The meadow below holds a gallery of contemporary outdoor sculpture, and is open for summer hiking and winter cross-country skiing.

The **Duncan House**, built in 1957 in the austere Usonian style, is one of only a few of the master architect's designs that are open to overnight guests. The home was relocated from its original Illinois site and reconstructed in Acme at **Polymath Park Resort**[23], a 125-acre spread designed by Wright apprentice Peter Berndtson. The resort is also home to two of Berndtson's designs, the Balter and Blum houses. Both are available for rent. (1 Usonian Drive, Acme; 877-833-7829; www.visitduncanhouse.com).

The **Compass Inn Museum**[4] in Laughlintown is a famous stagecoach stop built in 1799, when its patrons were young drovers bringing animals to market (1382 Route 30 East, Laughlintown; 724-238-4983; www.compassinn.com). Operated by the Ligonier Valley Historical Society, the Inn provides seasonal guided tours of the tavern (below), guest rooms, and outbuildings (above and left). The Country Store sells period reproductions.

## The Great Allegheny Passage

The **Great Allegheny Passage** (GAP) cuts a scenic 150-mile path from Pittsburgh to Cumberland, Maryland. Converted from an old railroad line and recently inducted into the Rails-to-Trails Hall of Fame, it is the longest recreational trail in the eastern United States. The trail connects to the C&O Canal Towpath in Cumberland, Maryland, providing a motor-free route for hiking and cycling from Pittsburgh to the District of Columbia. Much of the Pennsylvania route, a level crushed-limestone path, hugs the banks of the Casselman and Youghiogheny Rivers. It is part of a National Scenic Trail between the Appalachians and the Chesapeake Bay.

Hardy cyclists can cover the full route in as few as five days, but most recreational users tackle shorter sections. The most popular route, especially on weekends, is the ten-mile path along the Youghiogheny between Ohiopyle and Confluence. While the river gorge is almost always within view, with trains rumbling along the opposite riverbank, the most spectacular scenery lies on a twenty-mile section close to the Maryland border. That's where riders cross high over Somerset County fields at the Keystone Viaduct and pass under a mountain at the Big Savage Tunnel.

Small towns have embraced the GAP trail. Trailheads in Connellsville, Confluence, Rockwood, Meyersdale and other rural villages have sprouted bike stores, ice cream stands, and B&Bs that welcome cyclists. To plan a trip, visit www.gaptrail.org.

*Cyclists on the Great Allegheny Passage cross the Youghiogheny at Ohiopyle (below).*

## Great Outdoors

With elevations of nearly 3,000 feet, Laurel Highland peaks receive more natural snow than anywhere else in the state, making the area a perfect destination for winter sports.

Two major ski resorts, **Seven Springs**[9] and **Hidden Valley**[8], flank the Pennsylvania Turnpike in Somerset County. Each offers dozens of trails, golf, swimming, indoor activities and entertainment (Seven Springs Mountain Resort, 777 Waterwheel Drive, Seven Springs; 800-452-2223; www.7springs. com; Hidden Valley Resort, One Craighead Drive, Hidden Valley; 814-443-8000; www.myhiddenvalleyresort.com).

With over 22 miles of cleared trails for snowshoeing and cross-country skiing, and snowmobile trails through several state

forests, downhill isn't the only winter direction. Challenging trails for hiking and mountain biking are popular destinations year-round in **Forbes State Forest** and **Linn Run State Park**[6] (Rector; 724-238-6623; www.dcnr.state. pa.us/stateparks/parks/linnrun.aspx).

## Did You Know?

The Forbes Expedition tackled the Laurel Highlands: the 21st century tamed them, harnessing the steady winds of the summit for a source of renewable energy.

Four wind farms—groups of white fiberglass turbines that turn like giant windmills—now top Somerset County ridges. Two groups are seen easily from local roads. One set bristles above the Great Allegheny Passage near Meyersdale. Another group crests Route 31 just east of the Somerset interchange of the Pennsylvania Turnpike. Turning at a steady sixteen miles per hour 160 feet above ground, a group of six turbines provides electricity for 2,500 homes a year, saving nearly 16,000 tons of carbon dioxide emissions.

## Uniquely Laurel Highlands

History float trips down the Youghiogheny River explore the 1754 adventures of George Washington, local Indian lore, and the beginnings of the steel industry from the vantage of a comfortable raft. Contact **Wilderness Voyageurs** for details (800-272-4141; www.wilderness-voyageurs.com). Near Dunbar, named for the British colonel who stockpiled arms in the area in 1755, the Connellsville coal seam provided raw material for hundreds of beehive coke ovens in the mid 19th century. In the 1870s, a young Henry Clay Frick gained control of the region's coke production, supplying western Pennsylvania's burgeoning steel industry.

*Left: Laurel Summit State Park welcomes cross-country skiers and snowshoers; right, wind turbines power Somerset County; history float trips launch from Connellsville.*

# Plan a Visit

## Annual Regional Events

**Fort Necessity Battle Anniversary Commemoration,** Farmington, July
www.nps.gov/fone

**Ligonier Highland Games,** September
www.ligoniergames.org

**Stahlstown Flax Scutching Festival,**
September
ww.flaxscutching.org

**Fort Ligonier Days,** October
www.laurelhighlands.org

*right, Green Gables Restaurant offers fine wines in Jennerstown; Christian Klay Winery in Chalk Hill tends 200 acres of vineyards.*

## Laurel Highlands

For more information:
Laurel Highlands Visitors Bureau
120 East Main Street, Ligonier
www.laurelhighlands.org | (800) 333-5661

### DINING

**Green Gables[7]**
7712 Somerset Pike, Route 985 North, Jennerstown
(814) 629-9201
www.greengablesrestaurant.com
• Overlooking a scenic water view, this upscale dining room is next to the popular Mountain Playhouse, offering professional stock theater in a restored gristmill.

**Ligonier Tavern[3]**
137 West Main Street, Ligonier
(724) 238-4831 | www.ligoniertavern.com
• A Gay Nineties hotel turned casual pub. One block from the famous Diamond, or town square, with great specialty and antique stores.

**The River's Edge[13]**
203 Yough Street, Confluence
(814) 395-5059
www.riversedgecafebnb.com
• A favorite stop on the Great Allegheny Passage. Casual dining in a Victorian café on the banks of the Youghiogheny. Guest rooms available.

### LODGING

**Ligonier Country Inn[5]**
1376 Route 30, Laughlintown
(724) 238-3651
www.ligoniercountryinn.com
• An 18-room inn with dining, pub and outdoor pool convenient to Ligonier attractions.

**The Parker House[14]**
213 Yough Street, Confluence
(814) 395-9616
www.theparkerhousecountryinn.com
• The restored home of the town doctor is now a B&B that welcomes long-distance cyclists.

**Ohiopyle State Park[15]**
Route 381, Ohiopyle
(724)329-8591
www.dcnr.state.pa.us/stateParks/parks/ohiopyle.aspx)
• Reserve campsites, well-equipped cabins, and even yurts (platform tents with electric hook-ups) throughout the 19,000-acre state park. Open seasonally.

**Nemacolin Woodlands Resort[18]**
1001 LaFayette Drive, Farmington
(800) 422-2736
www.nemacolinwoodlands.com
• AAA five-diamond resort, the region's finest, on 3,000 acres near Ohiopyle.

# Preserving Wildlife Habitats

The ridges of the Alleghenies, with their deep forests and clear streams, provide havens for wildlife from tiny songbirds to gentle black bears. Pennsylvania's efforts to preserve that wilderness have helped several species to thrive.

More than three hundred species of birds—nearly half of all those found in North America—breed in Pennsylvania or travel here annually. The land bounded by the Chestnut and Laurel Ridges of the Laurel Highlands is a melting pot for birds that breed in the northern (boreal) and southern (austral) life zones.

Powdermill Nature Reserve has been tracking the Laurel Highlands' songbird visitors since 1961. The 2,200-acre biological research station of Pittsburgh's Carnegie Museum of Natural History is located in eastern Westmoreland County. Boreal birds from northern forests find the environmental conditions and high elevation habitats here similar to those in New England and Canada. Southern birds find Ligonier Valley surroundings that resemble the Virginias and Carolinas. Powdermill's Avian Research Center maintains one of the longest continuous bird banding programs of its kind in North America, collecting data that helps scientists understand the birds' longevity, migratory patterns, and population trends. The research also illuminates the connection between healthy bird populations and a healthy environment.

Much of the extensive forest in the Laurel Highlands is intact, protected as state parks, conservancies, and state forests. Below the treetops, the undisturbed core forest is home to a thriving black bear population.

Black bears grow to five feet in length and average 400 pounds, with some reaching 800 pounds or more. While they eat small mammals and fish if needed, Pennsylvania woods provide their favorite foods: berries, acorns and beechnuts, leaves, grasses, plant roots, and insects. In the mid 18th century, there were as many as two million black bears in North America. European settlers became their primary predator. Prized as a source of meat and fur, black bears were hunted nearly to extinction. Through the 19th century, the relentless pressures of human settlement turned forest to farmland. Extensive logging destroyed bear territory.

The creation of national and state parks, with protected forested habitats, helped to turn the tide. But even with Pennsylvania's active conservation of habitat, bear recovery stalled well into the 1970s. By the mid 1970s, some 250,000 people were pursuing a bear population of 4,000 during the state's annual hunting season. Changes in state hunting regulations limited hunting and allowed the population to rebound. Today, biologists with the Pennsylvania Game Commission track bears fitted with radio collars each year. Visiting dens, the scientists record health data on both mothers and cubs. The 14,000 black bears that now roam Pennsylvania constitute the largest population since the 18th century.

Powdermill's innovative nature center, on Route 381 south of Rector, introduces visitors to the biodiversity of the Laurel Highlands. Walking trails, hands-on programs and changing displays allow families to learn about the local environment, from wildflowers and trees to songbirds and salamanders.

**For more information:**

**Powdermill Nature Reserve**
1847 Route 381, Rector
(724) 593-4555 | www.powdermill.org

**Pennsylvania Game Commission**
www.pgc.state.pa.us

*Dependent on clean water and large tracts of unspoiled wilderness, poecile atricapillus and ursus americanus thrive in the Laurel Highlands.*

*Iroquois scouts, just joining the British advance, are stunned by a giant explosion that shatters the frontier stillness at the Forks of the Ohio.*

Pittsburgh

Forks of the Ohio
November 24, 1758

# General Forbes' Campaign Ends with a Bang

Reports of a big explosion drifted back to British army headquarters. Not since the firestorm that was Braddock's Defeat three years earlier had the valley's wild silence been so violated. On that cold, blustery November 24, 1758, the army's fast moving van was still twelve miles from the enemy fort.

The nervous redcoats were ready for a siege. They brought mortars and howitzers to lob exploding shells into Fort Duquesne. Confused by the sudden upheaval ahead, they sent Indian scouts to investigate. The scouts returned, reporting "a very thick smoke from the front extending in the bottom along the Ohio." A remarkable message soon arrived: "the enemies had abandoned their fort after having burned everything."

By the evening of November 25, the British army was standing in the ruins of Fort Duquesne. Astonished field officers sat down to pen the good news for leaders back east. Colonel George Washington wrote to the Virginia governor: "this fortunate, and indeed unexpected success of our arms, will be attended with happy effects." Colonel Henry Bouquet chose Miss Anne Willing, a Philadelphia lady friend, to express his delight at "the beauty of this situation, which appears to me beyond my description." General John Forbes, described as "ill and worn" by Colonel Washington, was carried in victory to the ruined French fort suffering with "the sharpest and most severe of all distempers." Writing to his commanders, he claimed "success in the face of almost insurmountable difficulties." Ravaged by chronic suffering, he predicted: "I shall leave this [place] as soon as I am able to stand, but God knows when or if I ever reach Philadelphia."

## The Final Assault

Armed with new information about the weakness of Fort Duquesne, General Forbes had chosen November 15 to launch 2500 redcoat and provincial troops for a final push to capture the Forks of Ohio. The column's first priority was to stay ahead of the winter weather. The next ten days became a flurry of felling axes and messengers carrying dispatches in all directions. Colonel John Armstrong was already twenty miles west with 500 men, hacking out a secure camp. Colonel Washington followed with 700 men. Colonel Montgomery was next with siege artillery, guarded by the Highlanders and the 2nd Virginia Regiment. Colonel Bouquet, with General Forbes in his litter, three battalions of Pennsylvanians, and the Royal Americans brought up the rear. Colonel James Burd stayed at Loyalhanna with 600 men, a rearguard should trouble develop ahead.

Hundreds of axmen, protected by a phalanx of muskets, feverishly chopped in rain and cold from dawn to dusk. The path had to be leveled, scraped and filled for the wagons, heavy guns and herds of beef cattle. Colonel Washington worked with boundless energy, regularly reporting his progress to General Forbes. Between November 15 and 18, he asked for more felling axes, complained of the road being "only very slightly blazed," pled for "Indian scouts to get intelligence to our front," requested more beef cattle for his hungry troops, and erected chimneys at the camps so the suffering General could stay warm. On November 20, General Forbes promised cattle and packhorses carrying flour along with thirteen Iroquois scouts arriving with Indian agent George Croghan. Constantly worried about an ambush, the General "never doubted that of the enemy's scouting parties discovering us."

The three British columns climbed 700 feet over Chestnut Ridge and descended 900 feet to the Pittsburgh Plateau, avoiding the wet, rocky ground in the Loyalhanna Creek water gap. The first camp (near Latrobe) had been an advance redoubt since work had begun on the Loyalhanna Post in September. Finally beyond the Allegheny Mountains, the redcoats cut through rolling hills to Colonel Armstrong's New Camp, near what would become the Hanna's Town settlement (near Greensburg). Colonel Washington's brigade established the Washington Camp at the head of Turtle Creek (Plum) and waited for the rest of the army to catch up. The road then continued to Camp Bouquet on Thompson Run just a dozen miles from Fort Duquesne.

## A Surprising Victory

During these tiring, suspense-filled days, General Forbes complained about the quality of work on the road and fretted over the continuing lack of intelligence: "I beg that some of the very best of your [Indian] scouters ought to be sent out." On November 24, as everyone puzzled over the sudden blast ahead, Colonel Washington gave his last written military orders, ordering his men to show "great precaution in case of a surprise." His next orders would be as rebel commander of the Continental Army seventeen years later.

Then, miraculously, the following evening, British soldiers were swarming over the Forks. The redcoats "found numbers of dead bodies, within a quarter of a mile of the fort, unburied, so many monuments of French humanity." Two weeks later, Philadelphia's *Pennsylvania Gazette* featured headline news from the front: "I have the pleasure to write this letter upon the spot where Ft. Duquesne once stood while the British Flag flies over the debris of its bastions in triumph. Blessed be to God, the long looked for day is arrived." General Forbes wrote to Secretary of State William Pitt: "I have used the freedom of giving your name to Fort Duquesne, as I hope it was in some measure actuated by your spirits that now makes us masters of the place."

Colonel Washington quickly left the army, his first military career at an end. Twenty-seven of his Virginia officers officially thanked the young colonel for

*General Forbes is briefed by his officers and staff as he sits among the ruins of French Fort Duquesne.*

his leadership, "so experienced in military affairs, so renowned for patriotism, courage and conduct." The Virginia war hero was preparing to marry and move his new bride into his Mount Vernon home. He wished General Forbes "a perfect return of health [that] contributes to crown your successes." The invalid General faced the long, uncomfortable trip east with most of the army. Colonel

Hugh Mercer and a small garrison were left in Pittsburgh facing a "sad state of affairs, camping 300 miles from Philadelphia, with neither tents nor baggage, and in need of clothing, with the weather bitter cold and getting supplies only with the greatest difficulty." They weathered the harsh winter by building a small stockade known to history as Mercer's Fort.

## Major Halkett Discovers His Father and Brother

While others celebrated the 1758 British victory, Major Francis Halkett, General John Forbes' aide, had important family business. The Major was part of a proud Scottish military family. His father, Sir Peter Halkett, was the magnet that drew the younger Halkett to a remote spot about eight miles from the Forks. A small party of Highlanders, Pennsylvanians and Indians accompanied him to a now deserted battlefield on the banks of the Monongahela River.

Moving quickly through the forest, the group followed Indian guides who had fought with the French three years earlier. The killing ground, undisturbed since the battle, was already a special place for Native Americans. Ghostly debris left by the violence stretched for over a mile. Decaying skeletons of humans and animals, mixed with bits and scraps of uniforms and equipment, were melting into the forest floor.

The Indian guides searched for a particularly memorable tree. Suddenly, with a shriek, they were at the base of a giant, gnarled, ancient tree. Major Halkett was close behind. As he kneeled and brushed away the leaves, two intertwined skeletons came to light. He reached down and picked up a skull. Examining it carefully, his tear-filled eyes lit up. "It is my father," he exclaimed to his stunned companions. A distinctive gold tooth told the tale. Sir Peter Halkett, Colonel of His Majesty's 44th Regiment of Foot, was lost and then found on the Battlefield of the Monongahela. A younger brother, James, was nearby, killed almost at the same moment during the firestorm of July 9, 1755.

The remains of father and brother were carefully gathered up, wrapped in Highland plaid, and buried with volleys of musketry. Major Francis Halkett, veteran of Braddock's defeat, left the battlefield for the second and last time. Two decades later, a horseman crossing the field was struck by how carefully his horse had to pick its way through the still unburied skulls and bones that littered the ground.

The world has moved on. The Braddock Battlefield has been forgotten for centuries, covered in part by a mill that has made the Monongahela River Valley famous for steel. Today, the Braddock's Battlefield Association, a subsidiary of Braddock's Field Historical Society and headquartered in America's oldest Carnegie Library, is dedicated to reviving the memories of a redcoat army lost long ago on the edge of the empire.

*Major Francis Halkett, Forbes' loyal Chief-of-Staff, returns to the Braddock Battlefield to find and bury the bones of his father and brother, both killed in the 1755 defeat.*

*Colonel George Washington has won favor for planning the British army's protected advance. He is tirelessly leading his men who are cutting the road to Fort Duquesne before winter sets in. Noisy dogs following Washington's Brigade have become a nuisance and leaders are threatening to hang them.*

## George Washington's Brigade

In the grey dawn of November 18, 1758, the fifes and drums that normally began a soldier's day were replaced by the dull thuds of a hundred axes. Limbs and trunks crashed down as mattocks and shovels clanged and scraped, striking stone and cold soil. The men of Washington's brigade had spent a restless night under the open sky. No doubt most were eager to shake off the cold by throwing their backs into the hard labor of road building, or shouldering their arms to guard against enemy attack. The long awaited advance on Fort Duquesne was underway, and Washington had assured Forbes in a letter written by candlelight, "All the men are in high spirits, and are anxious to get on."

The army's march across the low, undulating hills between Chestnut Ridge and the Forks of the Ohio marked George Washington's largest field command

before the American Revolution. Although he failed to achieve his youthful ambition to become a British officer, the seasoned Virginia commander was the highest-ranking provincial officer in Forbes' army. Washington's brigade, composed of Virginia, North Carolina, Maryland, and Delaware soldiers, led the army's advance from Loyalhanna, marching without tents, baggage, or women camp followers. For more than a week, the men labored to open a road for the army's artillery train, provisions, and supplies. At night, they huddled in shivering groups without shelter or adequate clothing.

As Forbes' army neared Fort Duquesne, the three brigades advanced in an "Order of March" that Washington had drawn up at Forbes' request. Worn down by professional disappointments and chronic sickness, Washington ended his first military career on a high note, with an independent command and a meaningful role in the fall of the French Fort Duquesne.

## Fort Duquesne - France's Precarious Outpost

Back in April of 1754, Ange Duquesne, Marquis de Menneville, an assertive Governor General of Canada, had launched 600 soldiers in a flotilla of canoes and bateaux to claim the Forks of the Ohio. A small contingent from Virginia, already there with designs on the same Ohio Country, was sent packing. Governor Duquesne gave his name to a new fort, the last in a string of four between Lake Erie and the Forks.

The Governor was pleased but almost everyone else, engineers and three fort commanders, had concerns. Fort Duquesne was too small and secure living space was cramped and primitive. All logs and dirt, it was poorly designed, poorly constructed, and almost impossible to defend. One good cannon shot from the surrounding heights and it might go up in smoke. During a flood in 1757, canoes could paddle entirely around the stockade. Although the garrison raised wheat, corn and vegetables, long supply lines remained vital but vulnerable.

The fort garrison, averaging 200, varied with the seasons and the dangers. Threats from the British brought reinforcements of hardened French frontier soldiers, paddling and portaging hundreds of miles from Canada, the Great Lakes and Illinois Country. Indian allies varied in numbers more than the garrison. Local Delaware and Shawnee allies complained when they were offered proselytizing Jesuit missionaries rather than gifts and trade goods. In any case, no Indian warrior had much patience with garrison life. They came and went on their own schedules.

## Defending the French Fort

In 1755, when General Braddock closed in with artillery and more than 2,000 men to destroy Fort Duquesne, the French were prepared to retreat. One brave French officer, Captain Daniel de Beaujeu, stripped down, applied war paint and coaxed his own men and hundreds of French Indians into the woods where they collided with Braddock's army. Beaujeu was soon killed, but the French and Indians defeated the English so completely that Fort Duquesne survived another three years. Indian warriors went home wearing captured red coats. The French attracted more Indian allies. The Delawares and Shawnees joined them in raiding parties that spread terror along the frontier.

Time ran out on France's far outpost in 1758. The Ohio Indians were being lured away by the English who offered what General Louis-Joseph de Montcalm, the French Commander-in-Chief, called "prayers, caresses, goods and brandy." Fort Frontenac, on Lake Ontario, was lost to a British attack during August, disrupting the supply line from Montreal. There was one more resounding French victory in September when Major James Grant's reconnaissance force strayed too close to Fort Duquesne and was overwhelmed. In October, reinforcements attacked the outpost at Loyalhanna but soon returned to Illinois. Another attack near Loyalhanna on November 12 was the last. After two years as fort commander, veteran François de Lignery "saw there was no longer reason to flatter himself that he would succeed."

On November 24, General Forbes, with his 6,000 man juggernaut, was marching ever closer. Lignery and his garrison loaded the cannons, munitions and prisoners on bateaux for a retreat down the Ohio River. They sent 192 men paddling north toward Venango, hoping there might be another opportunity to threaten the British. Everyone waited for sixty barrels of gun powder left in the magazine to reduce the burning fort to rubble. After the huge explosion reverberated through the valley, three men sent to investigate, reported the fort "entirely reduced to ashes." The French claim to the Forks of the Ohio was finished.

*Great Lakes Indian warriors, like the one tatooing this Canadian militiaman, have proven to be invaluable French allies. Their departure for their homes and winter hunting grounds after Grant's Defeat leaves Fort Duquesne vulnerable to Forbes' advance.*

## A Peace Envoy's Second Mission

Christian Frederick Post and his companions were carrying hopeful news to the Ohio Country Indians. It was so encouraging that Pisquetomen, the Delaware headman who had risked so much traveling with Post, "wanted to hear the writing from the General." After the party crossed the wide Allegheny River on a homemade raft, everyone sat in the open air and "we read to them to their great satisfaction." General Forbes ended his letter to Pisquetomen's brothers, Tamaqua and Shingas, "I write to you as a warrior should, that is, with candor and Love."

The party, on a peace mission quite different from the thousands of musket men assaulting the French, reached the Delaware Beaver Creek villages of Kuskuskies (New Castle) on November 16. Post watched many warriors return from war with bad notions that "the English only intended to cheat them; and that it was best to knock every one of us messengers in the head." The next three days, with returning warriors in a "murdering spirit, was precarious time for us." Post stayed in the background as a visiting French captain was telling the Indians that "the English were coming with an army to destroy both you and me." When the captain offered a string of wampum, the Delawares flung and kicked it "as if it was a snake," much to Post's delight and the French captain's mortification. Word arrived that the French were scuttling their fort and Post hoisted a British flag above the Indian council house. Tamaqua brought the best news, "that the English had the field. The Indians danced around the fire till midnight, for joy of their brethren the English coming." Pennsylvania's unarmed envoy had kept the Indian nations from fighting with the French. He and his Indian companions "end[ed] the day with pleasure and great satisfaction on both sides."

## A Humble Hero Returns Home

Christian Frederick Post rode south to the mouth of Beaver Creek at the end of November. Heading along the north side of the Ohio with a single Indian companion, he reached the banks of the Allegheny River, opposite newly-christened Pittsburgh. With no rafts available, he was unable to cross the river and watched General Forbes march off with much of his army on the other side. Post sat for a day and a half with no shelter or food. When forty Indian leaders arrived, the British fired twelve of their "great guns, and our Indians saluted three times round with their small arms." Post was finally ferried across, almost missing Colonel Bouquet's conference with Delaware leaders. The Colonel told the headmen that the English wanted extensive trade with Indian nations but did not want to possess their hunting lands.

His mission accomplished, Christian Frederick Post collected his horses, swimming them across the ice-filled Allegheny, and headed east with little recognition for his dangerous, important work. General Forbes had written, "I think he [Post] has execute[d] the commission he was sent upon, with ability and fidelity, and deserves a proper reward." Writing from England, Ben Franklin credited the honor of the Quakers and praised the "honest Frederick Post that completed those negotiations on foot with so much ability and success." On the trail home, this unassuming, valiant, and generous man spent Christmas alone in the woods at Loyalhanna, now christened Fort Ligonier. He asked Colonel Bouquet, who had traveled to the fort before him, for "some money, that we might buy necessaries." Riding over the mountains with General Forbes and his staff, Mr. Post lost his horse and trudged out of the historic events carrying "my saddle-bags and other baggage on my back. The burden was heavy, the roads bad, which made me very tired, and came late to Bedford."

*Upon hearing of the British victory at Fort Duquesne, envoy Christian Frederick Post wastes no time boldly raising a Union Flag over a Delaware Indian village.*

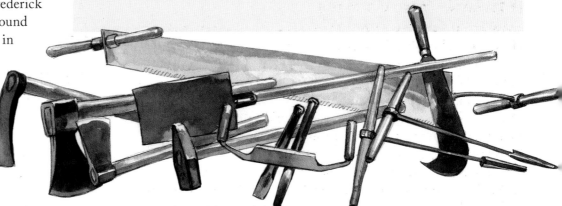

Soldiers labor for years to complete Fort Pitt, a massive symbol of British power in North America. Local Indians, told that the British army would leave Ohio Country, become suspicious and then defiant.

## Building Fort Pitt

During the summer following the Forbes Expedition, work began on what would become the most expensive and elaborate British fortification in North America—Fort Pitt. Chief Engineer Harry Gordon, a veteran of the 1755 Braddock expedition, and Brigadier General John Stanwix, who succeeded Forbes following his death in Philadelphia, presided over the September 3, 1759 groundbreaking. Hundreds of tradesmen and soldiers labored morning till night for two years on this massive public works project, moving 66,000 cubic yards of earth by shovel and wheel barrow alone. Little wonder that Colonel Henry Bouquet could report in June 1761, "The men begin to be a little discouraged to see no end to their fatigues."

Fort Pitt and its extensive outworks encompassed about twenty acres. Three massive angular bastions and the long curtain walls on the landward side were faced with brick and stone to a height of nearly 15 feet, surmounted with thick earthen parapets. Two additional earth bastions fronted the Allegheny and Monongahela Rivers. The entire pentagonal fort was surrounded by a deep defensive ditch. The town of Pittsburgh, 160 houses and more than 200 civilian men, women, and children, lay scattered outside the fort.

British troops occupied massive Fort Pitt for just fourteen years after the fall of Fort Duquesne. In the spring of 1772, the British high command ordered the destruction and abandonment of Fort Pitt to cut costs and move troops to troublesome eastern cities. Much of the fort's brick and stonework was still in place when the garrison departed for Philadelphia in November. Early Pittsburghers continued the unfinished work of hauling off building materials by the ton. Archeological excavations in the 1940s-1960s revealed that significant structural remains of Fort Pitt still lie beneath Point State Park.

## A Road and an Outpost

When General Forbes and his victorious army marched back over the mountains in December, 1758, they left behind a road and an outpost. The road that bore the General's name, following Indian trails many centuries old, was cut and filled with the hard labor of thousands. It was the first road in America that truly linked the coast with the interior. Christian Frederick Post and the Quakers saw it as a peaceful bond, creating a middle ground between cultures. Most other colonials saw it as a path to settlement in the back country.

Pittsburgh, the new British outpost, quickly made local Indians suspicious. The Indians were now dependent on European trade goods but wanted no more soldiers or settlers in Ohio Country. General Forbes advised his commander, General Amherst, "that you will not think triflingly of the Indians or their friendship. Twenty Indians are capable of laying half this province [Pennsylvania] waste."

With the main army's departure at the end of 1758, two hundred soldiers were left to defend Pittsburgh. Travelers to the outpost on the Forbes Road, still littered with ruined wagons and dead horses, endured fierce storms, swollen rivers, steep slopes, few shelters, lost horses, and howling wolves. The Quakers continued to reach out to Indian nations. They financed traders and needed supplies on the long trek to Pittsburgh and Ohio Indian villages.

1759 became a miraculous year for the British military. The French lost Fort Niagara and Quebec. Their supply lines to the Ohio Valley were permanently cut. In spite of these successes, life in Pittsburgh remained lonely and precarious. Soldiers were starving as the first cattle arrived from the east. When a Quaker trader lost his companion, a forlorn burial forced him to admit that "burying a dead man is thought but a light matter at garrisons."

The British were determined to stay. While disgruntled Indians watched, they replaced the small stockade built by Colonel Hugh Mercer with Fort Pitt, a great "emblem of empire," on the banks of the three rivers.

## War Trumps Peace

In 1763, the seven year French and British world war ended. Hardening attitudes of colonials and Indians made peacemaking ever more difficult in America. The old Indian agent Conrad Weiser had sadly observed that settlers "curse and damn the Indians and call them murdering dogs into their faces without distinction." The Delawares were listening to a prophet who preached separation from the whites and a return to the past without Europeans or their muskets, gunpowder, cloth, and alcohol. A charismatic Ottawa Indian leader named Pontiac picked up the call. He led a frontier firestorm, an Indian War of Independence. Fort Pitt was isolated and under siege for months. Marching a small army west on the Forbes Road, Colonel Henry Bouquet beat off an ambush at Bushy Run and saved the garrison at Fort Pitt. By 1764, the Colonel was deep in Ohio Country, retrieving white Indian captives and declaring, "if we choose, we can exterminate you [the Indians] from the earth."

While war raged on the American frontier, the British government signed the Treaty of Paris, ending the war with the French and inheriting a large piece of the North American continent. The English colonies would no longer be bottled up on the east coast and Pennsylvania had the first road to the American interior. Officials in London, however, decided to honor Indian treaties and protect Indian country. They drew a Royal Proclamation Line, separating colonial and Indian lands with a north-south line on a map through the Appalachian Mountains. A skeptical English officer said settlers

### The Battle of Bushy Run

Delaware Indian leader Keekyuscung warned prophetically in 1758 that should the British army remain at the Forks of the Ohio after driving the French away, "he was afraid it would be a great war, and never come to peace again." Keekyuscung, his son (known as the Wolf), and most of their countrymen embraced the peace that Christian Frederick Post helped to broker in 1758, but the soldiers stayed and a massive earthen fort and village rose on the ruins of Fort Duquesne. Keekyuscung's prophecy came true in the dramatic conflict known as Pontiac's War, an Anglo-Indian war that raged across the Great Lakes and Ohio Country in 1763-64.

Perhaps the most dramatic encounter took place west of Fort Ligonier on August 5-6, 1763, when Ohio Indian warriors attacked troops under Colonel Henry Bouquet near an abandoned British outpost called Bushy Run. Bouquet's column was trying to reach Fort Pitt, which had been besieged since May, when it was suddenly attacked at midday on August 5. Bouquet's force included many fellow veterans of the Forbes Expedition, including Highlander Robert Kirkwood, who had been

captured by Shawnee Indians at Grant's Defeat in September 1758, and fellow Scot John Peebles, who had been an army physician in 1758, caring for sick and wounded Virginians at Raystown. The leaders of the Ohio Indian force included Keekyuscung and his son, the Wolf, whose countrymen had fought tenaciously to defend their homes through force and diplomacy for more than a generation.

The Battle of Bushy Run was a struggle among familiars: Kirkwood later recalled that shouts from the Indian side threatened Bouquet and others personally. Another British participant reported that during the night of August 5 and the following morning, Keekyuscung himself "had been Blackguarding us in English." The British escaped Braddock's fate through an innovative tactical maneuver and more than a bit of luck. Keekyuscung, who had embraced peace in 1758 and feared "a great war," lay dead on the field as Bouquet's men marched west to Pittsburgh in the scorching August sun. None of the survivors knew that thirty years of conflict, culminating in the 1794 battle of Fallen Timbers, lay ahead for the Ohio Country and its peoples.

*The climactic clash between Indians (left) and the British army (right) for control of western Pennsylvania is fought at Bushy Run in 1763. British commander Colonel Henry Bouquet shows how much he has learned about fighting on the frontier.*

were "too numerous, too lawless and licentious ever to be restrained." Indian agent George Croghan, who had arrived at Pittsburgh in 1759 to sell goods to the Indians and land to settlers, scoffed at the paper document. George Washington called the Proclamation "a temporary expedient to quiet the minds of the Indians." It was the first of many British decisions that would alienate its American colonies.

## A Great City is Born
Pittsburgh started working on a town plan in 1764. With the sprawling Fort Pitt nearby, Colonel John Campbell surveyed four squares on the

Monongahela River side of the log village. From the beginning, Pittsburgh had abundant agricultural land in its river valleys. It had salt and sand to make glass and ore to make iron. Local coal and, later, gas and oil fed the furnaces of industry. Its waterways flowed to potential markets for its products in all directions. War and isolation, however, conspired against success for almost half a century.

By 1784, a United States congressman observed that "the place, I believe, will never be very considerable. [It] is inhabited entirely by Scots and Irish, who live in paltry log houses." War continued to intervene. The imperial struggle between England and France was soon followed by an American rebellion against its English cousins. The American Revolution spawned more frontier struggles. The new United States waged a war against Ohio Indians for twenty more years. Thousands of soldiers were trained at Fort Lafayette, built not far from Old Fort Pitt in the early 1790s. Pittsburgh was often an armed camp before 1800.

With peace, the frontier town quickly lived up to its promise. The turn of the 19th century was a time of breathtaking change for the young United States. Pittsburgh helped launch the Lewis and Clark Expedition. Ohio and Kentucky became new western states and President Thomas Jefferson pushed the American frontiers to the Pacific Ocean.

Pittsburgh became the gateway to the mighty Ohio River. The United States now had a suitable opening to the heart of the continent. Its population tripled in ten years. Thirteen thousand settlers a year were trekking through the mountains on the Forbes Road, buying supplies at the Forks of the Ohio as they pushed west. It was time for the manufacturing and commerce that would build Pittsburgh into the bedrock of America's Industrial Revolution.

## George Washington's Last Visit to Pittsburgh

Although he retired from military life in 1758, George Washington was determined to enjoy the fruits of the British victory. For Washington and other veterans, the rich lands along the rivers near Pittsburgh provided an opportunity to emulate the great Chesapeake planters whose ancestors had secured enormous estates in Virginia and Maryland. In August 1770, a veterans' group met near Fredericksburg, Virginia to press their claim for land grants in the west. They dispatched Washington to locate promising lands along the Ohio River.

Washington's journey must have brought back a flood of memories as he rode west along the road his soldiers first opened in 1754. On the afternoon of October 17, 1770, an "exceeding warm and very pleasant day," Washington arrived at Pittsburgh, a village of several dozen log buildings in streets along the Monongahela River. The Virginia commander was something of a celebrity, dining with the British officers of the Royal Irish Regiment at Fort Pitt and meeting a delegation of Ohio Indians. The Seneca chief Conengayote noted (and Washington recorded), "That I was a Person who some of them remember to have seen when I was sent on an Embassy to the French."

A week later and two hundred miles down the Ohio River, Washington's party encountered another figure from the past. The Seneca Guyasuta had guided Washington on his 1753 journey to the French Fort LeBoeuf, and like Washington, had become a leader during the conflict of the 1750s. Guyasuta and his companions "expressed their desire of having a trade opened with Virginia" and to live in "peace & friendship." Tragically, the following decades brought far more war and enmity than peace and friendship to the inhabitants of the Ohio Valley.

Colonel George Washington returns to the frontier village of Pittsburgh in 1770, accompanied by his recently purchased valet, the slave William Lee. Washington is scouting tracts of western land for himself and his fellow French and Indian War veterans.

# Roads West

A modern road map is a spider web of intersecting federal, state and local highways. If you pull out a colonial map of the Keystone State, however, the slate gets much cleaner. The famous Scull Map (in the front end papers of this book), one of the earliest comprehensive surveys of William Penn's Commonwealth, reduces trails west of the Susquehanna River to one bold line, the Forbes Road winding its way to the Forks of the Ohio. There is no evidence on the map that frontier travelers depended on a honeycomb of Indian trails crisscrossing the whole region.

Frontier travel was a daunting, dangerous ordeal and a horse could be a liability on narrow foot paths. Everyone got lost. Even Indians often "ran here and there in the forest, til at length they found a path." In 1758, envoy Christian Frederick Post faced the briars, bogs, toppled trees, slippery slopes, and swollen creeks that made the back country so challenging. No wonder pictures scratched on bare tree trunks received such notice. No wonder at journey's end, the Iroquois Wood's Edge Ritual solemnly cleared eyes, ears and mouth "from any evil matter that on your journey may have settled there."

The 1758 Forbes Road was a military road, built for expediency. The goal was to clear a 20-foot-wide path, fill in the holes, push aside the rocks, and plank the swampy bogs so heavy wagons and herds of cattle could move west. No great engineering breakthroughs improved on Indian trails but regular traffic kept the pathway open and free, except in bad weather, from trip-stopping impediments. The colonists accepted the dangers of travel, and as the Scull Map advertises, the Forbes Road pointed like a crooked arrow to the vast interior of the continent.

Improvements were slow in coming to American roads. As long as nothing moved faster than a horse, road surfaces remained vexingly uneven. Water routes, like the Ohio River flowing west from Pittsburgh or man made canals, were popular where practical. The 19th century saw a quest for speed and accessibility that has never stopped. When entrepreneurs built toll roads and turnpikes like the National Road and improved the next generation of the old Forbes Road, they introduced a compacted, all-weather crushed stone surface called Macadam. Six-horse freight wagons prospered. The next great step was "hell in harness" steam railroads that built their own roadbeds and reached lightning speeds of 30, even 40 miles-per-hour. Crowded, uncomfortable, bone-crunching stage coaches, along with freight wagons, soon became history.

After late 19th century bicycle clubs demanded better roads for excursions, the true road revolution arrived at the turn of the 20th century with the horseless carriage. At first suspicious of the quirky, noisy, and smelly machines, Americans were soon smitten and the romance continues unabated. Automobile adventurers took on the muddy, bumpy rural roads and wanted smoother motoring. The federal government and the states began a partnership that paved America, creating the legendary national highway systems like U.S. Route 30, the Lincoln Highway, which still largely follows the path of the Forbes Road across Pennsylvania. Today, hardly a road remains in the country that is not covered with concrete or asphalt, making speeds possible that were once unimaginable.

Pennsylvania's innovative contribution to the modern nation's infrastructure was laid down on an abandoned railroad bed. The Pennsylvania Turnpike, America's first super highway, promised an uninterrupted, high-speed magic carpet ride through the Allegheny Mountains when it opened in 1940. The features we now take for granted were breathtaking: four lanes, no cross streets, a 200-foot-wide right of way, wide curves with banking, three-percent grades and the ability to see ahead at least 600 feet. The Turnpike was the first practical example of what the 1939 New York World's Fair was predicting for the future. It is the surviving pioneer of our unmatched interstate road system.

Back in 1758, one of colonial America's historic achievements was a harbinger for the future of the continent. The Forbes Road blazed a path for all the country's frontier roads west.

Fort Pitt and the log cabin community of Pittsburgh in 1761.

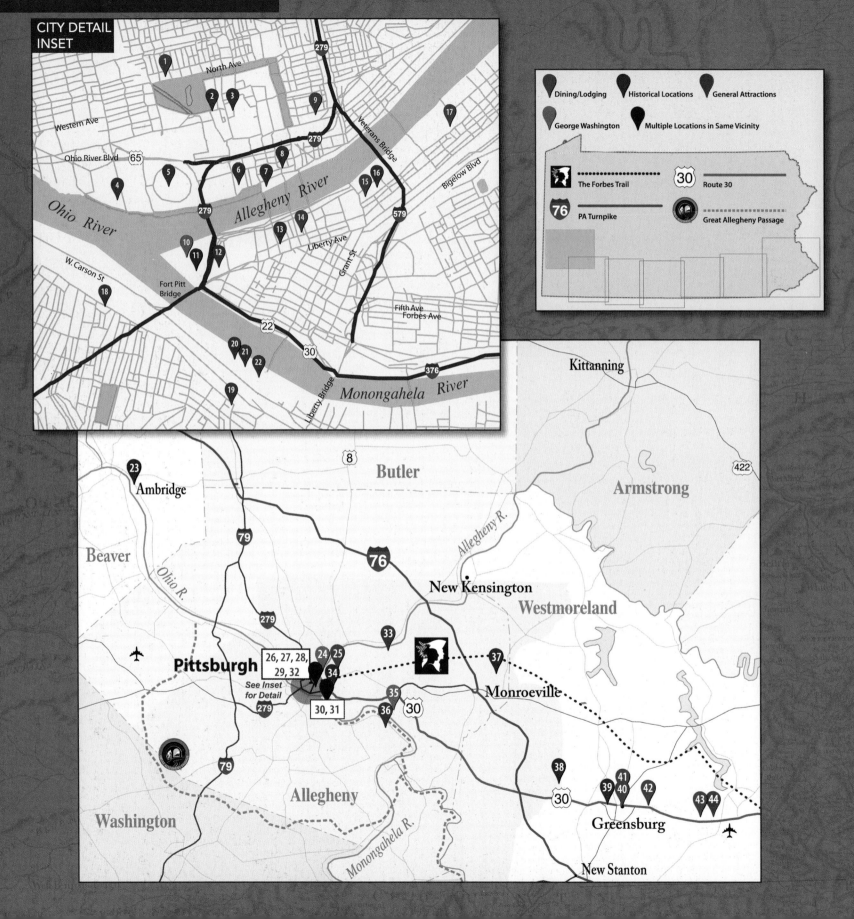

# Pittsburgh Regional Map

**CITY DETAIL INSET**

Western Ave
North Ave
Ohio River Blvd
65
Ohio River
W. Carson St
Fort Pitt Bridge
Allegheny River
Veterans Bridge
279
579
Bigelow Blvd
Liberty Ave
Grant St
Fifth Ave Forbes Ave
Liberty Bridge
Monongahela River
22
30
376

Dining/Lodging
Historical Locations
General Attractions
George Washington
Multiple Locations in Same Vicinity

The Forbes Trail
30 Route 30
76 PA Turnpike
Great Allegheny Passage

Kittanning
Butler
8
422
Armstrong
Ambrige
23
Beaver
79
Ohio R.
76
New Kensington
Westmoreland
Allegheny R.
279
33
26, 27, 28, 29, 32
24 25
34
Pittsburgh
See Inset for Detail
279
30, 31
35
36 30
37
Monroeville
38
39 40 41
42
43 44
30
Greensburg
79
Washington
Allegheny
Monongahela R.
New Stanton

## Visiting Pittsburgh

If geography is destiny, Pittsburgh was destined for greatness. Its mighty rivers reflect the steep hills that roll alongside. Over its 250-year history, the craft that ply the rivers have evolved from canoes to keelboats to coal barges to jet skis. But from several superb vantage points, a contemporary visitor can see exactly why the Forks of the Ohio were such a prize.

*The confluence of the Allegheny, Monongahela and Ohio Rivers lies at the center of Pittsburgh, where Point State Park retains a tracery of Fort's Pitt's music bastion.*

# See 1758 Today

George Washington viewed the confluence of the Allegheny, Monongahela and Ohio Rivers in several visits over two decades. He was here when General Forbes wrote to Secretary of State William Pitt on November 26, 1758, naming his location as Pittsburgh.

The historic site of Fort Pitt is now **Point State Park**[10]. With its broad lawns and stunning vistas, it is unique: it is the only downtown site for a Commonwealth-owned park. Pedestrians enter from Liberty Avenue, where the major downtown thoroughfares converge. The 36-acre commons are now the site of public celebrations from arts festivals to concerts, and its 150-foot fountain is the exclamation point on Pittsburgh's gleaming skyline.

When 19th century stockyards and slums were cleared from this site in 1950, Fort Pitt's original blockhouse and one bastion wall were preserved. The recreated Monongahela Bastion now houses the **Fort Pitt Museum**[12], which offers a comprehensive overview of the forces that gave birth to the city (101 Commonwealth Place; 412-281-9284; www.fortpittmuseum.com).

Walk first to the fountain, which operates in all but the coldest weather. An aquifer below the riverbeds, sometimes called Pittsburgh's fourth river, feeds the plume. From here the Ohio River begins a nearly 1,000-mile journey to the Mississippi. Originally called "the beautiful river" by the Seneca Indians, the Ohio merges the clear waters of the Allegheny with the darker-hued Monongahela, which flows north from West Virginia.

The Fort Pitt Museum offers the historical perspective of the Point. A second-floor gallery overlooks and interprets a stunning view of the confluence, orienting visitors to the landscape and its past. The adjoining exhibit answers the question "Whose Land?" by introducing the cultures and the characters that fought for control of the Forks in the French and Indian War. Short films illuminate the conflict, with displays on trade (explaining how deer hides were counted as "bucks") and period weapons adding depth.

A large-scale model dominates the first floor of the museum, showing the permanent fort the British built to replace the ruined remnants of Fort Duquesne. This massive brick fortification, enclosing more than two acres within its walls, remained in use until 1772; the model details its moat, fortifications, outbuildings and gardens. The gardens extended along the perimeter of the fort that now parallels Commonwealth Place at the park's entrance. The fort's immense size deterred attacks and attracted tradesmen and pioneers who settled nearby. By 1800, the city's population had leapt to 4,000 people.

The might of the three rivers makes Pittsburgh (pop. 300,000) one of the nation's largest inland ports with continuous traffic. Plan an afternoon on the water to view the Point. Options include sightseeing cruises aboard the **Gateway Clipper Fleet**[20] of riverboats that operate year-round (350 West Station Square Drive; 412-355-7980; www.gatewayclipper.com). **Just Ducky Tours**[22], aboard amphibian

vehicles, ride directly from downtown streets into the water (125 West Station Square Drive; 412-402-3825; www.justduckytours.com).

Pittsburgh believes in saving old buildings for new purposes. Its earliest settlers helped themselves to materials from the abandoned Fort Pitt as the city began to grow. A fine example of contemporary re-use is the **Senator John Heinz History Center**[16], a ten-minute walk from the Point (1212 Smallman Street; 412-454-6000; www.pghhistory.org). Anchoring one end of Pittsburgh's famous **Strip District**, a colorful food market, this 19th century ice factory has been handsomely converted to tell the stories of the city and the region, with a special installation on the French and Indian War. The exhibit includes video and superb art, including lifelike sculptures of key 1758 figures. A 26-foot-long birch bark canoe and hands-on activities in a miniature Fort Pitt compound engage young children.

In the eastern suburb of Plum Boro, a rough length of the Forbes Road runs through county-owned Boyce Park. The trail passes within a half-mile of the **Carpenter Log House**[37], an 18th century home reconstructed on its original site, and then crosses Pierson Run Road. (Get directions and details at www.plumhistory.org).

*pg. 184, left to right, A street vendor mans an outdoor stand in the Strip District, also the home of the city's History Center (far right pg. 185); below, Fort Pitt Museum interprets the French and Indian War with video, artifacts and interactive displays.*

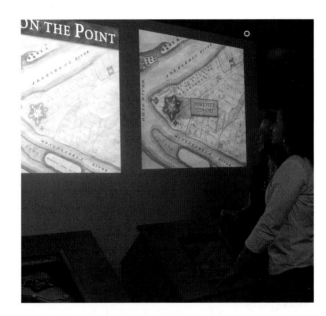

*William Pitt, 1st Earl of Chatham, (1708-1778) was the British Secretary of State during the 1758 campaign. Later Prime Minister, the politician known as the Great Commoner was almost solely responsible for the policies that won the French and Indian War and greatly increased the power and prestige of the British Empire. He was the logical choice for the new name of the Forks of the Ohio in November of 1758.*

## George Washington Was Here

Washington's assignments and business took him to the Forks on at least four occasions between 1753 and 1770. On the first three visits, he carried orders from the British Army: on the final trip, he surveyed land for investment.

George Washington first passed the Forks of the Ohio on his 1753 expedition to the French outpost near Erie. Follow his four-month trip along modern highways and scenic routes on **Washington's Trail**, running on a north-south axis through western Pennsylvania. Bright blue circular markers begin near the Maryland border and note the young colonel's path along what are now the National Road (Route 40) and other major routes. North of Pittsburgh, routes through Slippery Rock and Meadville meander past historic streams like French Creek, culminating at the Fort LeBoeuf Museum in Waterford. Download maps and travel suggestions at www. frenchandindianwar250.org.

A downtown Pittsburgh bridge commemorates Washington's return visit. Washington Crossing Bridge (31st Street) is named for the young emissary's December 1753 voyage south from Fort LeBoeuf, when he fell from his raft into the icy river. From observation decks at **Washington's Landing**[24], off Route 28 along the northern bank, visitors can survey the bridge and downtown Pittsburgh.

Again in 1755, Washington ventured to the region with the Braddock Expedition. On this occasion, the British drive towards Fort Duquesne was brutally thwarted ten miles south of the Forks. The Monongahela riverside town of Braddock marks the site of the July 9 battle in which General Braddock was mortally wounded. An exhibit with hundreds of artifacts recovered by archeologists, along with paintings and maps, is on display in the **Braddock's Field Historical Society** museum located within the **Braddock Carnegie Library**[35]

(419 Library Street; 412-351-5356). A statue of Washington stands across Library Street, at the spot where Braddock and the young colonel spent most of the battle. Local school children collected pennies to erect the statue in 1930.

Washington entered Pittsburgh with the British on November 25, 1758, after the French fled Fort Duquesne. In 1770, he returned to western Pennsylvania as a land speculator. On that trip he was reunited with Guyasuta, a Seneca who had guided him north in 1753. On Mt. Washington's **Grandview Avenue**, near the Duquesne Incline, their figures

appear deep in conversation, cast in bronze by sculptor James West.

Another statue of George Washington appears, somewhat incongruously, at **Kennywood Park**[36], Pittsburgh's beloved century-old amusement park (4800 Kennywood Boulevard, West Mifflin; 412-461-0500; www.kennywood.com). Among the classic roller coasters and gardens, the statue reminds visitors that he passed the park site with the Braddock Expedition in 1755.

*Rowers pull toward the Washington Crossing Bridge, the site where the future president forded the Allegheny River by raft in 1753. At right, sculptures commemorate the president's long friendship with Guyasuta, a Seneca chief, and Washington's role in the 1755 Battle of the Monongahela at Braddock.*

# History: Attacks and Independence in the Loyalhanna Valley

East of Pittsburgh, the Loyalhanna Valley towns of Greensburg and Latrobe offer a glimpse of the furious Indian response to British conquest and the stirrings of colonial independence.

The fierce black and red painted Mingo warrior, who stands in the visitor center at **Bushy Run Battlefield**[38] near Harrison City, offers a chilling reminder of Indian wrath in the woodlands (Route 993, Jeannette; 724-527-5584; www.bushyrunbattlefield.com). After the British took control of the Forks of the Ohio in 1758, Indians fought fiercely to regain their lands. Here, in deep forest 26 miles from the Forks, they ambushed British troops en route to the fort in August 1763, killing fifty men. Begin a visit to the site, now mostly grassy lawns, by viewing the short video. Narrated in the character of commander Henry Bouquet, it recounts how the British survived the assault, continued on to relieve Fort Pitt, and secure the frontier.

Five miles east of Bushy Run on Forbes Trail Road, a scarlet flag bears both a rattlesnake insignia and a Union Jack. Turn here for the entrance to **Hanna's Town**[39] (809 Forbes Trail Road, Hempfield Township; 724-836-1800; www.starofthewest.org). The section of Forbes Road that George Washington's brigade opened here on the morning of November 18, 1758 ran across ground that would play a significant role in the dramatic struggles of the American Revolution. Over the next dozen years or so, a growing stream of settlers and discharged soldiers built homesteads along what came to be called "the Great Road," leading to the fledgling town of Pittsburgh. By 1773, Hanna's Town had been chosen as the county seat over Pittsburgh, then part of vast Westmoreland County. After word of the battles of Lexington and Concord reached the town in 1775, the villagers protested British authority by issuing the Hanna's Town Resolves, which foreshadowed the Continental Congress' Declaration of Independence. A planned interpretive center will crest the hilltop overlooking the site.

*left to right, The deep forest battle of Bushy Run is reenacted each August; the original Hanna's Town flag of the Independent Battalion of Westmoreland County is now displayed at the State Museum.*

# Family Fun

Downtown Pittsburgh is the destination for world-class arts events. The famous Pittsburgh Symphony, theater, dance and opera companies share the thriving **Pittsburgh Cultural District**[13] centered on Penn Avenue (www.pgharts.com). The district offers over 300 evenings of performance a year, with galleries, cabarets, and restaurants for theatergoers.

Along the city's **North Shore**, a walkable loop of renovated landmarks beckons. The **Children's Museum of Pittsburgh**[3] (10 Children's Way; 412-322-5058; www.pittsburghkids.org) is a reconstituted, century-old post office that's young at heart. It has received national recognition for its innovative expansion, and youngsters—even toddlers—recognize it as a place to play with real things. On nearby Sandusky Street, the **Andy Warhol Museum**[8] (117 Sandusky Street; 412-237-8300; www.warhol.org), in a restored wedding-cake building, honors the hometown Pop Art icon in the country's largest museum devoted to a single artist. The **National Aviary**[2] is the country's premiere bird park, housed in an ornate Victorian glass house (700 Arch Street; 412-323-7235; www.aviary.org). The **Carnegie Science Center**[4] features more than 400 interactive exhibits, a Cold War submarine and Sports Works (1 Allegheny Avenue; 412-237-3400; www.carnegiesciencecenter.org).

All the museums are near the home fields of the **Pittsburgh Steelers**[5] and **Pirates**[6] along the Allegheny River waterfront.

To the east, **Forbes Avenue**, a major road named for the General, connects downtown Pittsburgh to the Oakland neighborhood. (Other distinguished names from the general's staff grace the nearby neighborhoods: Bouquet and Halkett intersect with Forbes, while Grant Street downtown marks the site of James Grant's disastrous defeat.) The district is home to the University of Pittsburgh, Carnegie Mellon University, and research hospitals. Landmarks include the **Cathedral of Learning**[26] and **Carnegie Library**. Don't miss the **Carnegie Museums of Art** and **Natural History**[28] (4400 Forbes Avenue, Pittsburgh; 412-621-3131; www.carnegiemuseums.org). The Museum of Natural History's world-renowned dinosaur collection is interpreted in a towering exhibit here.

*The Schenley Plaza carousel twirls in the shadow of the University of Pittsburgh's Cathedral of Learning; a skating rink punctuates downtown's PPG Place, architect Philip Johnson's collection of neo-Gothic glass skyscrapers.*

## The Great Road and the American Revolution

The section of Forbes Road that George Washington's brigade opened on the morning of November 18, 1758 ran across ground that would play a significant role in the American Revolution. Here, in a low spot nestled between sheltering hills, a spring of cool water had refreshed Native Americans for centuries. The weary horses that pulled Forbes' artillery and carried provisions and supplies, not to mention the ailing general himself, must have paused to drink here before climbing uphill to the plateau on which the army constructed a fortified encampment known as the Three Redoubts. Over the next dozen years, a growing stream of settlers built homesteads along the Great Road. Pennsylvania organized the region into Westmoreland County in 1773. For more than a decade, the courts met near the old spring in a tavern operated by Scots-Irish settler Robert Hanna, the proprietor of a town laid out nearby.

Westmoreland County settlers constructed a fort at Hanna's Town in 1774. They also served in the campaigns of the American Revolution. Community leader John Proctor, a French and Indian War veteran, organized local defenses and led a militia force to George Washington's aid in New Jersey during the winter of 1776-1777. Two locally-raised regiments served under Washington during the 1777 Philadelphia campaign and suffered through the Valley Forge winter before returning west for home defense. In one of the final battles of the American Revolution, Seneca Indian and British raiders almost totally destroyed Hanna's Town on July 13, 1782.

The entrance to **Schenley Park** beckons next to the museums. **Schenley Plaza**[27] draws visitors of all ages. A carousel, outdoor café, benches and lawns invite toddlers, students and researchers to relax. **Phipps Conservatory and Botanical Gardens**[29] boast indoor and outdoor displays (One Schenley Park, Pittsburgh; 412-622-6914; www.phipps.conservatory.org).

The **Pittsburgh Zoo and PPG Aquarium**[33], on the edge of Highland Park, exhibits wildlife in natural settings, from African savannas to an underwater polar bear tunnel that lets visitors view the bears from below (1 Wild Place, Pittsburgh; 800-474-4966; www.pittsburghzoo.org).

# Uniquely Pittsburgh

On the site of the former Jones and Laughlin steel mill, **SouthSide Works**[31] has reclaimed a 34-acre industrial brownfield as a thriving neighborhood with recreation, homes, and a bustling shopping district (www.southsideworks.com). The destination has become a nationally acclaimed example of adaptive re-use. The steel mill commanded two banks of the river, passing molten steel in buckets over the Hot Metal Bridge. Now the bridge includes a pedestrian lane connecting the **Great Allegheny Passage**, to the local Three Rivers Park Trail.

*below, the History Center's George Washasaurus, a triceratops in a tricornered hat, pays lighthearted tribute to young George Washington and the city's famous dinosaur collection; right, the town square at SouthSide Works replaces a steel mill with well-designed new public attractions; youngsters splash on the North Shore water steps overlooking downtown.*

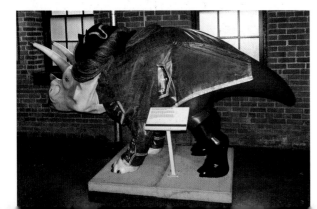

# Great Houses and Gardens

Pittsburgh's Penn Avenue cuts a straight asphalt line from the city's eastern border to its central Cultural District. The city has General Forbes to thank for the path—these six miles are the direct route of the 1758 expedition to its triumphant destination. Along the corner of Penn and Linden Avenues in residential Point Breeze in the city's East End (moved 1,200 feet to Mellon Park at Penn and Fifth Avenues on the 250th anniversary), a small historic marker memorializes a tree. The oak that shaded the passing Forbes troops is long gone, but a marker placed in 1914 recalls the expedition that founded the city.

Today, the east end of Penn Avenue reflects the city's brash 19th century swagger, when millionaire industrialists built mansions here. **Clayton**[34], the home of Henry Clay Frick, commands the corner of South Homewood Avenue (7227 Reynolds Street, Pittsburgh; 412-371-0600; www.frickart.org).

Frick's 1882 home is a showplace of perfectly preserved Victoriana—with the radical addition of whole-house electricity, arranged by Frick's neighbor George Westinghouse. The fantastic orchestrion, a huge musical invention, plays symphonic music rolls at ear-piercing levels. The backyard museum of European art treasures collected by Frick's daughter, Helen, flanks an automobile museum that will thrill car buffs. The **Frick Café**, in a cottage on the lawn, is an award-winning charmer.

Heading east towards Latrobe, a quiet garden on a college campus awaits where Route 30 turns rural. Next to St. Vincent's College,

founded as a Benedictine abbey in 1846, lies the **Winnie Palmer Nature Reserve**[44] (300 Fraser Purchase Road, Latrobe; 724-532-6600; www.stvincent.edu). The 50-acre sanctuary, named for the wife of hometown golfing legend Arnold Palmer, celebrates local ecology with peaceful walking trails and educational programs.

To the west of the city lies another historic settlement. The Harmony Society was one of the many communal German sects that sought Pennsylvania's religious freedom. The village they created as an industrial center in 1824 is a well-preserved state historic site, **Old Economy Village**[23] (270 Sixteenth Street, Ambridge; 724-266-4500; www.oldeconomyvillage.org). The museum, Feast Hall, gardens and other buildings host special events March through December.

*clockwise from lower left, Clayton, the 19th century home of millionaire Henry Clay Frick, is part of the Frick Art and Historical Center; Pittsburgh's oldest building, the **Fort Pitt Blockhouse11** was a dwelling throughout the 19th century, as this 1832 painting by Russell Smith shows; owner Mary Schenley later donated the Blockhouse to the Daughters of the American Revolution. The DAR opposed Henry Clay Frick's efforts to demolish it to make way for his Pennsylvania Railroad. Edith Ammon led the DAR's battle against Frick in Pennsylvania courts until 1907, when judges finally ruled in the DAR's favor. The landmark decision protected historic structures of the colonial period from being seized by eminent domain. The DAR still owns and operates the Blockhouse; call the Fort Pitt Museum for public hours; Interpreters staff Old Economy Village in Ambridge. The site of a German religious settlement is now a state museum; a marker erected by the Pennsylvania Society of the Colonial Dames of America marks General Forbes' route along Pittsburgh's Penn Avenue.*

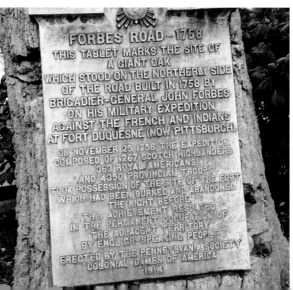

## Did You Know?

To reach observation points on Mt. Washington, board the incline railways (412-442-2000; www.portauthority.org). These unique cable cars are a Pittsburgh institution and a bargain to ride. From Carson Street, which runs along the south shore of the Monongahela River, choose either the **Monongahela**[19] or **Duquesne Incline**[18] (pronounced locally as IN-cline). The former is reached by subway to **Station Square**[21], a popular entertainment complex. The latter offers a higher elevation and a more direct view of the confluence. Both provide viewing decks and binoculars. A promenade along Grandview Avenue, with other platforms, connects the two upper stations. The street offers some of Pittsburgh's finest food-with-a-view, from casual pubs to elegant four-star restaurants (see the full listing at www.visitpittsburgh.com).

## Great Outdoors

Clean and green, Pittsburgh's environmental rebirth is best appreciated downtown. The city's riverfront, once used exclusively for industry, has been reclaimed for recreation over recent decades.

Downtown anglers congregate on the Monongahela side of Point State Park to cast their lines. Paddle the Point with **Kayak Pittsburgh**[7], which rents solo and tandem kayaks, canoes and hydrobikes seasonally: the rental shop is just below PNC Park on the North Shore of the Allegheny (412-969-9090; www.kayakpittsburgh.org). Currents are generally gentle, and children are welcome. For recreational boaters, the city's South Side **Riverfront Park** offers a launch ramp for watercraft. The **Three Rivers Park** Trail connects walkways, bridges and green spaces on both banks of all three rivers downtown (view the trail map at www.riverlifetaskforce.org).

*bottom left, the Monongahela Incline; right, Schenley Park's lush trails cut below bridges through Panther Hollow.*

# Plan a Visit

## Annual Regional Events

**Three Rivers Arts Festival,** June
www.artsfestival.net

**Battle of Bushy Run
Anniversary Reenactment,** August
www.bushyrunbattlefield.com

*right: In the city's Lawrenceville neighborhood, Church Brew Works transformed a 1902 church sanctuary into a contemporary restaurant.*

## Greensburg/Latrobe

For more information:
Laurel Highlands Visitors Bureau
120 East Main Street, Ligonier
(800) 333-5661 | www.laurelhighlands.org

### DINING
**Caffe Barista**[40]
7 West Otterman Street, Greensburg
(724) 837-8873
- Friendly downtown café next to Palace Theater.

**St. Vincent Gristmill and General Store**[43]
300 Fraser Purchase Road, Latrobe
(724) 537-0304
www.benedictine.stvincent.edu/gristmill/
- Coffeehouse open daily on college campus. Small historic display.

### LODGING
**Mountain View Inn**[42]
121 Village Drive (Route 30 East),
Greensburg
(800) 537-8709 | www.mountainviewinn.com
- Member, Historic Hotels of America. Packages combine admission to local attractions.

**Bed & Breakfast of Greensburg**[41]
119 Alwine Avenue, Greensburg
(866) 888-0303 | www.bbgreensburg.com
- Four guest rooms on quiet side street near courthouse.

## Pittsburgh

For more information:
Visit Pittsburgh
Liberty Avenue at Gateway Center
(800) 359-0758 | www.visitpittsburgh.com

### DINING
**Café Zao**[14]
649 Penn Avenue, Pittsburgh
(412) 325-7007 | www.cafezao.com
- Upscale restaurant with a Portuguese accent in the Cultural District.

**Eleven**[15]
1150 Smallman Street, Pittsburgh
(412) 201-5656 | www.bigburrito.com/eleven
- Five-star American cuisine near Heinz History Center.

**Kaya**[17]
2000 Smallman Street, Pittsburgh
(412) 261-6565 | www.bigburrito.com/kaya
- Informal Strip District pub with Caribbean and other world flavors.

**Church Brew Works**[25]
3525 Liberty Avenue, Pittsburgh
(412) 688-8200 | www.churchbrew.com
- Microbrew pub in the former St. John the Baptist Church.

### LODGING
**The Priory**[9]
614 Pressley Street, Pittsburgh
(412) 231-3338 | www.thepriory.com
- Former Benedictine monastery near the Warhol Museum.

**The Inn on the Mexican War Streets**[1]
604 West North Avenue, Pittsburgh
(412) 231-6544
www.innonthemexicanwarstreets.com
- Grand 19th century home.

**Sunnyledge**[32]
5124 Fifth Avenue, Pittsburgh
(412) 683-5014 | www.sunnyledge.com
- Five-star boutique hotel and restaurant in a historic 1886 mansion.

**Morning Glory Inn**[30]
2119 Sarah Street, Pittsburgh
(412) 431-1707 | www.gloryinn.com
- Victorian brick townhouse on Pittsburgh's eclectic South Side.

# Three Rivers

Pittsburgh is famous for its three rivers, but Pennsylvania has three legendary waterways that define the whole state. East to west, famous rivers flow through the history of Penn's Woods. As journalist Charles Kuralt might have said, "Pennsylvania is a great American story, and there is a river on every page of it." In a 1931 Supreme Court decision, Oliver Wendell Holmes, referring to the Delaware, said, "a river is more than an amenity, it is a treasure."

Once polluted and dying roads of commerce, Pennsylvania's signature rivers now have commissioners, keepers and untold fans devoted to giving the life-giving waters back to citizens. The Delaware, supplying drinking water to 15 million, is a study in contrasts on its 360 mile path between Pennsylvania, New York, New Jersey, and Delaware to the Atlantic Ocean. From its dual headwaters in the New York highlands, it is a protected wild and scenic river in beautiful valleys that feature two national parks, especially the Delaware Water Gap, a spectacular preserve where the river cuts through a ridge of the Appalachians. Adventurers, paddling in canoes, discover the valley's wild charms during the annual Delaware River Sojourn in June.

At the Trenton fall line, fresh meets salt water and the river becomes a wide, lazy estuary flowing past the gigantic port of Philadelphia, the world's largest twin suspension bridges, and refinery cities to ports around the globe. That window to the world became General Forbes' lifeline of redcoat troops, equipment, and supplies in 1758. After Hog Island, near Philadelphia, became a major world shipyard in 1915, the Delaware River Port Complex grew into the world's largest freshwater port. Today a strategic military port, called critical to the nation, it accounts for $19 billion annual dollars of economic activity. Among its major

importers of steel, paper, meat, cocoa beans and fruit, the nation's main depot for bananas is located in Wilmington.

In mid-state, the Susquehanna, ancient home of the powerful Susquehannock Indian Nation and important water barrier on the 1758 Forbes Trail, gives special meaning to the term "Old Man River." At 300 million years plus, it may be the oldest river system in the world. It has another special distinction. After cutting Pennsylvania almost in two and flowing past the state capital, it ends a 444 mile run as the headwaters of the Chesapeake Bay, contributing half of the estuary's fresh water. The Bay, in fact, is part of the Susquehanna River valley, drowned after the last Ice Age. Like other major waterways, this 16th largest American river has suffered from abuse and neglect.

The Susquehanna's many rapids and its shallow water, except during spring thaws, frustrated early exploiters. Two successful canals, however, sparked the industry that eventually left it polluted and endangered, even enduring the worst American nuclear accident at Three Mile Island. Many devoted government agents, admirers and recreational users now look after the Susquehanna's welfare. The Susquehanna River Trail Association sponsors an annual Great River Adventure on a beautiful 51 mile stretch between Sunbury and Harrisburg.

Western Pennsylvania may have the most spectacular river story of all. Two major rivers, the Allegheny and the Monongahela, launch another, the Ohio, known to French Canadian settlers as *La Belle Riviere* (Beautiful River). The 981-mile-long Ohio, fiercely contested at the time of the Forbes Campaign, flows through much of eastern America and is the largest tributary of the mighty Mississippi. Thus Pittsburgh, the Forks of the Ohio, became the open door to America's vast interior. Along with the industry that built America, Pittsburgh became one of the

country's largest inland ports. Today, the Port of Pittsburgh has 200 river terminals with access to a 10,000 mile waterway system, stretching to Sioux City, Iowa, and New Orleans.

The inevitable price for industry and commerce was life-threatening pollution, but, as Pittsburgh has changed gears from heavy industry to high tech, the miles of dirty waterfront and poisoned rivers are becoming a model of renewal. Building out from a renovated Point State Park, an urban renaissance begun after World War Two, the Riverlife Task Force is reviving the river banks with a 13 mile loop called Three Rivers Park. Ambitious plans call for 128 miles of green space along local rivers. Crowds are now flocking to the rivers, heeding the call of Friends of the Riverfront and Venture Outdoors to bike, hike, rollerblade, row, paddle and swim under the famous bridges of the Steel City.

### The Delaware River

- Delaware River Sojourn (The Delaware River Basin Commission's public page with information on the annual Sojourn) (609) 883-9500 www.nj.gov/drbc/sojourn.htm

- Delaware Riverkeeper Network (215) 369-1188 www.delawareriverkeeper.org

- Delaware River Recreation Page www.delawareriver.net

### The Susquehanna River

- Susquehanna River Basin Commission (717) 238-0423 www.srbc.net

- Susquehanna River Trail Association (Great Trail Adventure) (717) 737-8622 www.susquehannatrail.org

## The Three Rivers of Pittsburgh

- The Port of Pittsburgh Commission
  (412) 201-7330
  www.port.pittsburgh.pa.us

- The Riverlife Task Force
  (412) 258-6636
  www.riverlifetaskforce.org

- Friends of the Riverfront
  (412) 488-0212
  www.friendsoftheriverfront.org

- Venture Outdoors
  (412) 255-0564
  www.ventureoutdoors.org

*clockwise from lower left, Moored at Philadelphia's exciting waterfront, the tall ship Moshulu, a Seneca Indian word for fearless, is now a fine restaurant. Once named the Kurt, the Moshulu sailed around Cape Horn 54 times and is an apt symbol of the Quaker City's long and fruitful relationship with the Delaware River and the oceans of the world; the wide, shallow, and rocky Susquehanna River is still a formidable dividing line between Pennsylvania's east and west; the once polluted Three Rivers of Pittsburgh have become a playground for kayakers and triathlete swimmers along a revitalized riverfront; the view of Pittsburgh's historic Forks of the Ohio from Mount Washington is always spectacular.*

# EPILOGUE

Events in 1758 provide a snapshot, a moment in time, during the tidal wave of historic events that was building on the east coast of North America. The front edge of that wave was the string of British victories, first at Louisburg and Pittsburgh then later, at Quebec and Montreal, defeating the French and opening the interior in America.

For redcoat leaders, victory verified their aspirations of empire, their new possessions spreading English virtues around the world. For American colonials, it meant something quite different. **Ben Franklin** was among the first to see a new empire of freedom, of self-sufficiency, of opportunity in the vastness of America. Almost three decades later, the French observer, Crevecoeur, summed up the new United States: "The American is a new man, who acts upon new principles… Here individuals of all nations are melted into a new race of men, whose labors and posterity will one day cause great changes in the world."

The many characters in this story were players caught up in the great wave of change. Some soon disappeared from the stage. The veteran French Fort Duquesne commander, **Lignery**, abandoning and destroying his post to fight another day, was killed less than a year later in an ambush near Fort Niagara. **General John Forbes** was already dying during his moment of triumph. Carried back over the mountains on the road his army had so arduously built, the General lingered for six more weeks in Philadelphia, an active correspondent to the end. When his body was carried with full military honors to its final resting place in Christ Church, the *Pennsylvania Gazette* remembered his "steady pursuit of well concerted measures, in defiance of disease, and numberless obstructions…" His premature death, however, robbed this capable, valiant man of what he deserved: the fame, the promotions, the portraits that would today grace museum walls.

**Colonel Henry Bouquet**, the loyal deputy commander, continued to serve with the Royal American Regiment in Pennsylvania. Five years after the Forbes victory, Bouquet was again in a frontier war, winning a singular victory of his own at Bushy Run. In 1765, the Swiss hero, now a respected old hand at woods fighting, died suddenly of yellow fever at his new post in Pensacola, Florida.

After victory at the Forks of the Ohio, Quartermaster **Sir John St. Clair** was soon in New England doing what he did best, telling the new British commander how he would have improved on General Forbes' performance. In spite of his well known dislike of colonials, Sir John married an American and settled in New Jersey. He still sought military advancement during the decade left to him, but he also became something of a homebody, pursuing landscape gardening and collecting an impressive library.

The Highlander **James Grant** recovered quickly from his career-threatening defeat and capture near the gates of Fort Duquesne. The French paroled him and, by 1761, he was leading a 2,600 man army against the Cherokee nations in the Carolinas. Grant later became the governor of East Florida and then a determined foe of the American rebellion, commanding redcoats at the Battles of Long Island and Brandywine. The high-living Laird of Balindalloch was a celebrated epicure to the end, living well into his 80s on his Scottish estate.

The Delaware leader **Teedyuscung** exemplified the enduring perils for Native Americans. Eastern Woodland nations were being overrun by European immigrants. They were dependent on the trade goods of settlers who kept pushing them west. Teedyuscung responded by adopting many English ways and seeking a preserve for his people among the intruders. His reward was a puzzling death in 1763, dying in a burning house built for him by Pennsylvanians but destroyed by Connecticut settlers who claimed the land. His Delaware cousins who had fled west fared no better. They needed trade but drew a line and wanted no truck with settlers. They tried everything: diplomacy, war, even pleas to the spiritual world. Still striving to stem the tide of settlers in the 1760s, the western Delaware nations faced challenges that would vex Native Americans across the continent.

Immigrants **George Croghan** and **Christian Frederick Post** followed different paths to the Pennsylvania frontier. The hardy trader Croghan was the opportunist with few scruples, tirelessly claiming millions of acres farther and farther west. The selfless missionary Post returned to his new found Indian friends and converts in Ohio Country. When his mission failed, a victim of yet another Indian war in 1763, he sailed to Honduras to live among the natives on the Mosquito Coast.

**Israel Pemberton**, the "King of the Quakers," took stands on pacifism and fairness to Native Americans that were too enlightened for the age. His lifelong efforts, however, to bring tolerance and charity to the public arena helped define the American spirit. The two Scots-Irish leaders, **John Armstrong** and **James Burd**, were more grounded in the growth and success of their adopted frontier communities. Important founding fathers in Lancaster and Cumberland Counties, they helped incite Americans to rebellion. In spite of brief military careers during the Revolution, these hometown heroes devoted most of their full lives to local affairs.

Soldier and physician **Hugh Mercer**, the refugee from a 1745 Scottish rebellion, left Pennsylvania in 1760 to live among other Scots in Fredericksburg, Virginia. When another rebellion called him to arms, he led Virginia troops in the Continental army, again serving with his friend **George Washington**. On a cold January morning in 1777, the brave General Mercer became a much lamented martyr, mortally wounded during the American victory at Princeton. **Benjamin Franklin** gained immortality in many ways. During his 84 years of achievement, he saved the best for last. Between long stays overseas as a diplomat, Franklin was intimately involved in the creation of both the Declaration of Independence and the Constitution, the bookends of the Revolutionary era. In 1758, **George Washington** chose to abandon the military life. A second military career, fifteen years later, made the Virginia citizen soldier one of the most famous men in the world.

Through it all, the **Forbes Road** pointed the way to the future. It carried the colonies west and introduced the world to the big idea of a limitless America. When the tidal wave of events created the United States, the Forbes Road took the new country to Benjamin Franklin's empire of opportunity and self-sufficiency and through George Washington's "wide door and smooth way" to unimagined prosperity. Its descendants, Lincoln Highway and Pennsylvania Turnpike, continue the mission today, carrying millions of always restless, always striving Americans to the shared history, opportunities and ideals that still define this nation.

*right, Rohr's Gap*

## Suggestions for Further Reading

Armchair historians can explore a wide choice of books about a worldwide war that Americans call the French and Indian War. J. Martin West, ed., *War for Empire in Western Pennsylvania*, (Ft. Ligonier Association, 1993) and Ruth Sheppard, ed., *Empires Collide: The French and Indian War, 1754-63*, (Oxford: Osprey Publishing. Ltd., 2007) introduce the American campaigns. Walter O'Meara, *Guns at the Forks* (Pittsburgh: University of Pittsburgh Press, 1965), and Alfred P. James and Charles M. Stotz, *Drums in the Forest* (Pittsburgh: Historical Society of Western Pennsylvania, 1958) are popular standards about the war in Pennsylvania. Robert Leckie, *"A Few Acres of Snow, The Saga of the French and Indian Wars* (New York: John Wiley & Sons, Inc., 1999) places the war in the whole sweep of European settlement. Other overviews include: William M. Fowler, Jr., *Empires at War: The French and Indian War and the Struggle for North America* (New York: Walker & Company, 2004), and Seymour I. Schwartz, *The French and Indian War, 1754-63: The Imperial Struggle for North America* (New York: Simon & Schuster, 1994; reprinted Edison, NJ: Castle Books, 2000).

Any venture into the growing collection of scholarly books and articles about the French and Indian War should begin with the recent work of Fred Anderson. *Crucible of War: The Seven Years' War and the Fate of Empire in British North America, 1754-1766* (New York: Alfred A. Knopf, 2000) is the latest comprehensive treatment of the French and Indian War. Professor Anderson condensed his authoritative study in *The War That Made America: A Short History of the French and Indian War* (New York: Viking Penguin, 2005), a volume that accompanied the PBS production of the same name. A collection of recent French and Indian War articles, Warren R. Hofstra, ed., *Culture in Conflict: The Seven Years' War in North America* (Lanham, MD: Rowman & Littlefield Publishers, Inc., 2007) expands on an introductory essay by Anderson.

The famous 19th century French and Indian War chronicler Francis Parkman, *Montcalm and Wolfe* (Boston: Little, Brown & Company, 1884), still "gives the dry fact the magic of style." Lawrence Henry Gipson wrote most of his monumental *The British Empire Before the American Revolution*, 15 Volumes, (Idaho and New York: Caxton Printers and Alfred A. Knopf, 1936-1970) (Vols. 6-8 address the French and Indian War) at Lehigh University near the historic Moravian settlement in Bethlehem.

Francis Jennings, *Empire of Fortune: Crowns, Colonies and Tribes in the Seven Years War in America* (New York: W.W. Norton, 1988) brought Native Americans to the center of the story. Many studies including Daniel K. Richter, *Facing East from Indian Country: A Native History of Early America* (Cambridge, Mass: Harvard University Press, 2001), James H. Merrell, *Into the American Woods: Negotiators on the Pennsylvania Frontier* (New York: W.W. Norton, 1999), Michael N. McConnell, *A Country Between: The Upper Ohio Valley and Its Peoples* (Lincoln: University of Nebraska Press, 1992), and Matthew C. Ward, *Breaking the Backcountry: The Seven Years' War in Virginia and Pennsylvania, 1754-1765* (Pittsburgh: University of Pittsburgh Press, 2003) have ably continued and expanded those efforts. Paul A. W. Wallace, *Indians of Pennsylvania* (Harrisburg; The Pennsylvania Historical and Museum Commission, 1989) is a favorite introduction, while C. A. Weslager, *The Delaware Indians, A History*

(New Brunswick, NJ: Rutgers University Press, 1972) follows Delaware fortunes to present day Oklahoma.

The Forbes Campaign is rich in primary sources. General Forbes and Colonel Bouquet were relentless and talented letter writers and their correspondence was skillfully collected and edited in two now rare editions: Alfred Procter James, ed., *Writings of General John Forbes Relating to his Service in North America* (Menasha, Wisconsin: The Collegiate Press, 1938), S.K. Stevens et al., eds., *The Papers of Henry Bouquet,* Volume II, *The Forbes Expedition* (Harrisburg: The Pennsylvania Historical and Museum Commission, 1951). An abbreviated edition of the Forbes papers, Irene Stewart, ed., *Letters of General John Forbes*, (Pittsburgh: Allegheny County Committee, 1927) is available from the Pennsylvania State University Press (www.psupress.org) which has an excellent collection of titles about western Pennsylvania.

George Washington kept no surviving diaries or journals in 1758, but his letters and orderly books are exhaustively collected and edited in W. W. Abbot, ed., *The Papers of George Washington*, Colonial Series, Volumes 5 & 6 (Charlottesville: University of Virginia Press, 1988). The lively journal of British army chaplain Thomas Barton, edited by Gettysburg Professor James P. Myers, Jr., is now available in *Adams County History*, Volume 8 (Gettysburg: Adams County Historical Society, 2002). An edited version of Christian Frederick Post's 1758 Journal is in John W. Harpster, ed., *Crossroads, Descriptions of Western Pennsylvania 1720-1829* (Pittsburgh: University of Pittsburgh Press, 1938).

Among the vast collection of George Washington biographies, some studies that look at his early career include: Fred Anderson, ed., *George Washington Remembers: Reflections on the French and Indian War* (Lanham, MD: Rowman & Littlefield Publishers, Inc., 2004), Hugh Cleland, *George Washington in the Ohio Valley* (Pittsburgh: University of Pittsburgh Press, 1955), Paul K. Longmore, *The Invention of George Washington* (Berkeley: University of California, 1988), and Thomas A. Lewis, *For King and Country : The Maturing of George Washington, 1748-1760* (New York: Harpers Collins Publishers, 1993). Joel Achenbach, *The Grand Idea: George Washington's Potomac and the Race to the West* (New York: Simon & Schuster, 2004) is an engaging look at Washington's interest in western expansion.

Benjamin Franklin, also the object of much scholarly attention, is best represented in his own writings: Kenneth Silverman, ed., *The Autobiography and Other Writings* (New York: Penguin Books, 1986). Several less familiar characters in this story have biographies: Anthony F. C. Wallace, *King of the Delawares, Teedyuscung, 1700-1763* (Syracuse University Press, 1949, 1990), Theodore Thayer, *Israel Pemberton, King of the Quakers* (Philadelphia: The Historical Society of Pennsylvania, 1943), Lily Lee Nixon, *James Burd, Frontier Defender, 1726-1793* (Philadelphia: University of Pennsylvania Press, 1941), and Nicholas B. Wainwright, *George Croghan: Wilderness Diplomat* (Chapel Hill: University of North Carolina Press, 1959). Ian McCulloch and Timothy Todish, editors, *Through Many Dangers, The Memoirs and Adventures of Robert Kirk, Late of the Royal Highland Regiment* (Fleischmanns, NY: Purple Mountain Press, 2004) is a rare memoir of a redcoat enlisted man who served in the 1758 campaign.

Life in 18th century British armies is richly documented in Richard Holmes, *Redcoat: The British Soldier in the Age of the Horse and Musket* (New York: W.W. Norton & Company, 2001) and Stephen Brumwell, *Redcoats: The British Soldier and War in the Americas, 1755-1763* (Cambridge University Press, 2002). Simon Schama, *A History of Britain*, Volume II, *The Wars of the British, 1603-1776* (New York, Hyperion, 2001) is an overview of the 17th and 18th century British wars for empire. The relationship of war and empire in America is explored, especially through the career of George Washington, in Fred Anderson and Andrew Cayton, *The Dominion of War: Empire and Liberty in North America, 1500-2000* (New York: Viking, 2005). Pennsylvania's role in the war is exhaustively treated by William A. Hunter, *Forts on the Pennsylvania Frontier, 1753-1758* (Harrisburg: The Pennsylvania Historical and Museum Commission, 1960). Charles M. Stotz, *Outposts of the War for Empire* (Historical Society of Western Pennsylvania and the University of Pittsburgh Press, 2005) spent a lifetime studying Pennsylvania forts. Colonial military uniforms, weapons, and equipment are featured in Harold L. Peterson, *Arms and Armor in Colonial America, 1526-1783* (Harrisburg: Stackpole Company, 1956), R. Scott Stephenson, *Clash of Empires, The British, French and Indian War, 1754-1763* (Pittsburgh: Historical Society of Western Pennsylvania, 2005), and the military uniform series available from www.ospreypublishing.com.

Local histories play a large role in studies of the 1750s. Readers can begin with an up-to-date history of the entire state: Randall M. Miller and William Pencak, editors, *Pennsylvania: A History of the Commonwealth* (Pennsylvania Historical and Museum Commission and Pennsylvania State Press, 2002). Philadelphia is well-documented in Chapter Three, Russell F. Weigley, editor, *Philadelphia: A 300-Year History* (New York: W. W. Norton 7 Company, 1982). Lancaster gets a thorough look in Jerome H. Wood, Jr., *Conestoga Crossroads, Lancaster, Pennsylvania, 1730-1790* (Harrisburg: Pennsylvania Historical and Museum Commission, 1979). Pittsburgh has two studies of its beginnings: Leland D. Baldwin, *Pittsburgh: The Story of a City, 1750-1865* (Pittsburgh: University of Pittsburgh Press, 1947 and 1995), and Stefan Lorant, *Pittsburgh: The Story of an American City* (Pittsburgh: Esselmont Books, 5th Edition, 1999). The influence of immigrants is documented in James G. Leyburn, *The Scotch-Irish: A Social History* (Chapel Hill: The University of North Carolina Press, 1962), Senator James Webb, *Born Fighting: How the Scots-Irish Shaped America* (Broadway, 2004), and Aaron Spencer Fogleman, *Hopeful Journeys: German Immigration, Settlement, and Political Culture in Colonial America, 1717-1775* (Philadelphia: University of Pennsylvania Press, 1996). The frontier communities along the Forbes Trail have several local chroniclers and two captivity narratives are excellent introductions to the 1755-1758 terror: James E. Seaver, *A Narrative of the Life of Mrs. Mary Jemison* (BiblioBazaar, 2006), and James Smith, *Scoouwa: James Smith's Indian Captivity Narrative* (Columbus: Ohio Historical Society, 1976).

A wealth of information on the natural history of the Keystone State can be found on the Pennsylvania Department of Conservation and Natural Resources website (www.dcnr.state.pa.us). An attractive introduction to the outdoors is Lisa Gensheimer, *Pennsylvania Wilds: Images from the Allegheny National Forest* (Bradford, PA: Forest Press, 2006). Pennsylvania's important role in forestry is discussed in Lester A. DeCoster, *1895-1995: The Legacy of Penn's Woods, A History of the Pennsylvania Bureau of Forestry* (Harrisburg: Commonwealth

of Pennsylvania, 1995), R. R. Thorpe, *The Crown Jewel of Pennsylvania: The State Forest System* (Harrisburg: Commonwealth of Pennsylvania, 1997), and Eric Sprague et al., editors, *The State of Chesapeake Forests* (Arlington: The Conservation Fund, 2006). Charles H. Shultz, editor, *The Geology of Pennsylvania* (Harrisburg: Commonwealth of Pennsylvania, 2002) is one of several natural history titles available on the Pennsylvania Historical and Museum Commission website (www.pabookstore.com).

Robert B. Swift, *Mid-Appalachian Frontier: A Guide to Historic Sites of the French and Indian War* (Gettysburg: Thomas Publications, 2001) is a thorough introduction to historic sites in the region. Another good source is the series of Trail of History guidebooks to the Pennsylvania Historical and Museum Commission sites available on the PA Bookstore website. General Introductions to Pennsylvania travel include: Christine H. O'Toole, *Pennsylvania: Off the Beaten Path* (Guilford, CT: Globe Pequot Press, 9th Edition, 2007), Joanne Miller, *Moon Handbooks Pennsylvania* (Emeryville, CA: Avalon Publishing Company, 3rd Edition, 2005), and Faith and Emily Paulsen, *Fun with the Family: Pennsylvania*, revised and updated by Christine H. O'Toole (Guilford, CT: Globe Pequot Press, 2007). Special travel studies are Tom Huntington, *Ben Franklin's Philadelphia: A Guide* (Mechanicsburg, PA: Stackpole Books, 2006), Tom Huntington, *Pennsylvania's Civil War Trails: The Guide to Battle Sites, Monuments, Museums and Towns* (Mechanicsburg, PA: Stackpole Books, 2007), and Helene Smith and George Swetnam, *A Guidebook to Historic Western Pennsylvania* (Pittsburgh: University of Pittsburgh Press, 1991).

The French and Indian War 250 website (www.frenchandindianwar250.org) has a substantial list of recommended readings with special emphasis on Native Americans, for all ages: elementary, middle school, high school and adult. Some highlights of that list for elementary and middle school students: Kris Hemphill, *Ambush in the Wilderness* (Silver Moon Press, 2003), Alden R. Carter and Bill Clipson, *Colonial War: Clashes in the Wilderness* (Scholastic Library Publishing, 1993), Craig A. Doherty and Katherine M. Doherty, *The Iroquois* (Illustrated Series: First Books, 1989), Rayna M. Gangi, *Mary Jemison: White Woman of the Seneca* (Clear Light Publishers, 1997), and Richard Kozar, *Fort Duquesne and Fort Pitt* (Mason Crest Publishers, 2004). Titles for middle and high school readers are; Albert Marrin, *Struggle for a Continent: The French and Indian Wars, 1690-1760* (London: Macmillan Publishers, Ltd., 1987), Robert M. McClung, *Young George Washington and the French and Indian War, 1753-1758* (Linnet Books, 2002), James Fenimore Cooper's 1826 classic, *Last of the Mohicans* (Barnes & Noble Classics, 2004), and Alfred A. Cave, *The French and Indian War* (Connecticut: Greenwood Press, 2004).

## Acknowledgements

Pennsylvania's Forbes Trail has been several years in the making, and there are many who have contributed to its completion. We thank especially Donna Panazzi, John Rohe and the Colcom Foundation for their wonderful enthusiasm and support for this project. We also thank Scott Izzo and Mike Watson from the Richard King Mellon Foundation for their unflagging interest, commitment and generous help. And we thank the directors of French and Indian War 250, Inc. for their guidance and leadership: C.J. Queenan, Jr., Jim Broadhurst, Linda Boxx, Jane Burger, George Greer, Harry Thompson and Mike Watson.

We are especially grateful to Fred Anderson. Exceptionally generous with his time and interest, he has brought the story of this global conflict to a broad audience and is responsible for generating much long overdue interest in the French and Indian War.

This book has been a team effort: Burton Kummerow has written the history text, Scott Stephenson has written historical sidebars and coordinated the marvelous work of Gerry Embleton with the text, and Christine O'Toole has written the travel sections.

The authors and editor have had a superb team to work with, including Debbie Corll, our tireless production manager; Tricia Kummerow and Melissa Tower from Historyworks, Inc.; David Dixon, Slippery Rock University, author of the web content for the Forbes Trail story; Karen Lightell, public relations and marketing; Virginia Deily, corporate sales; Rachel McCool, intern; Diana Reibling and Lindy Kravec, creative consultants; Tom Woll, Cross River Publishing Consultants, Inc.; The YGS Group: Brian Flaherty, Jim Kell, Jr., Renae Meckley, Jenelle Rittenhouse, Brian Smith and Jonpaul Terwilliger.

We are delighted to publish this book as an imprint of Rowman Littlefield, Inc., and especially thank Jed Lyons for his generous assistance.

And we are grateful for the help of the following individuals and institutions:

The Allegheny Conference on Community Development: James E. Rohr, Chairman; Mike Langley, Bill Flanagan, Barbara McNees, Janel Skelly, Catherine DeLoughrey, Jim Evangelista, Pam Golden, Robert Petrilli, Karen Adkins, Terry Tylka, Eric Chaikowsky, Cindy Bowers, Claudia Graitge, and Val Jones; Pennsylvania's Department of Conservation and Natural Resources: Michael DiBerardinis, John Norbeck, Larry Williamson, Gretchen Leslie, Chris Novak, Sarah Hopkins, Roy Brubaker, Ed Callahan, Ron Hermany, Jim Hyland, Jim Bubb; The Pennsylvania Historical and Museum Commission: Wayne Spilove, Chairman; Barbara Franco, Howard Pollman, Donna Williams. And at the Pennsylvania Department of Community and Economic Development: Dennis Yablonsky, Mickey Rowley; the Pennsylvania Game Commission: Gerald Feaser.

Allegheny Foothills Historical Society: Tom Whanger, Gary Rogers; Army Heritage Education Center: Martin Andresen, Jack Giblin, Mike Perry; Bartram's Garden; Bedford County Visitors Bureau: Dennis Tice; Bedford Springs Resort: W. Courtney Lowe; Borough of Bedford: John Montgomery, Joel Riggle; Boswell Historical Society: Georgia Sheftic; Braddock's Field Historical Society: Bob Messner; Chambersburg Chamber of Commerce: Jean Newvine; The

Chancellor's House B&B: Steve and Lynn George; Christ Church, Philadelphia: Neil Ronk; City Tavern, Philadephia: Paul Bauer; Clark Productions: Jerry Clark; Conococheague Institute: Walter Powell, Mary Hartmann; Cumberland Valley Visitors Bureau: Lynn Bubb; Cumberland Valley Historical Society: Merri Lou Schaumann, Richard Tritt; Family Heirloom Weavers: David Kline; Fort Ligonier Association: Martin West, Penny West; Fort Loudoun State Historic Site: Anna Rotz; Fort Pitt Blockhouse: Kelly Linn; Fort Pitt Museum: Chuck Smith, Doug MacGregor, Fred Threfall; Fort Ticonderoga: Christopher Fox, Mark Turdo; Franklin County Visitors Bureau: Janet Pollard; The Garamond Agency: Lisa Adams; Gettysburg College: James P. Myers, Jr.; Greater Philadelphia Tourism Marketing Corporation: Cara Schneider; Green Gables Restaurant and Mountain Playhouse: Teresa Marafino; Hammond Pretzel Bakery staff; Senator John Heinz History Center: Ned Shano; Heritage Center of Lancaster County: Erika Belen, Peter Seibert; Historic Bethlehem Partnership, Inc.: Kathryn Lynch; Hope Lodge; Independence National Historical Park: James Mueller, Coxey Toogood; Jacob's Resting Place B&B: Marie Hegglin; Johns Hopkins University Press: Robert Brugger; LJ Aviation: Ed Kilkeary; Landis Valley Museum: Craig Benner, James F. Cauley; Laurel Highlands Visitors Bureau: Annie Urban, Julie Donovan; Ligonier Valley Historical Society, Compass Inn: Tina Yandrick; Lincoln Highway Heritage Corridor: Olga A. Herbert; Loyalhanna Watershed Association: Drew Banas; McLean House B&B: Jan Rose; National Museum of the American Coverlet: Melinda Zongor; National Park Service: Joanne Hanley; Old Bedford Village: Roger Kirwin; Old Economy Village; Once Upon a Nation, Inc.: Sandra M. Lloyd; Pennsylvania Educational Alliance for Citizenship: Jim Wetzler; Pennsylvania State Senate, Office of the Secretary: Andrea Faber; Pittsburgh Post-Gazette: David Bear; Quaker Information Center: Chel Avery; Renfrew Museum and Park: Bonnie Iseminger; Somerset Historical Center: Charles Fox; Susquehanna Glass Company; Swarthmore College, Friends Historical Library: Christopher Densmore; U.S. Army Center of Military History: Joseph Seymour; Venture Outdoors: Sean Brady, Rob Walters; Visit Pittsburgh: Lynne Glover, Tinsy Lipchak, Colleen Kalchthaler; Wheatland: Patrick Clarke; Whispering Brook Farm: Ed Brechbill; Wilderness Voyageurs.

We also thank Merlin Benner; Ellen Brooks; Steve and Jacquie Delisle; Charles A. Fagan, III; Diane and Paul Gormley; Alan Gutchess; Barry Haver; James Hostetler; Larry Nehring; Roger Moore; Abby Smith and David Rumsey; Richard Sturtz; Lenora Vesio.

And finally, we thank our families for their patience and support: Dan, Eric, Heidi, Jeremy and Joe Corll; Aiken, Maddy and Chet Fisher; Judy Parfitt, Donna, Evans and Ellie Stephenson, Robert C. Stephenson and Judith Regina Stephenson (1941-2007).

## Mapping Forbes' Route West

No sooner had John Forbes returned from the Forks of the Ohio than his wilderness road became a bustling avenue of commerce. As the years passed, merchants, soldiers, settlers, and travelers continued to use the trail blazed by Forbes' army. During this time, variants to the original trace were constructed to avoid various obstructions and ease travel. Despite such efforts, a journey over the rugged mountains proved grueling.

Over the years, the trace of John Forbes' original path to the Ohio was either paved over or by-passed. It was not until the early 20th century that historians made any serious attempt to locate the trail. In 1909, a Harvard University professor named John Laycock hiked the path from Bedford to Pittsburgh. The professor was guided during his trek by a crude map that had been drawn during the Forbes Expedition by a Pennsylvania soldier named John Potts. Twenty-five years later, Lewis C. Walkinshaw, William Laughner, and David Rial again traced the route. The three men made extensive notes and Rial drew a map of the route. Later, Walkinshaw incorporated his field notes from the excursion into his monumental four-volume study entitled, *Annals of Southwestern Pennsylvania*, published in 1936.

Perhaps the best study of the actual route taken by Forbes' army was done by Edward G. Williams after more than thirty years of research. Williams built upon the earlier investigations of the trail and utilized land records and survey plats that contained dotted representations of road. Like Laycock, Walkinshaw, and others, Williams found scars from the old path still evident in some locations. He also took note of "two tracks in use simultaneously by Forbes' army in several places," and variants to the original route that were constructed in later years. Williams' findings were published in 1975 by the Historical Society of Western Pennsylvania in a small volume entitled, *Bouquet's March to the Ohio: The Forbes Road*. The book, which is long out of print and highly sought by collectors, contains seven detailed maps that trace the route of Forbes' army.

With the commemoration of the 250th anniversary of the Forbes Campaign and the naming of Pittsburgh in 2008, it was important to bring modern technology to bear upon tracing this historic trail. As a result, a number of dedicated historians and trail buffs gathered with a team from the Pennsylvania Department of Conservation and Natural Resources, led by GIS specialist Ron Hermany, to once again plot the route Forbes took from Philadelphia to the Forks of the Ohio. The group poured over existing maps, descriptions, and landmarks that had been established by earlier historians and used global positioning software to plot a new map of the route, located inside the back cover. Interestingly, this new map, like previous efforts, cannot be considered definitive since it is still impossible to discern with precision trail variants and locations where all vestiges of the road have been obliterated through mining operations, road construction, and modern improvements.

David Dixon
Slippery Rock University

## Artwork and Photo Credits

**Artwork**, The authors gratefully acknowledge the always lively and fascinating artwork of Richard Schlecht and Gerry Embleton that fills the pages of this book. All artwork is by Gerry Embleton with the exception of the illustrations on pages 11, 12-13, 38-39, 180-181, which are by Richard Schlecht.

**Photography Credits,** The authors gratefully acknowledge the use of images and photography from the following sources:

**Historical Images, Front end papers** The David Rumsey Map Collection, Scull Map, 1775. **Philadelphia** Courtesy Fort Ligonier, General John Forbes, artist unknown, p. 14. **Lancaster** Courtesy of the Historical Society of Pennsylvania Collection, Atwater Kent Museum of Philadelphia, Henry Bouquet, by J. Wollaston, 1759, p. 46; Courtesy Fort Ligonier, John St. Clair, by Allan Ramsay, 1754, p. 46. **Carlisle** Courtesy Winterthur Museum, Benjamin Rush, by Charles Willson Peale, Gift of Mrs. T. Charleton Henry, p. 75. Courtesy Cumberland County Historical Society, Sea of Faces, 1892, p. 78; Courtesy United States Army Heritage Education Center, MOLLUS-MASS Collection of Civil War Era Photographs, p. 80, p. 81. **Fort Loudoun** Courtesy Fort Ligonier, Earl of Loudoun, by Allan Ramsay, p. 102. **Bedford** Collection of the Maryland State Archives, Washington, Lafayette, and Tilghman at Yorktown, by Charles Willson Peale, 1784, p. 124; Collection of the New-York Historical Society, George Washington, by Charles Willson Peale, 1795, #1867.299, p. 125; Courtesy Winterthur Museum, George Washington Reviewing the Troops, at Fort Cumberland, by Frederick Kemmelmeyer, p. 130. **Ligonier** Courtesy Washington-Custis-Lee Collection, Washington and Lee University, Lexington, Virginia, George Washington 1772, by Charles Willson Peale, p. 148; Courtesy Fort Ligonier, Lord Ligonier, by Joshua Reynolds, 1760, p. 153. **Pittsburgh** Courtesy Fort Ligonier, William Pitt, George Knapton, p. 185; Courtesy Chatham College, The Block House, by Russell Smith, 1832, p. 191.

**Photographs, Philadelphia** Photograph by Laura Fisher, p. 23; Clark Productions, Aerial Photography, p. 23; National Constitution Center in Philadelphia, Signers Hall, p. 28; GPTMC, Photograph by J. Holder, Franklin Square, p. 31; Concepts by Staib, Ltd., City Tavern, p. 34. **Lancaster** von Hess Foundation, Wright's Ferry Mansion, Interior, p. 57; Clark Productions Aerial Photography, p. 63. **Carlisle** Juniata College, Founders Hall, p. 74; Dickinson College, Old West, Photograph by A. Pierce Bounds, p. 74; Wilson College, Photograph by Afton Unger, p. 75; University of Pennsylvania, "Ben on the Bench," Photograph by Steven Minicola, p. 75; Franklin and Marshall College, Old Main, p. 75; United States Army Heritage Education Center: Reenactors, p. 82; Pennsylvania Historical and Museum Commission, Curiosity Connection, p. 83; Pennsylvania Capitol Building, Photograph by Dave Fetter, p. 86. **Fort Loudoun** Clark Productions, Aerial Photography, p. 101, p. 112; Murray Schrotenboer, Grouseland Tours, Pike to Bike Trail, p. 108; Merlin Benner, Wildlife, p. 108, p. 113. **Bedford** Clark Productions, Aerial Photography, p. 123, p. 134; Bedford Springs Resort, Pool, p. 133, Entrance, p. 137. **Ligonier** Permission Courtesy Allegheny Trail Alliance, Logo, p. 150; Clark Productions, Aerial Photography, p. 154, p. 155, p. 161, p. 162; Merlin Benner, Wildlife, p. 164, p. 165. **Pittsburgh** Clark Productions, Aerial Photography, p. 179; Permission Courtesy Allegheny Trail Alliance, Logo, p. 182; Photographs by Archie Carpenter, p. 184, p. 185; Westmoreland County Historical Society, Westmoreland County Flag, p. 188; Denise Garrott, "Approach," p. 188; The Soffer Corporation, Southside Works, p. 190; Sports and Exhibition Authority of the City of Pittsburgh and Allegheny County, North Shore Water Steps, p. 190; Pittsburgh Parks Conservancy, Photograph by Melissa McMasters, Schenley Park, p. 192; Friends of the Riverfront, Kayakers and Swimmers, p. 195. **Epilogue** Clark Productions, Aerial Photography, p. 197.

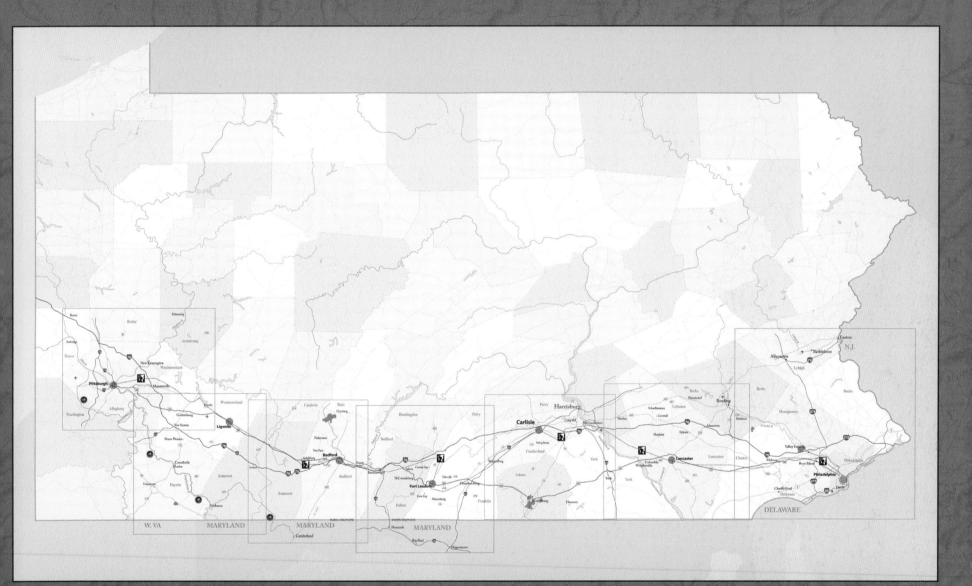

PITTSBURGH

LIGONIER

BEDFORD

FORT LOU